WORK-FAMILY RESEARCH

Recent Titles in
Bibliographies and Indexes in Sociology

Violence and Terror in the Mass Media: An Annotated Bibliography
Nancy Signorielli and George Gerbner, compilers

Latin America, 1983–1987: A Social Science Bibliography
Robert L. Delorme, compiler

Social Support Networks: A Bibliography, 1983–1987
David E. Biegel, Kathleen J. Farkas, Neil Abell, Jacqueline Goodin, and Bruce Friedman, compilers

Diffusion of Innovations: A Select Bibliography
Klaus Musmann and William H. Kennedy, compilers

Native American Youth and Alcohol: An Annotated Bibliography
Michael L. Lobb and Thomas D. Watts

The Homosexual and Society: An Annotated Bibliography
Robert B. Marks Ridinger, compiler

Pro-Choice/Pro-Life: An Annotated, Selected Bibliography (1972–1989)
Richard Fitzsimmons and Joan P. Diana, compilers

Sikhs in North America: An Annotated Bibliography
Darshan Singh Tatla

Adoption Literature for Children and Young Adults: An Annotated Bibliography
Susan G. Miles

Homelessness in America, 1893–1992: An Annotated Bibliography
Rod Van Whitlock, Bernard Lubin, and Jean R. Sailors, compilers

The Multilevel Design: A Guide with an Annotated Bibliography, 1980–1993
Harry J. M. Hüttner and Pieter van den Eeden

Pro-Choice/Pro-Life Issues in the 1990s: An Annotated, Selected Bibliography
Richard Fitzsimmons and Joan P. Diana

WORK-FAMILY RESEARCH

An Annotated Bibliography

Compiled by
Teri Ann Lilly,
Marcie Pitt-Catsouphes,
and Bradley K. Googins

Prepared under the Auspices of
The Center for Work & Family at Boston College
The Wallace E. Carroll School of Management

The Center for
Work & Family
BOSTON COLLEGE
CARROLL SCHOOL OF MANAGEMENT

Bibliographies and Indexes in Sociology, Number 25

GREENWOOD PRESS
Westport, Connecticut • London

Library of Congress Cataloging-in-Publication Data

Work-family research : an annotated bibliography / compiled by Teri
Ann Lilly, Marcie Pitt-Catsouphes, and Bradley K. Googins.
    p.   cm.—(Bibliographies and indexes in sociology, ISSN
0742–6895 ; no. 25)
    "Prepared under the auspices of the Center for Work & Family at Boston
College, the Wallace E. Carroll School of Management."
    Includes bibliographical references and index.
    ISBN 0–313–30322–3 (alk. paper)
    1. Work and family—United States—Bibliography.   I. Lilly, Teri
Ann.   II. Pitt-Catsouphes, Marcie.   III. Googins, Bradley K.
IV. Wallace E. Carroll School of Management.   V. Series.
Z7165.U5W65   1997
016.3063'6'0973—dc21   97–24357

British Library Cataloguing in Publication Data is available.

Library of Congress Catalog Card Number: 97–24357
ISBN: 0–313–30322–3
ISSN: 0742–6895

First published in 1997

Greenwood Press, 88 Post Road West, Westport, CT 06881
An imprint of Greenwood Publishing Group, Inc.

Printed in the United States of America

The paper used in this book complies with the
Permanent Paper Standard issued by the National
Information Standards Organization (Z39.48–1984).

10 9 8 7 6 5 4 3 2

Contents

Contents

Preface

Work-Family Research: An Annotated Bibliography is a collection of 934 entries providing bibliographic information and annotations for selected articles, books, chapters in books, reports, and papers that present information about work and family research. Given the expansive nature of the work-family field, it was somewhat difficult to decide which literature to include. We began with the identification of the primary thematic and topical strands that have contributed to the understanding of the work-family field. The thematic strands served as an organizational framework for our literature searches which mined voluminous literature in particular areas and a dearth in others, reflective of the nature and growth of the area studied. Using an academic screen, we focused on research articles written within the last eight years, reports from independent research groups, selected papers, and a sampling of classic studies that have guided work and family research.

The scope of *Work-Family Research: An Annotated Bibliography* is rather daunting considering the diverse disciplines addressing work-family issues, the broad range of topics covered, and the multiplicity of research approaches. Given the size and nature of the project, therefore, the thematic sections are not exhaustive, and we apologize for the many deserving works not included. We believe, however, the strength of the bibliography rests with this broad sweep of the work-family literature, because it promotes a preliminary mapping of the field. Our intent is to provide a multidisciplined and representative sampling of academic research-oriented work in each thematic strand.

Organization
This bibliography has been organized to help you find information as readily as possible. The primary thematic and topical strands of the work-family field serve respectively as parts and chapters. For example, the thematic strand, "Work and Family Roles" (part 3), contains several topical chapters, among them, "Role Conflict/ Strain/ Stress and Well-being" (chapter 10). Overall, the arrangement of the

thematic strands reflects the historical progression of the development of the work-family field.

Author Index
The author index lists the names of all authors whose works are represented in the bibliography. Next to the name is a number corresponding to the citation in the text, not the page number.

Entries
In an effort to present the information in a consistent and efficient manner, we have followed the author-date system prescribed by the *Chicago Manual of Style*, 1993, 14th edition, University of Chicago Press. It should be noted, however, that specific database restrictions necessitated certain adjustments. The formats for the six types of citations are as follows:

> JOURNAL ARTICLES: Name of Author(s). Date. Title of article: Subtitle. *Journal Name.* Volume No.: Page numbers.

> BOOKS: Name of Author(s). Date. *Title of Book: Subtitle.* Place Published: Publisher.

> CHAPTERS IN BOOKS: Name of Author(s). Date. Title of article. In *Name of Work.* Place Published: Publisher. Page numbers.

> ARTICLES IN EDITED BOOKS: Name of Author (s). Date. Title of article. In *Name of Work*, edited by Editors' Name. Place Published: Publisher. Page numbers.

> PAPERS OR REPORTS: Name of Author(s). Date. *Title of Paper or Report: Subtitle.* Place Published: Publisher.

> UNPUBLISHED PAPERS: Name of Author(s). Date. *Title of Paper or Report: Subtitle.* Information.

Although the majority of entries are annotated, we decided not to annotate books since space limitations would not allow us to fully capture the nature of the research.

Acknowledgments

The Center for Work & Family at Boston College wishes to express sincere appreciation to the Alfred P. Sloan Foundation for its support of *Work-Family Research: An Annotated Bibliography*. In particular, we wish to acknowledge the contribution and vision of Dr. Kathleen Christensen, a program officer at the Sloan Foundation. As the convener of the Sloan Work Research Network on Work Redesign and Work-Family, Dr. Christensen recognized the need for a thorough compilation of the work-family research literature.

The Center is also grateful to a number of people who made significant contributions to this work. Many of the authors cited within gave generously of their time and knowledge. In addition, several members of the Sloan Network assisted in reviewing sections of the bibliography. The authors of this bibliography, however, take full responsibility for the content of the book.

Many staff members at the Center for Work & Family made substantial contributions to the compilation and preparation of this bibliography. We would like to thank Charlene Broock who helped to initiate the computer searches and subsequently contributed to the editing tasks. Jamie Johnson-Riley and Sarah Stanczak helped to get the project off the ground in setting up the database. Under Jamie's supervision, Sarah and the other students at the Center — Laura Kropinack, Andrea LaBounty, Katherine Rand, Trupi V. Rao — labored patiently, making it possible to collect the database. We also thank Irene Fassler, research assistant, for her significant contribution in annotating several chapters. Of special note is Rachel Kohn, research assistant, for her writing skills, her computer skills, and her organization skills.

Finally, preparation of *Work-Family Research: An Annotated Bibliography* would have stalled without some critical technical expertise and programming assistance. Daniel Juliana, computer analyst-consultant, compiled the author index and stretched the capacity of the existing computer program, creatively scripting every letter, period, and space of the bibliographic entries. Julianne Gray, research associate, was tireless with her "on-the-spot" trouble shooting and her gracious assistance in pulling the final product together. Our heartfelt thanks to both of them.

Work-Family Research: An Annotated Bibliography is an expansion of the collection of academic articles and resources maintained at the

Center for Work & Family at Boston College. The Center was founded in 1990 as the first academic center which focused on research and policy assessments of work and family issues. We anticipate that this bibliographic database will continue to grow and be updated. The combined effort of everyone involved has made this a successful project and has created a valuable tool for use by researchers, students, and professionals working toward greater understanding of the intersection between work, life, and community.

Teri Ann Lilly
Marcie Pitt-Catsouphes
Bradley K. Googins, Ph.D.

Introduction

Over the past decade, work and family experiences have become "front-burner" issues in community discourse, corporate decision making, public policy debates, and our reflections of everyday life. Cover stories in prominent business and professional journals, weekly columns in *The Wall Street Journal*, coverage in local newspapers, and feature spots on radio and television coverage speak to the coming of age of work and family priorities.

The work and family revolution of the latter part of the 20th century has profoundly changed the social structures, institutions, and cultures that constitute the fabric of our lives. Work and family transformations have begun to redefine our most basic social processes. Fundamental characteristics of families, the organization of work, and the social contracts which individuals and families have with their communities and their workplaces have been drastically altered within a relatively brief time frame. New gender roles have been tested, enabling us to break away from traditional structures that have determined social constructs of gender. Technology has virtually outpaced the abilities of human systems to adapt, integrate, and utilize its benefits. Global economies have made it necessary for us to redefine citizenship and create new relationships between nations and their social and economic systems. Changing workforce demographics, the disappearance of boundaries between the worlds of work and family, and the metamorphosis of basic social values and attitudes have stimulated change throughout society. Tremors from the work and family revolution have been felt in nearly every aspect of our social and our private lives.

Responses to social changes have emerged more slowly and hesitantly. Perhaps most noticeable has been the development of the concept of "family-friendly" corporations. In comparison to other social institutions, the workplace has assumed significant leadership for responding to work and family changes. The development of an ever-expanding cluster of employer-sponsored programs, benefits, and policies has precipitated the articulation of new corporate roles and increased corporate involvement in employees' personal and family issues.

Given the profound nature of work and family changes, it is little wonder that numerous social science researchers have studied these changes and their impacts on society. At the most basic level, the work and family arenas have been seen as interlocking, semi-independent spheres. Understanding the complex dynamics that link work and family is difficult, at best. The multiple dimensions within each sphere frustrate attempts to compartmentalize and simplify issues. However, the potential subjects for exploration and research within each of these life areas quickly expands so that the work-family field appears to have no boundaries and seems to encompass all of human existence.

There has been an incredible growth in the attention that academic literature has devoted to work and family issues during the past decade. The avalanche of articles and books that have appeared provide evidence of the extent to which work and family issues are perceived to be significant social concerns. Ironically enough, the expansive nature of the work-family topic has presented a conceptual challenge to researchers. In fact, researchers interested in entering the work-family field must face a formidable task of trying to understand the literature and become familiar with the research. The expanse of the two domains of work and family greatly surpasses the scope of most other fields.

Many researchers have expressed support for the development of conceptual guides that could help to categorize work and family issues into a more cogent field of study. Researchers have attempted to introduce some coherence into the field (c.f., Barnett, 1996; Greenhaus, 1988; Pleck, 1992; Voydanoff, 1988). However, given the recent pro-fusion of studies and contributions to the literature, this challenge has remained daunting. *Work-Family Research: An Annotated Bibliography* is an attempt to organize the rich work and family literature. It reflects three major perspectives of the work-family field: the developmental perspective, the work and the family focus, and work-family interaction focus.

A Developmental Perspective
As a field, the study of work and family is a relatively new arena that has evolved incrementally along focused areas of interest. The outline

for this bibliography indicates the discrete categories that have emerged over the years. These categories reflect the developmental stages of the work and family field as it has moved through key issues and as researchers have expanded their lines of inquiry.

Much of the early literature was rooted in changing gender roles, particularly those of women. A voluminous literature arose on the determinants and correlates of women's labor force attachment, for example (c.f., Kahn, 1975). As the characteristics of women's participation in the workforce changed, the focus broadened to issues such as dual career families (c.f., Hall and Hall, 1979; Perry-Jenkins, 1988; Rapoport and Rapoport, 1977; Young and Wilmont, 1973). Soon, the concept of stress became prominent in the literature—stress between work roles and family/home roles as well as stress between men and women as they attempted to fulfill their own roles (c.f., Rook, et al., 1991; Cooke and Rousseau, 1984).

Many studies conducted during the early years of work and family research examined issues related to child care. Some would claim that concerns about the care for children and the conflicts that working mothers experienced about their roles as mothers and workers were the primary factors that catapulted the widespread awareness of work-family issues. Concomitantly, there was an intense examination of the impacts of maternal employment on children (c.f., Belsky, 1988; Hoffman, 1989). The dependent care priorities of working families emerged as a subfield when eldercare concerns were documented.

Much of the early work and family literature had centered on individual and family roles, and workplace experiences and responses soon became the focus of many studies. The relevance of using a work-family lens to consider issues such as careers, organizational commitment, flexibility, and alternative organizational arrangements was recognized. Eventually, researchers began to explore and depict the concept, nature, and boundaries of family-friendly corporations.

Although this summary of the development of work-family research highlights just a few of the research streams, it illustrates how the number of issues has expanded and how subconcentrations have evolved.

Work Focus, Family Focus

Another framework of the work and family literature emerges from the perspectives about the outcomes of work and family experiences. One body of literature has explored the effects of work experiences on family life, while another focuses on the impacts of family life on work experiences. Although the research questions and the methodologies of these two approaches vary, both are concerned about quality of work life and family life. A number of studies have documented stress that originates in one domain and then impacts the other. Burke and Greenglass (1987) provided one of the first reviews of this literature and concluded that most of the literature has depicted the negative impacts work can have on family life.

Within the past decade, there has been more research attention devoted to how employees' lives outside of work impact on the workplace. Kanter (1977), among others, has lifted up the prevailing dominance of the work paradigm which asserts the centrality of work as establishing the conditions of family life. Kanter observes that a major deficiency of the work and family field is the lack of a tested framework which captures the impact of family life on work. It is telling that, in our country the term "work and family" is rarely reversed to "family and work," in contrast to European nations where family is emphasized over work.

Some of the more recent research developments have started to examine the outcomes of the dramatic changes in the workplace (c.f., Friedman, 1991; Gonyea and Googins, 1992; Lambert, 1993). The Alfred P. Sloan Foundation recently funded a project that focused on the impact of work redesign on families and family life. Over the course of eighteen months, a group of researchers examined this topic from a number of different perspectives. It became evident that there has been only minimal attention devoted to an examination of how workplace transformation, including reengineering and redesign, has impacted families.

Interaction Focus

Perhaps one of the more conceptually challenging aspects of work and family research has been the examination of the interaction between these two life domains. A number of researchers have developed models that depict the dynamic relationship between work and family experiences. For example, Pleck (1995) uses the interaction perspective to discuss the job demands model, a conceptual framework used for research such as that conducted by Guelzow et al., 1995. Many of the empirical studies reflect the influence of spillover theories, compensation theories, and role conflict theories (Lambert, 1990; Staines, 1980). Most of the early research examined the spillover from work to home. More recently, there has been a recognition that home experiences, such as the emotional climate of the family, can influence work experiences as much as workplace culture can affect family experiences (c.f. Crouter, 1984; Greenhaus and Parasuraman, 1987; Westman and Etzion, 1995).

Cross-Disciplinary Perspective

A broad range of disciplines speak to and contribute to work and family inquiries. In assembling this bibliography, it was readily apparent that the work-family literature draws from a number of social science traditions (including sociology, psychology, management, political science, and, to some extent, economics) as well as fields such as family studies, management, social work, education, nursing, labor and industrial relations, and women's studies. This academic and professional diversity has introduced a healthy spectrum of perspectives about work and family issues. However, it has been difficult for work-family researchers to have an awareness and appreciation of the findings in so many different fields. As a consequence, the work and family field has struggled to establish and build on a scientific base of knowledge.

It is curious that, despite the vast body of research highlighted in *Work-Family Research: An Annotated Bibliography,* there currently is no academic journal which focuses exclusively on this field. The findings of work and family studies are scattered throughout journals associated with virtually every profession. While this can help to stimulate widespread discussion about and interest in work and family issues, the fragmentation of the work and family literature has made it difficult to identify a primary source for the publication of scholarly work. Not surprisingly, there is no professional association for work and family researchers where academic work is routinely presented.

In light of the dispersed nature of the work and family field, this bibliography should be seen as more than a unique source of information. It has the potential to serve as a guide for work and family researchers that can help them begin to codify findings and build stronger theoretical perspectives. This bibliography increases the access researchers have to each others' work, making it easier to promote interdisciplinary, collaborative work that will be the future of the work and family field.

Bradley K. Googins, Ph.D.

PART 1

WOMEN AND WORK

CHAPTER 1

Wages and Benefits

1   Acker, J. 1989. *Doing Comparable Worth: Gender, Class, and Pay Equity.* Philadelphia, PA: Temple University Press.

In this book, Acker presents a large study of a comparable worth project—the Oregon project. Acker's account reflects the underpinnings of her theoretical stance, that is, that gender is built into the class structure. Acker summarizes: " ... economically, culturally, and socially constituted differences between men and women are the medium through which class processes are played out."

2   Acker, J. 1987. Sex bias in job evaluation: A comparable worth issue. In *Ingredients for Women's Employment Policy*, edited by C. Bose and G. Spitze. Albany, NY: State University of New York Press. 183-196.

3   Bamberger, P., M. Admati-Dvir, and G. Harel. 1995. Gender-based wage and promotion discrimination in Israeli high-technology firms: Do unions make a difference? *Academy of Management Journal* 38(6): 1744-1761.

The effectiveness of unions to protect women from gender-based wage and promotion discrimination is examined in this study of two matched firms in Israel (one unionized and one not). Overall, the authors conclude that women in unionized firms experience no less discrimination. The most notable difference between the matched firms was that in the unionized firm, the impact of promotion discrimination was less severe. The researchers discuss the findings in terms of future research and union policy.

4   Baron, J. N., and A. E. Newman. 1990. For what it's worth: Organizations, occupations, and the value of work done by

women and nonwhites. *American Sociological Review* 55: 155-175.

5 Baron, J. N., B. S. Mittman, and A. E. Newman. 1991. Targets of opportunity: Organizational and environmental determinants of gender integration within the California Civil Service, 1979-1985. *American Journal of Sociology* 96(6): 1362-1401.

An examination of gender integration among the California Civil Service state agencies in 1979 and 1985 is linked to theories of organizational change and organization-environment relations. The first section of the paper develops hypotheses regarding gender integration based on a review of the literature. The second section analyzes and tests the hypotheses using the California case. The analysis reveals that progress toward gender integrations is influenced by the following: (1) the degree of external pressure; (2) the numbers of internal groups (e.g., unions, women); (3) characteristics of leadership; and (4) particular structural characteristics inherent in the company (e.g., resistance to any change). The discussion further links organizational studies and social inequality.

6 Bellas, M. L. 1994. Comparable worth in academia: The effects on faculty salaries of the sex composition and labor-market conditions of academic disciplines. *American Sociological Review* 59: 807-821.

Bellas explores the relationship between lower salaries and academic disciplines with higher proportions of women on faculty. Using a contextual model, the analysis confirms Bellas' hypothesis that disciplines with higher proportions of women experience wage penalties. Issues of comparable worth and cultural devaluation of work performed by women are discussed.

7 Bergmann, B. R. 1986. *The Economic Emergence of Women.* New York: Basic Books.

8 Berheide, C. W., C. H. Chertos, L. Haignere, and R. J. Steinberg. 1987. A pay equity analysis of female-dominated

and disproportionately minority New York state job titles. *Humanity and Society* 11: 465-485.

9   Bielby, W. T., and J. N. Baron. 1987. Undoing discrimination: Job integration and comparable worth. In *Ingredients for Women's Employment Policy,* edited by C. Bose and G. Spitze. New York: State University of New York Press. 211-229.

This chapter presents evidence that argues against supply-side economic explanations of sex segregation in organizations. The authors use data from recent research to substantiate their explanations of sex segregation, thereby providing evidence in opposition to human capitalist explanations.

10   Blau, F. D., and L. M. Kahn. 1992. The gender earnings gap: Learning from international comparisons. *The American Economic Review* 82(2): 533-538.

This analysis examines the gender pay gap among eight industrialized countries. The study, using micro data, finds that the U. S. experiences greater wage inequality compared to other industrialized countries. The authors consider this to be the major finding of the study because it underscores the importance of wage structure.

11   Blau, F. D., and M. A. Ferber. 1986. *The Economics of Women, Men, and Work.* NJ: Prentice Hall.

12   Bridges, W. P., and R. A. Berk. 1978. Sex, earnings, and the nature of work: A job-level analysis of male-female income differences. *Social Science Quarterly* 58(4): 553-565.

This study examines the income disparities between men and women using survey data from 1,308 white collar employees and 130 supervisors in 20 firms in Chicago. The unit of analysis is the job type. This study found that income disparities between male- and female-typed jobs are almost as sizable as the measured income disparities between males and females.

13   Bridges, W. P., and R. L. Nelson. 1989. Markets in hierarchies: Organizational and market influences on gender inequality in a State pay system. *American Journal of Sociology* 95(3): 616–658.

This paper focuses on the nature of income discrepancies between jobs held by men and women within the same organization. The authors develop two models of the market-organization relationship: (1) an administered-efficiency model; and (2) a bureaucratic politics model. An analysis of gender inequality in a bureaucratic employer, the state of Washington, demonstrates that both market and organizational influences interact and contribute to pay inequity.

14 Clark, T. A., and F. J. James. 1992. **Women-owned businesses: Dimensions and policy issues.** *Economic Development Quarterly* **6(1): 25-40.**

Clark and James explore the nature and implications of women-owned business in the U. S. over the past few decades. The analysis indicates women earn more money in management positions than when they own their own businesses. Additionally, the analysis underscores care responsibilities as an impetus to become self-employed. Issues addressed include (1) constraints on women-operated businesses; and (2) federal policy and women-owned businesses.

15 Cohen, C. F. 1983. **The impact on women of proposed changes in the private pension system: A simulation.** *Industrial and Labor Relations Review* **36(2): 258-270.**

Cohen tests effects of barriers for women in attaining pension benefits by creating benchmark estimates and comparing them with predicted benefits that would result from changes recommended by the President's Commission on Pension Policy. The analysis finds significant differences, in other words, proposed changes in women's pension benefits would greatly benefit women. Based on the analysis, argues for a need to combine a policy of greater coverage and lower vesting standards.

16 Cook, A. H. 1985, 1986. *Comparable Worth: A Casebook of State and Local Experiences.* **Honolulu, HI: Industrial Relations Center.**

17   Coyle, A. 1995. *Women and Organisational Change.*
      Manchester, U. K.: Equal Opportunities European Commision.

      Based on five organizational case studies, this report examines
      the effects of organizational changes and restructuring of work
      on women's employment opportunities. Policy implications are
      considered within the European context.

18   England, P., and D. Dunn. 1988. Evaluating work and
      comparable worth. *Annual Review of Sociology* 14: 227-248.

      England and Dunn address the interdisciplinary approaches to
      evaluating work and comparable worth and, then, link the
      various discussions to sociological theory. This paper is
      divided into four sections which address the following topics
      and approaches: (1) methods and findings of job evaluation
      (industrial psychologists); (2) job evaluation methods
      (sociology); (3) theories of setting compensation levels
      (neoclassical economic views); and (4) pay equity debates
      (social science theories).

19   Evans, S. M., and B. J. Nelson. 1989. *Wage Justice: Comparable
      Worth and the Paradox of Technocratic Reform.* Chicago, IL:
      The University of Chicago Press.

20   Gerhart, B. A., and G. T. Milkovich. 1989. Salaries, salary
      growth, and promotions of men and women in a large, private
      firm. In *Pay Equity: Empirical Inquiries,* edited by R. T.
      Michael, H. I. Hartmann, and B. O'Farrell. Washington, DC:
      National Academy Press. 23-45.

      In this chapter, the authors investigate gender-based
      differences in annual salaries, salary growth, and promotions.
      The longitudinal data used are from the personnel information
      system of a Fortune 500 firm and focus on professional,
      managerial, sales, and technical jobs. Findings are discussed,
      including the following: (1) narrowing differentials among
      female/male salaries; (2) women's increasing number of
      promotions; and (3) women's larger percentage of salary
      increases.

21   Hakim, C. 1988. Women at work: Recent research on women's employment. *Work, Employment and Society* 2(1): 103-113.

This review article covers seven books from an interdisciplinary group of scholars who address women's position in the labor market.

22   Halaby, C. N. 1979. Job-specific sex differences in organizational reward attainment: Wage discrimination vs. rank segregation. *Social Forces* 58(1): 108-127.

This study investigates within employer differences in women's and men's salaries for the same management personnel job in a large company. Findings indicate that rank segregation contributes to sex differences in salaries to a much greater extent than discrimination. Simply put, lower salaries for women result from the way promotions are given.

23   Hartmann, H. I., and R. M. Spalter-Roth. 1992. *Women in Telecommunications: An Exception to the Rule of Low Pay for Women's Work.* Washington, DC: Institute for Women's Policy Research (IWPR).

This IWPR study documents women's recent job and wage losses in the telecommunications industry which had previously been an anomaly in terms of women's jobs and wages. This analysis, however, illuminates a pattern of race and gender segmentation.

24   Hartmann, H. I., and S. Aaronson. 1994. Pay equity and women's wage increases: Success in the States, a model for the nation. *Duke Journal of Gender Law & Policy* 1: 69-87.

This study evaluates the effects of pay equity programs in twenty states. The female-male wage gap improved with the pay equity program in all states studied. However, the study found the impact differed based on the following identified factors: (1) amount of money spent; (2) number of women affected; and (3) standard set for wages for females. The report found no evidence of predicted negative side effects, such as increased unemployment and rampant escalation of wages in the private sector.

25   Hartmann, H. I., R. E. Kraut, and L. A. Tilly, eds. 1986. *Computer Chips and Paper Clips: Technology and Women's Employment.* Volumes I and II. Washington, DC: National Academy Press.

26   Hartmann, H. I., R. M. Spalter-Roth, and N. Collins. 1994. What do unions do for women? *Challenge* July-August: 11-18.

This analysis of the role of unions in addressing women's issues considers, among others, the following two issues: (1) union membership by gender, occupation, and education level; and (2) effects of union membership on women's wages and job tenure. Following an outline of the results, recommendations for unions are made, including training women for leadership roles, and including women in key union activities.

27   Hartmann, H. I., Y. H. Yoon, R. M. Spalter-Roth, and L. B. Shaw. 1995. *Temporary Disability Insurance: A Model to Provide Income Security for Women over the Life Cycle.* Presented at "Women's Lives and Economic Participation," 1995 Annual Meeting of the American Economics Association, Allied Social Science Associations.

A model of temporary disability insurance (TDI) is presented that will provide paid pregnancy/ childbirth/ child care leave. The paper presents TDI feasibility data from an on-going project conducted by the Institute for Women's Policy Research (IWPR).

28   Hersch, J., and S. I. White-Means. 1993. Employer-sponsored health and pension benefits and the gender/race wage gap. *Social Science Quarterly* 74(4): 851-866.

Differences between the hourly wage differentials and total compensation, including in-kind pension and health care benefits, are examined. Using data from the 1988 CPS Survey of Employee Benefit, differences are compared by race and gender. The authors conclude that examining total compensation accounts for only a slight difference in the earnings gap. Between white men and black men, although half of the total compensation gap is related to worker qualifications, the rest is unexplained.

29   Jackson, L. A. 1989. Relative deprivation and the gender wage
        gap. *Journal of Social Issues* 45(4): 117-133.

        A survey of the research provides a framework for an analysis
        of the relationship between gender and pay satisfaction. A
        model is presented that integrates the value-based and
        comparative-referents explanations of the contented woman
        worker (Fig. 1, p. 128). Implications and conclusions from the
        analysis are discussed in terms of comparable worth issues.

30   Jacobs, J. A., and R. J. Steinberg. 1990. Compensating
        differentials and the male-female wage gap: Evidence from
        the New York State Comparable Worth Study. *Social Forces*
        69(2): 439-468.

31   Korczyk, S. 1992. Gender and pension coverage. In *Trends in
        Pensions,* edited by J. Turner and D. Bell. Washington, DC:
        The Government Printing Office. 119-133.

        This analysis of gender differences in pension coverage in full-
        time private sector jobs uses data from the May 1988 Current
        Population Survey. The report discusses and presents data on
        the following topics: (1) pension coverage and vesting; (2)
        pension coverage by industry; and (3) mobility and pension
        coverage. Detailed tables are provided.

32   Krecker, M. L., and A. M. O'Rand. 1991. Contested milieux:
        Small firms, unionization, and the provision of protective
        structures. *Sociological Forum* 6(1): 93-117.

        The authors examine firm size and the influence of unionization
        on provision of pensions. Data from two sources were used to
        support the analyses: The 1983 Current Population Survey and
        the Pension Supplement. Results suggest unionizations were
        more influential in small firms. Labor market theory frames
        the discussion.

33   Lee, D. J. 1981. Skill, craft, and class: A theoretical critique
        and a critical case. *Journal of the British Sociological
        Association* 15(1): 56-78.

        Lee posits that it is impossible to get at skill and class directly.

Using the case of the 'deskilling' of craft labor in twentieth-century Britain, Lee shows that labor market processes are "intervening social filters."

34   **Madden, J. F., and L. C. Chiu. 1990. The wage effects of residential location and commuting constraints on employed married women.** *Urban Studies* **27(3): 353-369.**

Quantifies the effects of residential location and commuting restrictions which would inhibit labor market opportunities. Data on dual-earner households from The 1980 Public Use Microdata Sample (PUMS) of the US Census for Detroit and Philadelphia SMSAs are used to study commuter behavior. No effects for gender gap were found.

35   **Marini, M. M. 1989. Sex differences in earnings in the United States.** *Annual Review of Sociology* **5: 343-380.**

This paper presents a description of the characteristics, size, life course variations, and racial differences in the gender gap in wages. Also included is a detailed consideration of explanatory theories of both supply-side and demand-side approaches.

36   **Meyer, M. H. 1990. Family status and poverty among older women: The gendered distribution of retirement income in the United States.** *Social Problems* **37(4): 551-563.**

This review of U. S. and British feminist works reveal the gendered nature of old-age income schemes. An examination of U. S. programs, specifically Social Security, private pensions, and personal pensions show gender discrimination.

37   **O'Neill, J., and S. Polachek. 1993. Why the gender gap in wages narrowed in the 1980s.** *Journal of Labor Economics* **11(1): 205-228.**

38   **O'Rand, A. M. 1986. The hidden payroll: Employee benefits and the structure of workplace inequality.** *Sociological Forum* **1(4): 657-683.**

O'Rand's analysis supports the argument that fringe benefits combine with earnings to stratify the workplace.

39   **Perman, L., and B. Stevens. 1989. Industrial segregation and the gender distribution of fringe benefits.** *Gender and Society* **3(3): 388-404.**

This paper focuses on fringe benefits (e.g., health coverage) as a factor in gender differences in job rewards. Three models are presented: (1) the direct discrimination model; (2) the occupational segregation model; and (3) the industrial segregation model. Based on the findings, the authors posit that industrial segregation of women workers may be more instrumental in gender differences in work rewards than occupational segregation.

40   **Peterson, R. R. 1989. Firm size, occupational segregation, and the effects of family status on women's wages.** *Social Forces* **68(2): 397-414.**

Peterson examines a structural explanation of family status on women's work outcomes. Using data from the National Longitudinal Surveys of Mature Women, Peterson finds that large firms and male-dominated occupations appear to give promotions and wage increases to single and childless women to a greater extent than their married and married with children counterparts.

41   **Quadagno, J. 1988. Women's access to pensions and the structure of eligibility rules: Systems of production and reproduction.** *Sociological Quarterly* **29(4): 541-558**

A case study of pension negotiation in two unions—the United Auto Workers and the International Ladies Garment Workers Union—presents a historical look at the way rules are structured to penalize women for their reproductive labor.

42   **Quadagno, J. 1988.** *The Transformation of Old Age Security: Class and Politics in the American Welfare State.* **Chicago, IL: The University of Chicago Press.**

43   Quadagno, J., and M. H. Meyer. 1990. **Gender and public policy.** *Generations* **14(3): 64-66.**

This article examines ways that women are penalized through pension structures.

44   Reeves, J. B., and R. L. Darville. 1991. **Gender-related worker characteristics: Their effect on income in a dual-career family.** *Free Inquiry in Creative Sociology* **19(2): 155-159.**

Examines the income of men and women in dual-earner families and gender-related characteristics, (e.g., gender/child, divorce, age, and age at first marriage).

45   Roos, P. A. 1981. **Sex stratification in the workplace: Male-female differences in economic returns to occupation.** *Social Science Research* **10: 195-224.**

46   Shelton, B. A., and J. Firestone. 1988. **An examination of household labor time as a factor in composition and treatment effects on the male-female wage gap.** *Sociological Focus* **21(3): 265-278.**

This study assesses the effects of household labor time on women and men's earnings. The authors conclude that presence of children affects earnings for women more than men.

47   Spalter-Roth, R. M. 1988. *Feminism vs. Familism: Research and Policy for the 1990's.* **Paper presented at the National Council on Family Relations Annual Meeting, Philadelphia, Pennsylvania. Washington, DC: Institute for Women's Policy Research (IWPR).**

Spalter-Roth argues for a feminist based research agenda and offers specific avenues for future research. One suggestion is to deconstruct "the family" as a unit of analysis because its usage masks basic inequalities or problems for women.

48   Spalter-Roth, R. M., and H. I. Hartmann, with C. A. Andrews, L. M. Andrews, M. Danner, and U. Sunkara. 1991. *Increasing Working Mothers' Earnings.* **Washington, DC: Institute for Women's Policy Research (IWPR).**

The researchers hypothesize that socioeconomic trends have impacted working mothers' wages to a greater degree than specific family structures. The study examines the variables of human capital, family characteristics, race/ethnicity, marital status, and education levels on the hourly wages of working mothers.

49   Spalter-Roth, R. M., and H. I. Hartmann, with D. Clearwaters. 1992. Raising women's earnings: The family issue of the 1990s. In *Buying America Back, Economic Choices for the 1990s*, edited by J. Greenberg and W. Kistler. Tulsa, OK: Council Oak Books. 384-397.

This paper connects two trends affecting women's and children's lives, that is, the increase in poverty and the increase in women's labor force participation. The researchers make the point that when the low income wages of women is ignored, then, explanations of changes in family status dominate. Strategies for raising women's economic status are presented.

50   Spalter-Roth, R. M., and Y. H. Yoon. 1995. *Women and Minorities in Telecommunications: An Exception to the Rule: The Mid-Atlantic Region.* Washington, DC: Institute for Women's Policy Research (IWPR).

51   Spalter-Roth, R. M., D. M. Pearce, H. I. Hartmann, L. M. Andrews, and S. Hopkins. 1989. *Low-Wage Jobs and Workers: Trends and Options for Change.* Washington, DC: Institute for Women's Policy Research (IWPR).

This study conducted in 1989 by National Displaced Homemakers Network and Institute for Women's Policy Research examined the prevalence and characteristics of low-wage jobs. In particular, the report focuses on the risks inherent in low-wage employment for women and minorities and the factors that could increase opportunities for them. Recommendations for policies and programs are made.

52   Spalter-Roth, R. M., H. I. Hartmann, and L. M. Andrews. 1990. Mothers, Children, and Low-Wage Work: The Ability to Earn a Family Wage. Selected Papers: 1989 Meeting of the

American Statistical Association. Washington, DC: Institute for Women's Policy Research (IWPR).

This study examines women's wages by race, ethnicity, and children. Using panel data from the 1984 Survey of Income and Program Participation (SIPP), the researches use a logistic regression model to predict factors that will increase the likelihood that women will earn a family wage, that is, a wage substantial enough to support a family of four.

53   Steinberg, R. J. 1995. Gendered instructions: Cultural lag and gender bias in the hay system of job evaluation. In *Gender Inequality at Work*, edited by J. A. Jacobs. Thousand Oaks, CA: Sage Publications. 57-92.

In this chapter, Steinberg critiques the Hay Guide Chart-Profile Method (of job evaluation), and concludes that this commonly used form of job evaluation reflects the cultural assumptions about gender, occupations, and the distribution of wages. The system does not recognize characteristics associated with work that women commonly perform. Steinberg examines an application of the Hay System by looking at public sector jobs in the state of Minnesota. The results indicate a strong male bias.

54   Steinberg, R. J. 1990. Social construction of skill: Gender, power, and comparable worth. *Work and Occupations* 17(4): 449-482.

This paper provides an in-depth description and exploration of the definitions of skill, illustrating how definitions of skill are socially constructed. Further, these "invisible" cultural assumptions have been intricately built into the technical matrices for measuring. Steinberg uses the theoretical and actual practice of comparable worth to expose the subtle gender biases and the power relations inherent in the labor market.

55   Steinberg, R. J. 1986. The debate on comparable worth. *New Politics* Summer: 108-126.

This paper addresses the debate on comparable worth, presents the historical background, and explores the arguments. Three basic arguments against comparable worth are countered: (1) no problem exists; (2) impossible to measure; (3) consequences are dire; and (4) it's not a serious reform. Steinberg also posits that pay equity is both a working class and feminist issue.

56   Steinberg, R. J. 1984. "A want of harmony": Perspectives on wage discrimination and comparable worth. In *Comparable Worth and Wage Discrimination: Technical Possibilities and Political Realities,* edited by H. Remick. Philadelphia, PA: Temple University Press. 3-27.

This chapter presents an historical overview, including identification of recent key events, of wage discrimination, and the policy of comparable worth. Also discussed are the characteristics inherent in wage discrimination; the methodologies used for identifying systematic undervaluation; and the underlying reasons for the fierce opposition to comparable worth.

57   Steinberg, R. J., and L. Haignere. 1987. Equitable compensation: Methodological criteria for comparable worth. In *Ingredients for Women's Employment Policy,* edited by C. Bose and G. Spitze. Albany, NY: State University of New York Press. 157-182.

58   Steinberg, R. J., V. M. MacLean, and H. Smith. *What Do We Know about Women and Pensions and What Do We Need to Know?* Paper presented March 1995 at the Eastern Sociological Society, Philadelphia, PA. Ronnie Steinberg, Temple University, New York.

This working paper critically examines the social organization of both the private and public pension systems focusing on a high-risk population, women, particularly women of color. The stated intent of the paper is to extend past research and to develop a theoretically framed research agenda.

59   Stoper, E. 1991. Women's work, women's movement: Taking stock. *The Annals of the American Academy* 515: 151-162.

This paper discusses policies and programs used to reduce the wage gap: (1) affirmative action; (2) pay equity; and (3) work-family programs. Stoper explores the strategies, then, discusses the implications in context of the women's movement.

60   Stromberg, A. H., and S. Harkess, eds. 1978. *Women Working: Theories and Facts in Perspective.* Palo Alto, CA: Mayfield Publishing.

61   Vallas, S. P. 1990. The concept of skill: A critical review. *Work and Occupations* 17(4): 379-398.

62   Waite, L. J., and S. E. Berryman. 1986. Job stability among young women: A comparison of traditional and nontraditional occupations. *American Journal of Sociology* 92(3): 568-95.

Explores retention in military and in civilian firms of young women employees. The study uses data from the Longitudinal Survey of Youth Labor Market Behavior to examine career mobility of young women in nontraditional occupations.

63   Wellington, A. J. 1994. Accounting for the male/female wage gap among whites: 1976 and 1985. *American Sociological Review* 59: 839-848.

The effects of differences in employment history and training on the wage gap are examined using data from the Panel Study of Income Dynamics. Interview data from the 1976 and 1985 waves concerning employment history and on the job training are drawn to examine human capital differences between white men and white women. The author concludes than human capital theory alone can not explain the differences.

64   Woods, J. 1986. Summaries of recent research: Working women and pensions. *Social Security Bulletin* 49(5): 33-34.

65   Woody, B. 1992. Wages and Benefits. In *Black Women in the Workplace: Impacts of Structural Change in the Economy.* New York: Greenwood Press. 93-125.

In this chapter, Woody examines the effects of industry and sector hiring patterns on black women's wages. Following a theoretical and research review on wage variation, the chapter addresses the growth of nonwage compensation and part-time work.

66   Yoon, Y. H., R. M. Spalter-Roth, and M. Baldwin.   1995. *Unemployment Insurance: Barriers to Access for Women and Part-Time Workers.* Research Report No. 95-06. Washington, DC: National Commission for Employment Policy.

This report provides a historical background of Unemployment Insurance (UI) and identifies barriers and eligibility characteristics for individuals.

CHAPTER 2

Sex Segregation/Occupation Segregation/Glass Ceiling

67   Amott, T., and J. A. Matthaei. 1991. *Race, Gender and Work: A Multicultural Economic History of Women in the United States.* Boston, MA: South End Press.

This book traces women's work lives through capitalist development. In addition to providing a broad overview of the contributions of women's work to U.S. economic history, the economic histories of major racial-ethnic groups are treated separately.

68   Baron, J. N., A. Davis-Blake, and W. T. Bielby. 1986. The structure of opportunity: How promotion ladders vary within and among organizations. *Administrative Science Quarterly* 31: 248-273.

An analysis of data describing jobs in 100 California firms suggest that job ladders are linked to firm-specific skill, the interests of unions, and the institutional environment. The authors conclude that the results indicate that gender influences the clustering of jobs, and the position of those jobs, in the promotion ladders. Recommendations for future research are made.

69   Bielby, W. T. 1991. The structure and process of sex segregation. In *New Approaches to Economic and Social Analyses of Discrimination,* edited by R. R. Cornwall and P. V. Wunnava. New York: Praeger Publishers. 97-112.

70   Bielby, W. T., and J. N. Baron. 1984. A woman's place is with other women: Sex segregation within organizations. In *Sex Segregation in the Workplace: Trends, Explanations, Remedies,* edited by B F. Reskin. Washington, DC: National Academy Press. 27-55.

This chapter examines the manner in which sex segregation is achieved in various institutions. The researchers analyzed data from over 500 firms and determined that the size of the organization is important because almost all large organizations are sex-segregated. Small businesses, however, are also segregated by sex which is established and maintained by patriarchal control.

71   Blum, T. C., D. L. Fields, and J. S. Goodman.   1994. Organization-level determinants of women in management. *Academy of Management Journal*   37(2): 241-268.

Resource dependence and institutional theories underpin the rationales for promoting or hiring women into management positions. Specifically, the study examines the association of organizational characteristics that influence the number of women placed in management positions in over 200 workplaces in Georgia. Support for the theoretical underpinnings of the study were found. The organizational level is where the primary gender segregation differences occur.

72   Brown, C., and J. A. Pechman, eds.   1987.   *Gender in the Workplace.* Washington, DC: Brookings Institution.

73   Cabral, R., M. A. Ferber, and C. A. Green. 1981. Men and women in fiduciary institutions: A study of sex differences in career development. *The Review of Economics and Statistics*   63(4): 573-580.

Examines differentials of women and men in fiduciary institutions. The results show that although the male employees have more education and experience, the difference does not account for the size of the differential in terms of career development.

74   Cockburn, C. 1991. In the Way of Women: Men's Resistance to Sex Equality in Organizations. Ithaca, NY: ILR Press.

A feminist perspective frames this examination of four organizational case studies. Interview data were gathered from males, females, blacks, gays, people with disabilities within the organizations and without regarding "equality policies."

Chapter six specifically addresses ethnicity and racism. The thematic findings of this qualitative study are discussed.

75   DiPrete, T. A. 1989. *The Bureaucratic Labor Market: The Case of the Federal Civil Service.* New York: Plenum Press.

76   DiPrete, T. A. 1987. Horizontal and vertical mobility in organizations. *Administrative Science Quarterly* 32: 422-444.

DiPrete considers the filling of vacancies in four bureaus of the federal government on career trajectories and the constraints of job ladders. Overall, employees most likely to get the job were on the same job ladder and division. The study showed boundary crossing did occur within bureaucratized organizations; there was a significant relationship between grade and boundary crossing.

77   DiPrete, T. A., and W. T. Soule. 1988. Gender and promotion in segmented job ladder systems. *American Sociological Review* 53: 26-40.

This paper discusses gender differences in promotion rates within a highly bureaucratized white collar labor market. An analysis of the promotion rates in the federal civil service (during the middle 1970s) reveal that the greatest difference in promotion rates for females occurred at the boundary between the lower- and upper-tier grades. Findings and policy implications are discussed.

78   Gaskell, J. 1986. Conceptions of skill and the work of women: Some historical and political issues. In *The Politics of Diversity: Feminism, Marxism and Nationalism,* edited by R. Hamilton and M. Barrett. Canada: Book Center. 361-380.

The focus of this chapter is on training of women. Gaskell describes how some male workers get restricted and lengthy apprenticeships, while women's training is short and widely available. The process illustrates how training programs create skill. Hence skill, Gaskell argues, is a political process.

79   Haignere, L., and R. J. Steinberg. 1989. Nontraditional training for women: Effective programs, structural barriers, and

political hurdles. In *Job Training for Women: The Promise and Limits of Public Policy*, edited by S. L. Harlan and R. J. Steinberg. Philadelphia, PA: Temple University Press. 333-358.

This study focuses on Comprehensive Employment and Training Act (CETA) funded programs and their impact on women's entry into nontraditional occupations. The authors identify factors that maintain occupational segregation, such as men's resistance, inequalities that women bring to the labor market, and structural barriers.

80   Harlan, S. L., and B. O'Farrell. 1982. After the pioneers: Prospects for women in nontraditional blue-collar jobs. *Work and Occupations* 9(3): 363-386.

This study examines success of job integration after the pioneering movements in the 1970s. Organizational changes are studied using data from an industrial firm study: (1) interview data with 75 blue-collar employees and 27 union officials; (2) survey data from 388 blue-collar respondents; and (3) plantwide data on employment status and job classifications of workers.

81   Harlan, S. L., and R. J. Steinberg, eds. 1989. *Job Training for Women: The Promise and Limits of Public Policies.* Philadelphia, PA: Temple University Press.

82   Hartmann, H. I. 1990. Capitalism, patriarchy, and job segregation by sex. In *Women, Class, and the Feminist Imagination: A Socialist-Feminist Women Reader*, edited by K. V. Hansen and I. J. Philipson. Philadelphia, PA: Temple University Press. 146-181.

Within the context of an historical and anthropological framework, Hartmann examines the division of labor by sex. The basic thesis of the paper is that capitalism and patriarchy are intertwined after years of coexistence. The point is also made that gender division of labor is psychologically internalized.

83   Jacobs, J. A., ed. 1995. *Gender Inequality at Work.* Thousand Oaks, CA: Sage Publications.

84   Jones, E. B., and J. D. Jackson. 1992. **Gender differences in business school graduates' opportunity to advance.** *Journal of Socio-Economics* 21(2): 125-141.

This study examines differences between men and women (in the early work-life opportunities for promotion) using survey data from a sample of 801 business graduates five years after graduation from a large southern state university. Findings show men reported more optimism than women about their opportunities for advancement. Differences by occupation occurred when women spent less time on the job than men. The authors urge that the time dimension (i.e., weekly work hours) be considered when looking at differences in labor market attachment.

85   Kaestner, R. 1994. **Some empirical evidence on the use of gender specific promotion rules.** *Eastern Economic Journal* 20(2): 201-218.

Kaestner examines the glass ceiling phenomenon by exploring the Lazaer and Rosen (1990) 'jobs' theory of discrimination. A test of the model supports the model, that is, the firm considers the employee's probability of leaving the firm when making decisions. The author concludes that this phenomenon may not be discriminatory; rather it is a decision based on productivity criteria.

86   Kessler-Harris, A. 1988. **The just price, the free market, and the value of women.** *Feminist Studies* 14(2): 235-250.

This edited volume addresses issues from the gender gap in wages, authority, and sex segregation.

87   King, M. C. 1992. **Occupational segregation by race and gender, 1940-1980.** *Monthly Labor Review* 115: 30-37.

88   Loscocco, K. A., and J. G. Robinson. 1991. **Barriers to women's small-business success in the United States.** *Gender and Society* 5(4): 511-532.

The authors examination of women in small business revealed that women-owned businesses are nested within traditionally female-typed fields. Not only do female-typed businesses generate smaller profits, but even within the same type, women-owned businesses make less. Women, the authors conclude, experience the same labor market disadvantages and institutional barriers.

89   Markham, W. T., and J. H. Pleck. 1986. **Sex and willingness to move for occupational advancement: Some national sample results.** *Sociological Quarterly* **27(1): 121-143.**

This study found that sex differences continue to explain willingness to move for occupational advancement. Women were less willing to move for advancement.

90   Markham, W. T., S. J. South, C. M. Bonjean, and J. Corder. 1985. **Gender and opportunity in the federal bureaucracy.** *American Journal of Sociology* **91(1): 129-150.**

91   Matthaei, J. A. 1982. *An Economic History of Women in America: Women's Work, the Sexual Division of Labor, and the Development of Capitalism.* **New York: Schocken Books.**

92   McGuire, G. M., and B. F. Reskin. 1993. **Authority hierarchies at work: The impacts of race and sex.** *Gender and Society* **7(4):487-506.**

Using 1980 survey data for 1,216 employed workers, the researchers examine how sex and race affect access to and rewards for skill, effort, and responsibility. The authors note their analysis focuses on black women. The study found significant race interaction for both black men and women. The authors conclude that employers failed to reward black women at the same level as white men and women.

93   Morrison, A. M., and M. A. Von Glinow. 1990. **Women and minorities in management.** *American Psychologist* **45(2): 200-208.**

This extensive review of the literature encompasses theoretical perspectives from multiple disciplines covering individual and systemic factors. Current data on the status of women and minorities in management is presented. Additionally, the authors outline remedies for the glass ceiling and offer research directions to pursue.

94   Morrison, A. M., R. P. White, E. Van Velsor, and The Center for Creative Leadership. 1987. *Breaking the Glass Ceiling: Can Women Reach the Top of America's Largest Corporations?* Reading, MA: Addison-Wesley .

Morrison and colleagues present and examine interview data from 76 women managers in 25 Fortune 100 sized companies.

95   Ohlott, P. J., M. N. Ruderman, and C. D. McCauley. 1994. Gender differences in managers' developmental job experiences. *Academy of Management Journal* 37(1): 46-67.

96   Olson, C. A., and B. E. Becker. 1983. Sex discrimination in the promotion process. *Industrial and Labor Relations Review* 36(4): 624-641.

Olson and Becker compare the earnings and promotion experiences of men and women drawing on longitudinal interview data at two time periods, 1973 and again in 1977, from the Quality of Employment Panel. The authors report the results and conclude that promotion process is a determinate in the wage gap between men and women.

97   Olson, J. E., I. H. Frieze, and E. G. Detlefsen. 1990. Having it all? Combining work and family in a male and a female profession. *Sex Roles* 23(9/10): 515-533.

A comparison of a female-dominated profession (MLAs) (i.e., women librarians) and a male-dominated profession (MBAs), focuses on the difficulties of combining work and family obligations. This study compares the family status and professional careers of 449 women MBAs and 747 women MLAs. The authors observe that the study reveals few differences in the ability of the two professional groups in combining work and family, although MBAs experienced somewhat more difficulty.

98   Perry, E. L., A. Davis-Blake, and C. T. Kulik. 1994. Explaining gender-based selection decisions: A synthesis of contextual and

cognitive approaches. *Academy of Management Review* 19(4): 786-820.

Personnel selection in organizations are examined in this study. The authors integrate two explanations, cognitive (i.e., schemas) and contextual (e.g., characteristics of groups in and out of company applicant pools). The authors argue that the persistence of gender segregation may be related to the interaction between contextual features and schemas. Implications for research are discussed.

99   Phelan, J., E. J. Bromet, J. E. Schwartz, M. A. Dew, and E. C. Curtis. 1993. **The work environments of male and female professionals: Objective and subjective characteristics.** *Work and Occupations* 20(1): 68-89.

This study examines the relationships among subjective job characteristics of male and female employees to objective job characteristics, such as family circumstances and personality characteristics. Interview data from 1,115 male and 271 female professional employees of a technology-based corporation were analyzed using multiple regression equations. For both men and women, the factors associated with subjective job characteristics were similar. However, reports of objective job characteristics varied on earnings and authority.

100   Powell, G. N., and D. A. Butterfield. 1994. **Investigating the "glass ceiling" phenomenon: An empirical study of actual promotions to top management.** *Academy of Management Journal* 37(1) 68-86.

This study presents an analysis of the records of 258 applicants for 32 senior management positions in a cabinet-level department of the U. S. federal government. An examination of promotion decisions reveals that women received significantly higher performance ratings, evaluations, and referrals than men.

101   Ratner, R. S. 1981. *Barriers to Advancement: Promotion of Women and Minorities into Managerial Positions in New York State Government.* **Albany, NY: Center for Women in Government at the State University of Albany.**

This study identifies the institutional barriers to advancement of women and minorities in the four-stage promotion process in the state of New York. The primary institutional barrier was the lack of eligibility to compete for promotions.

102   **Ratner, R. S., ed. 1980.** *Equal Employment Policy for Women: Strategies for Implementation in the United States, Canada, and Western Europe.* **Philadelphia, PA: Temple University Press.**

103   **Reskin, B. F. 1988. Bringing the men back in: Sex differentiation and the devaluation of women's work.** *Gender and Society* **2(1): 58-81.**

Reskin argues that men's desire to maintain their hegemony is the cause of the wage gap and job segregation, therefore strategies of sex-integrating jobs and comparable worth are doomed to fail because men control the rewards. The causal model of the traditional explanations of the wage gap and job segregation are critiqued from a methodological stance on Lieberson's critique of causal analysis. Reskin concludes her analysis with a call for political solutions.

104   **Reskin, B. F., and H. I. Hartmann, eds.** *1986. Women's Work, Men's Work: Sex Segregation on the Job.* **Washington, DC: National Academy Press.**

This report examines the effects of occupational segregation and presents evidence from case studies and empirical analyses to substantiate ways to reduce sex segregation in the workplace.

105   **Reskin, B. F., and I. Padavic. 1994.** *Women and Men at Work.* **Thousand Oaks, CA: Pine Forge Press.**

106   **Reskin, B. F., and P. A. Roos. 1990.** *Job Queues, Gender Queues: Explaining Women's Inroads into Male Occupations.* **Philadelphia, PA: Temple University Press.**

107   **Reskin, B. F., ed. 1984.** *Sex Segregation in the Workplace: Trends, Explanations, Remedies.* **Washington, DC: National Academy Press.**

108   Robinson, J. G., and J. S. Mcilwee. 1989. **Women in engineering: A promise unfulfilled?** *Social Problems* **36(5): 455-472.**

Compares a cohort of female and male engineers across two engineering specialities, mechanical and electrical, in both the aerospace and high tech industries. An examination of job status reveals that women held fewer high status jobs, even though they were similar to men on educational variables and time on the job. A structural and interactional perspective informs the authors' report of the findings.

109   Roos, P. A., and B. F. Reskin. 1992. **Occupational desegregation in the 1970s: Integration and economic equity?** *Sociological Perspectives* **35(1): 69-91.**

Internal labor market theory guides an analysis of workplace mechanisms that act as barriers to women's entry into traditional male occupations. The authors use case studies of fourteen occupations that became feminized to show that women gained access to them because the occupations were less attractive to men. Additionally, the authors suggest that in occupations where the wage gap declined, the reason was a decline in men's real earnings, not an increase in women's earnings.

110   Rosenbaum, J. E. 1984. *Career Mobility in a Corporate Hierarchy.* Orlando, FL: Academic Press.

111   Rosenbaum, J. E. 1979. **Tournament mobility: Career patterns in a corporation.** *Administrative Science Quarterly* **24(2): 220-241.**

This examination of career mobility describes two conflicting models of mobility: (1) the path independence model which is an ahistorical model; and (2) the tournament model which is a historical model. Rosenbaum's analysis of the career mobility of a cohort of employees over a 13 year period supports the tournament model. The analyses, as Rosenbaum notes, indicate that the initial period in an employee's career is an important selection period.

112   Rosenfeld, R. A. 1980. Race and sex differences in career dynamics. *American Sociological Review* 45: 583-609.

113   Rossi, A. S. 1965. Barriers to the career choice of engineering, medicine or science among American women. In *Women in the Scientific Professions*, edited by J. A. Matfield and C. G. Van Aken. Cambridge, MA: MIT Press. 51-127.

This paper presents an overview of women's positions in the fields of engineering, medicine, and science. Also included is a report of women college graduates who have chosen careers in fields traditionally male.

114   Schneer, J. A., and Reitman, F. 1994. The importance of gender in mid-career: A longitudinal study of MBAs. *Journal of Organizational Behavior* 15: 199-207.

This longitudinal study surveyed women and men MBAs in 1984 and 1990. Statistical analyses reveal no gender differences in early careers. However by mid-career, women experienced a less supportive work environment (e.g., lower income, lower reports of career satisfaction, and lower appreciation from boss).

115   Schwartz, D. B. 1995. *An Examination of the Impact of Family-Friendly Policies on the Glass Ceiling.* New York: Family and Work Institute.

This monograph explores the relationship between the glass ceiling and family-friendly policies, (e.g., flexible work arrangements, leaves, and dependent care benefits. Debra Schwartz integrates data with a review of the literature, as well as analyzing data from the National Study of the Changing Workforce. Research findings are reported on (1) the use of leaves and flexible work arrangements; (2) the career impact of using leaves and flexible work arrangements; and (3) the influence of supervisors and corporate culture on the use of policies. Responds to the "mommy track" debate.

116   Schwartz, F. N. 1989. Management women and the new facts of life. *Harvard Business Review* 67: 65-74.

This is the article that ignited the "mommy track" debate. Felice Schwartz posits that companies must address the "immutable enduring difference between men and women," that is, pregnancy, childbirth, and motherhood. Some women are career-primary, or willing to make the same trade-offs as men, but most women are career-family, that is, they desire both family and career. Schwartz, therefore, suggests that businesses distinguish between the two types of women and provide appropriate tracks for each.

117   Shepela, S. T., and A. T. Viviano. 1984. **Some psychological factors affecting job segregation and wages.** In *Comparable Worth and Wage Discrimination: Technical Possibilities,* edited by H. Remick. **Philadelphia, PA: Temple University Press. 47-58.**

In this chapter, the authors argue that women earn less because women's work is characterized as less valuable in our society simply because it is done by women. Citing anthropological and sociological data, the researchers explore this psychological argument and conclude that there are "... deeply ingrained, pervasive psychological biases that affect decisions made about the competence and work of women."

118   Snyder, N. M. 1994. **Career women in perspective: The Wichita Sample.** In *Women and Careers: Issues and Challenges,* edited by C. W. Konek and S. L. Kitch. **Thousand Oaks, CA: Sage Publications. 1-18.**

This chapter presents an economic and demographic profile of young women in nontraditional careers drawn from the Wichita Sample. The analysis reveals that more young women are becoming better educated and entering professional and managerial careers. Snyder notes the importance of studying this group for several research related reasons: (1) for young women, occupational segregation is decreasing; and (2) the labor force will be increasingly female.

119   Sokoloff, N. J. 1992. *Black Women and White Women in the Professions: Occupational Segregation by Race and Gender, 1960-1980.* **New York: Routledge.**

120   Spalter-Roth, R. M, and H. I. Hartmann. 1990. *Raises and Recognition: Secretaries, Clerical Workers and the Union Wage Premium.* Washington, DC: Institute for Women's Policy Research (IWPR).

This article focuses on the low wages of undervalued secretarial and clerical occupations that have recently benefited from "union premium to wages." This study examines the wage benefits of unionization.

121   Steinberg, R. J. 1994. Pay equity in nonprofit organizations: Making women's work visible. In *Women, Status, and Power in the NonProfit Sector,* edited by M. O'Neill and T. Odendahl. New York: John Wiley and Sons.

122   Steinberg, R. J., L. Haignere, and C. H. Chertos.   1990. Managerial promotions in the public sector: The impact of eligibility requirements on women and minorities. *Work and Occupations* 17(3): 284-301.

This study examines the institutional barriers blocking the managerial advancement of women and minorities in the New York State government work force. Steinberg and colleagues analyze two sources of data related to the promotional process: (1) a data set of individuals promoted through a formal competitive examination process; and (2) a data set of individuals promoted through non-examination administration transfer.   Unlike previous studies, findings indicate that eligibility requirements constitute the primary institutional barrier to the promotion of women and minorities. Moreover, findings suggest that internal labor markets "define" and "constrain" career paths.

123   Steinberg, R. J., L. Haignere, S. Petersen-Hardt, and H. Smith. Forthcoming.   Career ladders and promotion: A structural analysis.   In *Women's Careers: Research and Strategies for Change,* edited by R. J. Steinberg and S. Harlan.

124   Stover, D. L. 1994. The horizontal distribution of female managers within organizations. *Work and Occupations* 21(4): 385-402.

This study investigates the factors that influence horizontal distribution of female managers within organizations on a sample of 99 university departments from two universities in the Northwest. Archival and survey data were collected on the following independent variables: (1) departmental power; (2) departmental growth; (3) departmental founding period; (4) gender of previous manager; and (5) departmental proportion of female nonmanagerial workers. Findings reveal women work in different departmental contexts than their male counterparts.

125   **Strober, M. H. 1984. Toward a general theory of occupational sex segregation: The case of public school teaching.** In *Sex Segregation in the Workplace: Trends, Explanations, Remedies,* edited by B. F. Reskin. **Washington, DC: National Academy Press. 144-156.**

Strober describes a theory of occupational segregation within paid employment. It is the interaction of patriarchy and utility maximization by the male workers' that explains how an occupation becomes gendered, how it maintains that gender primacy, and how occupations can change. Strober uses the case of public school teaching in the nineteenth century to illustrate the theory.

126   **Tharenou, P., S. Latimer, and D. Conroy. 1994. How do you make it to the top? An examination of influences on women's and men's managerial advancement.** *Academy of Management Journal* **37(4): 899-931.**

The researchers investigated the differences in managerial advancement between men and women. Models of situational and individual influences were tested on a sample of 513 female and 501 male managers in Australian public and private organizations. Confirmatory modeling showed that separate models by gender were most revealing. Although training and development (and work experience) predict women's managerial advancement, the effect is greater for men.

127   **Tomaskovic-Devey, D. 1993.** *Gender and Racial Inequality at Work: The Sources and Consequences of Job Segregation.* **Ithaca, NY: ILR Press.**

128   Ward, K. 1990. *Women Workers and Global Restructuring.* Ithaca, NY: ILR Press.

129   White, R. W., and R. P. Althauser. 1984. Internal labor markets, promotions, and worker skill: An indirect test of skill ILMs. *Social Science Research* 13: 373-392.

This study investigates the determinants of promotions in the commercial banking industry using data from job histories of 193 employees of a large metropolitan bank and 64 employees of a smaller bank, both were in the Midwest. The authors contrast their findings with those of Baron and Bielby (1980). The finding suggest that in skill internal labor markets, promotions will be a positive function of employees' duration. The study shows that for men, movement up the job ladders are associated with the development of worker skill.

130   Williams, C. L. 1992. The glass escalator: Hidden advantages for men in the "female" professions. *Social Problems* 39(3): 253-267.

Williams examines the question of whether men are discriminated against in the hiring and promotion practices in four predominately female professions, (i.e., nursing, social work, elementary school teaching, and librianship). Additionally, the research focuses on the workplace culture and interactions with clients and those on the "outside." Interview data were gathered from 76 men and 23 women in the four occupations in four metropolitan areas representing variation in the proportions of men in the field. The study found men were not discriminated against, rather they experienced structural advantages. However, the men experienced prejudice from those outside the profession.

131   Williams, C. L. 1989. *Gender Differences at Work: Women and Men in Nontraditional Occupations.* Berkeley, CA: University of California Press.

132   Woody, B. 1995. *Women Corporate Directors and New England Companies.* Special report CRW 11. Wellesley, MA: Center for Research on Women at Wellesley College.

Woody summarizes the results of a survey of 33 women corporate directors and 66 women CEOs in major New England companies. Women directors, the survey found, are less likely than men to head companies than male directors. However, the survey showed that the number of women directors has increased over the last decade and women "hold a stronger position on New England boards than the nation as a whole."

133   **Zimmer, L. 1988. Tokenism and women in the workplace: The limits of gender-neutral theory.** *Social Problems* **35(1): 64-77.**

Zimmer assesses the value of the concept "tokenism" as an explanation for women's occupational problems. Following a critical review of the research concerning tokenism, Zimmer concludes that "tokenism" is of little value, primarily because the concept neglects the broad structural and cultural systemization of gender inequality.

CHAPTER 3

Women's Employment and Well-Being

134   Barnett, R. C., H. Davidson, and N. L. Marshall.   1991.
       Physical symptoms and the interplay of work and family roles.
       Health Psychology 10(2): 94-101.

This study focuses on the quality of work and family roles for
403 employed women (social workers or licensed nurses) and the
relationship with mental health. Quality of work roles was
assessed by a rewards and concerns scale and operationalized as
the difference between the two. Work concerns, such as
overload, were associated with reported physical symptoms.
However work rewards, such as helping others at work, were
associated with low levels of physical symptoms. The
researchers emphasize the importance of studying the absence
of work rewards, not just studying job concerns.

135   Barnett, R. C., N. L. Marshall, and J. D. Singer. 1992. Job
       experiences over time, multiple roles, and women's mental
       health: A longitudinal study. *Journal of Personality and
       Social Psychology* 62(4): 634-644.

The relationships between job role quality (i.e., the balance of
rewards and concerns) and mental health or psychological
distress were examined. Data from a 2-year 3-wave study of a
sample of 403 employed women were used to study the changes
of job role quality at three points in time. The findings on job
role quality varied by family status. For example, when job role
quality decreased over time, single women and women without
children   reported   experiencing   increased   psychological
distress; whereas married women with children did not.

136   Gray, E. B., M. C. Lovejoy, C. S. Piotrkowski, and J. T. Bond.
       1990. Husband supportiveness and the well-being of employed

mothers of infants. *Families in Society: The Journal of Contemporary Human Services* 71(6): 332-341.

Based on a secondary analysis of Mothers in the Workplace project, this study examines the relationship of husbands' supportiveness and wive's well-being. The researchers operationalized well-being with two scales: (1) stress and coping; and (2) life satisfaction. Reports of well-being were significantly related to wife's perceptions of husband supportiveness.

137   Kibria, N., R. C. Barnett, G. K. Baruch, N. L. Marshall, and J, H. Pleck. 1990. **Homemaking-role quality and the psychological well-being and distress of employed women.** *Sex Roles* 22(5/6): 327-347.

The researchers examine the relationship between quality of the homemaking role (and quality of the work role) with the psychological well-being of 403 women employed as social workers or licensed practical nurses. The women reported rewarding aspects of homemaking (e.g., having other people enjoy your home) and distressing aspects (e.g., work is never done). Overall, the results indicate that women view the homemaking role more positively than negatively. Further, the study found that when homemaking experiences were positive, psychological well-being increased.

138   Lerner, J. V., and N. L. Galambos. 1988. **The influences of maternal employment across life: The New York Longtitudinal Study.** In *Maternal Employment and Children's Development: Longitudinal Research*, edited by A. E. Gottfried and A. W. Gottfried. New York: Plenum Press. 59-83.

Data drawn from the New York Longitudinal Study provide the researchers with the opportunity to examine the influences of the mother's employment on child's development from the early life stages of infancy, adolescence, and through early adulthood. This chapter presents a sampling of the available data and the findings.

139   Marshall, N. L., and R. C. Barnett. 1992. **Work-related support among women in caregiving occupations.** *Journal of Community Psychology* 20: 36-42.

This research examined a model of job stress and work-related support for women using data from the third year of a longitudinal study (n = 362 women employed as social workers or licensed practical nurses). Job stress was measured in terms of job demands, that is, concerns about workload and emotional demands. The study found a direct effect for work-related support on employed women's mental and physical health. On the other hand, there was no support for work-related support as a buffer for job demands on health.

140   **Martikainen, P. 1995. Women's employment, marriage, motherhood and mortality: A test of the multiple role and role accumulation hypotheses.** *Social Science and Medicine* **40(2): 199-212.**

This study analyzes the effects of combining women's employment, marriage, and motherhood on mortality. The analysis is based on data from the 1980 census records in Finland during the period 1981-1985. The census records are linked with mortality records. The study finds that women with three simultaneous roles (i.e., employee, spouse, and mother) had lower mortality rates.

141   **Miller, M. L., P. Moen, and D. Dempster-McClain. 1991. Motherhood, multiple roles, and maternal well-being: Women of the 1950s.** *Gender and Society* **5(4): 565-582.**

This study focuses on the psychological well-being and the number of roles women occupy. A secondary analysis of data drawn from a 1956 archive assessed the effects of number of roles on a sample of 358 married mothers with children under age 13. The results indicate that number of roles, in addition to wife and mother, are positively related to psychological well-being (i.e., self-esteem and life satisfaction). However, the results also indicate that the paid worker role was related to maternal discontent and maternal inadequacy.

142   Moen, P. 1992. Women's Two Roles: A Contemporary Dilemma. New York: Auburn House Publishing.

143   Ozer, E. M. 1995. The impact of childcare responsibility and self-efficacy on the psychological health of professional working mothers. *Psychological of Women Quarterly* 19(3): 315-335.

Ozer investigated how child care responsibility and self-efficacy relate to a new mother's psychological well-being. The sample consisted of 42 married women who recently gave birth to their first child and returned to work full-time. These mothers were of similar professional status as their husbands and contributed approximately half of the family income. The study found that child care responsibilities were related to greater psychological distress. However, a sense of efficacy or mastery over the responsibilities mediated the distress.

144   Repetti, R. L., K. A. Matthews, and I. Waldron. 1989. Effects of paid employment on women's mental and physical health. *American Psychologist* 44(11): 1394-1401.

This article reviews the empirical research and longitudinal data on the effects of paid employment on women's health. Also addressed are intervening variables that might contribute to the effects of employment on health (e.g., social support, overload, job demands, and multiple role strain). The authors raise methodological issues and offer recommendations for future research.

145   Schwartzberg, N. S., and R. S. Dytell. 1988. Family stress and psychological well-being among employed and non-employed mothers. In *Journal of Social Behavior and Personality: Work and Family: Theory, Research, and Applications*, edited by E. B. Goldsmith. Corte Madera, CA: Select Press. 175-190.

This study assesses family stress and psychological well being in two groups of mothers (n = 94 employed, 68 nonemployed). Psychological well-being was measured by scales of depression, self-esteem, and psychological disturbances. Results indicate no significant difference on psychological well-being for the two groups. For unemployed mothers, however, stress from family roles and the specific stress of nonchallenge accounted for a greater proportion of the variance.

146   Spitze, G. 1995. **Women's employment and family relations: A review.** In *The Work and Family Interface: Toward a Contextual Effects Perspective,* edited by G. L. Bowen and J. F. Pittman. Minneapolis, MN: National Council on Family Relations. 230-250.

This article reviews the more recent research literature concerning the effects of women's employment on families. Spitz observes that research in general focuses on differences by employment status, rather than focusing on characteristics of particular employment experience. Spitz also laments the lack of research on minority, working-class, and single-parent families. Areas of review addressed by Spitz include: (1) marital quality and spouses' well-being; (2) family work and power; (3) combined effects of husbands' and wives' employment; and (4) effects of employment status on children. Spitz recommends future research topics.

147   Voydanoff, P. 1987. **Women's work, family, and health.** In *Working Woman: Past, Present, Future,* edited by K. S. Koziara, M. H. Moskow, and L. D. Tanner. Washington, DC: Bureau of National Affairs. 69-96.

Voydanoff reviews and synthesizes research on the effects of work on health and family life among married women who have children. Voydanoff also reviews the outcome data on the following: (1) the effects of work-role characteristics on health and family life of employed women; and (2) the combined effects of husbands' and wives' work-role characteristics on family life.

148   Waldron, I., and J. A. Jacobs. 1989. **Effects of multiple roles on women's health--evidence from a national longitudinal study.** *Women and Health* 15(1): 3-19.

Waldron and Jacobs draw from the National Longitudinal Surveys of Labor Market Experience, utilizing data from the 1977-1982 interval to comprise a sample of 2,392 white women and 890 black women. The researchers examine the women's initial role status and change in health. Regression analyses indicate that multiple roles did not contribute to women's poor health. Conversely, the authors conclude that involvement in multiple roles generally led to better health. Some differences by race are reported.

149   Weatherall, R., H. Joshi, and S. Macran. 1994. **Double burden or double blessing? Employment, motherhood and mortality in the longitudinal study of England and Wales.** *Social Science Medicine* **38(2): 285-297.**

Investigates the effect of combining two roles, motherhood and paid worker, on women's mortality. The study draws on data from the OPCS Longitudinal Study, which is a dataset linking census records to death registrations. The analysis is guided by two theoretical perspectives, role overload and role enhancement. The researchers conclude that whatever the effects of combining the two roles, they did not lead to an early death. Results also showed that unemployed women with no children experienced poorer health.

150   Wethington, E., and R. C. Kessler. 1989. **Employment, parental responsibility, and psychological distress: A longitudinal study of married women.** *Journal of Family Issues* **10(4): 527-546.**

The researchers studied the mental health effects of employment and parenting status changes, at two time periods, using panel data from 745 married women. Change in employment status was measured as movement from homemaker to full-time worker from Time 1 to Time 2. Also examined was change in parental status, for example, giving birth, from Time 1 to Time 2. The study found that women who increased labor force participation reported lower levels of psychological distress, whereas women who decreased their labor force participation reported higher levels of psychological distress.

151   Wolfer, L. T., and P. Moen. *Staying in School: Maternal Employment and the Timing of Black and White Daughters' School Exit.* **Unpublished paper. L. T. Wolfer, Department of Sociology, Rowan College of New Jersey, Glassboro, NJ 08028**

and P. Moen, Brofenbrenner Life Course Center, Cornell University, Ithaca, NY 14853.

This longitudinal study examines the influences of maternal employment on daughters during three stages of the child's life: (1) early childhood; (2) preadolescence; and (3) adolescence. The researchers draw on data from the 1968-1990 waves of the Panel Study of Income Dynamics to constitute a sample of 246 white and 188 black daughters. The basic research question is how temporal and status characteristics of mother's jobs affect the rate that daughters leave school. Results indicate maternal employment does not influence white daughters decision to remain in school. However, maternal employment at any point in childhood increases the likelihood that black daughters will stay in school.

CHAPTER 4

Women's Employment and Effect on Children
(annotated by Irene Fassler)

152   Armistead, L., M. Wierson, and R. Forehand.   1990.
Adolescents and maternal employment: Is it harmful for a
young adolescent to have an employed mother? *Journal of
Early Adolescence* **10(3): 260-278.**

The effect of maternal employment on adolescent
development was explored using a sample of 63 young
adolescents. A second sample of 96 young adolescents
underwent a maternal and paternal prestige rating. No
differences in adolescent functioning or the mother-adolescent
relationship were noted for employed or nonemployed
mothers. Further, while the prestige of father's employment
predicted adolescent functioning, the prestige of mother's
employment did not.

153   **Chase-Lansdale, P. L.   1994.   Families and maternal
employment during infancy: New linkages. In *Exploring
Family Relationships with other Social Contexts*, edited by
R. D. Parke and S. G. Kellam.   Hillsdale, NJ: Lawrence
Erlbaum Associates.   29-47.**

The author presents the conclusions of several teams of
investigations who analyzed data from the National
Longitudinal Survey of Youth and applied it to topics such as
maternal employment, child care and interventions. In
addition, the author reviews research in child care and
intervention programs (e.g., early childhood education
programs and employment training programs). Suggestions for
future research are made.

154   **Crockenberg, S., and C. Litman. 1991. Effects of maternal
employment on maternal and two-year-old child behavior.**
Child Development **62: 930-953.**

Interviews and observations of 94 mothers and their two-year-old children regarding maternal employment, role satisfaction, and social support are analyzed. The findings indicate that specific aspects of work and family contexts influence the nature of the impact of maternal and child behavior. For instance, role satisfaction and social supports have a greater positive effect on parenting for employed than nonemployed mothers.

155   Crouter, A. C., and S. M. McHale. 1993. The long arm of the job: Influences of parental work on childrearing. In *Parenting: An Ecological Perspective,* edited by T. Luster and L. Okagaki. 179-202.

The authors observe that research concerning employment and parenting are driven by multiple perspectives. Following a critical review of these diverse approaches, noting their strengths and frontiers, the authors suggest a synthesis.

156   Gottfried, A. E., and A. W. Gottfried, eds. 1988. *Maternal Employment and Children's Development: Longitudinal Research.* New York: Plenum Press.

157   Greenstein, T. N. 1995. Are the "most advantaged" children truly disadvantaged by early maternal employment? Effects on child cognitive outcomes. *Journal of Family Issues* 16(2): 149-169.

The data analysis is drawn from the National Longitudinal Survey of Youth (n = 2,040). The study examines the effects of early maternal employment on the cognitive ability of 4 to 6 year olds. The findings suggest that maternal employment during early childhood does not negatively affect the cognitive abilities of children.

158   Heyns, B., and S. Catsambis. 1986. Mother's employment and children's achievement: A critique. *Sociology of Education* 59: 140-151.

The authors critique prior research related to maternal employment that found a small negative effect of maternal employment on children's achievement. Data were gathered from over 3,500 respondents. The study showed that when strucutral, attitudinal, and socioeconomic variables are controlled, the negative effect of mother's employment is much smaller.

159   **Hoffman, L. W. 1989. Effects of maternal employment in the two-parent family.** *American Psychologist* **44(2): 283-292.**

Research regarding the effects of maternal employment is reviewed. The data suggest that maternal employment may increase the morale of mothers and offset other day-to-day anxieties; however, stress of a dual role can minimize this advantage.

160   **Hong, G., and S. I. White-Means. 1993. Do working mothers have healthy children?** *Journal of Family and Economic Issues* **14(2): 163-186.**

Data are analyzed from the 1981 National Health Interview Survey conducted by the U. S. Bureau of the Census for the National Center for Health Statistics. The relationship between maternal employment and children's health was studied. Findings suggest that maternal employment has a significant negative effect on a child's physical health.

161   **Joebgen, A. M., and M. H. Richards. 1990. Maternal education and employment: Mediating maternal and adolescent emotional adjustment.** *Journal of Early Adolescence* **10(3): 329-343.**

The Experience Sampling Method (ESM) was utilized to assess the lives of adolescents in 52 families. A mother's day-to-day functioning in relation to her education and employment influenced her adolescent's well-being.

162   **Kalmijn, M. 1994. Mother's occupational status and children's schooling.** *American Sociological Review* **59: 257-275.**

This study examines the influence of mother's occupational status on children's schooling. A large national cross-sectional data set is utilized. The author concludes that the occupational status of employed mothers has a significant positive effect on their children's schooling. This effect is independent of, and about equivalent in strength as, the influence of father's occupation in dual-earner families.

163   **Key, R. J., and M. M. Sanik. 1990. The effect of homemaker's employment status on children's time allocation in single-and two-parent families.** *Lifestyles: Family and Economic Issues* **11(1): 71-88.**

Time use data were collected from 210 two-parent, two-child families over the course of two days. A sample of 81 single parent, two-child households were surveyed as well. The study explores the effect on children's use of time, in families in which the mother is employed professionally. The findings suggest that a mother's employment status does not have a significant effect on an older child's (age 10 or above) allocation of time.

164   **Mannheim, B., and T. Seger. 1993. Mothers' occupational characteristics, family position, and sex role orientation as related to adolescents' work values.** *Youth and Society* **24(3): 276-298.**

A sample of 93 adolescents and their mothers completed questionnaires regarding their work values. Significant differences were found for intrinsic work values and attitudes of earnings between male and female adolescents. In addition, maternal work values of pride in work and humanism were found to be similar for both male and female adolescents.

165   **Menaghan, E. G., and T. L. Parcel. 1995. Social sources of change in children's home environments: The effects of parental occupational experiences and family conditions.** *Journal of Marriage and the Family* **57: 69-84.**

The mother and child supplements (1986 and 1988) to the National Longitudinal Survey of Youth were used as a sample to inquire about what, if any, effect changes in parental employment status and family composition had on children's home environments. While parents occupational changes were not found to have an effect on children's home environment, maternal job entry was found to have negative effects on the environment. Single motherhood for mothers employed in high wage, high status jobs were found to have a more positive effect than mothers who remain single without employment.

166   Menaghan, E. G., and T. L. Parcel. 1991. Determining children's home environments: The impact of maternal characteristics and current occupational and family conditions. *Journal of Marriage and the Family*   53: 17-431.

Data were gathered from the mother and child supplements (1986) of the National Longitudinal Survey of Youth (NLSY). Maternal characteristics, such as initial self-esteem and locus of control, were found to be important predictors of a child's home environment. Maternal employment in environments which involved complex work activities was found to have a positive effect on children's home environment.

167   Muller, C. 1995. Maternal employment, parental involvement, and mathematics achievement among adolescents. *Journal of Marriage and the Family*   57: 85-100.

Data collected from the National Educational Longitudinal Study of 1988 using a two-stage stratified probability design indicate that youth with mothers working part-time scored higher than youth with mothers working full-time and youth with mothers who did not work outside of the home. Further, the amount of after-school unsupervised time that a youth experiences may have an impact on the effect maternal employment has on mathematics achievement of youth.

168   Parcel, T. L., and E. G. Menaghan. 1990. Maternal working conditions and children's verbal facility: Studying the intergenerational transmission of inequality from mothers to young children. *Social Psychology Quarterly*   53(2): 132-147.

A sample of 697 mothers and children taken from the National Longitudinal Survey's Youth Cohort (1986) was analyzed. Maternal employment conditions had a significant effect on children's verbal facility. Additional factors that were found to have an effect on children's verbal facility include: child's home environment, number of children in the household, maternal AFQT (Armed Forces Qualification Test) score and ethnicity.

169   **Paulson, S. E., J. J. Koman, and J. P. Hill. 1990. Maternal employment and parent-child relations in families of seventh graders.** *Journal of Early Adolescence* **10(3): 279-295.**

A sample of 200 seventh grade youth and their parents were surveyed using, among others, measures of maternal employment status. The effects of maternal employment were reported by both parents and children, as different for young adolescent boys and girls.

170   **Pett, M. A., B. Vaughan-Cole, and B. E. Wampold. 1994. Maternal employment and perceived stress: Their impact on children's adjustment and mother-child interaction in young divorced and married families.** *Family Relations* **43: 151-158.**

A sample of 104 married and 99 divorced families were randomly selected and videotaped in their homes on two occasions. Maternal employment alone was not found to have an effect on children's psychosocial adjustment. Demographic and psychosocial conditions, such as maternal stress (divorce, everyday hassles), were found to be significant predictors of a child's adjustment and maternal-child interactions.

171   **Richards, M. H., and E. Duckett. 1991. Maternal employment and adolescents. In** *Employed Mothers and their Children,* **edited by J. V. Lerner and N. L. Galambos. New York: Garland Publishing.**

This chapter explores the effects of maternal employment during the early and mid developmental periods of adolescents. The authors consider family environment as an intervening variable between maternal employment and adolescent well-being. Other factors considered important to the child's well-being are discussed, for example support, guidance, and after-school activities.

172   Williams, E., and N. Radin. 1993. Paternal involvement, maternal employment, and adolescents' academic achievement: An 11-year follow-up. *American Journal Orthopsychiatry* 63(2): 306-312.

An original sample of 59 families with preschool aged children were interviewed (1977) to understand the impact of high father involvement in two parent families. A second interview (1981) was conducted with 47 families four years later and a third interview (1988) was conducted with 32 families eleven years later. The third interview addressed the children's (now adolescents) academic achievement and expectations. Maternal employment was found to be a long term predictor of the academic achievements of children.

173   Youngblut, J. M., C. J. Loveland-Cherry, and M. Horan. 1993. Maternal employment, family functioning, and preterm infant development at 9 and 12 months. *Research in Nursing and Health* 16: 33-43.

Data were collected from a sample of 67 families through home interviews. Maternal employment was not found to have a significant effect on a child's mental and psychomotor development. Consistency between employment and attitude was found to be more of a predictor of infant development than maternal employment alone.

174   Zaslow, M. J., F. A. Pedersen, J. T. D. Suwalsky, and B. A. Rabinovich. 1989. Maternal employment and parent-infant interaction at one year. *Early Childhood Research Quarterly* 4: 459-478.

Middle-class families (n = 34) were recruited and observed in their homes on four occasions. During the employed mother-father-infant interactions, there were fewer attempts to engage the infant with objects and less engagement in mutual visual regard than in homemaker-father-infant interactions. When observed alone (mother-infant), there was little difference in the interactions between employed and nonemployed mothers and their infants.

PART 2

WORK-FAMILY AS STRUCTURAL AND DEVELOPMENTAL CONCEPTS

CHAPTER 5

Single Parent Families

175   Amott, T. 1988. Working for less: Single mothers in the workplace. In *Women as Single Parents*, edited by E. A. Mulroy. Dover, MA: Auburn House Publishing. 99–122.

Amott identifies and examines the barriers single mothers face in entering and staying in the labor market (e.g., child care costs and inadequate or no health insurance). Additionally, Amott posits that the structure of the labor market presents a barrier to single mother's earning a sufficient income. Policy implications are considered.

176   Ballweg, J. A., and L. Li. 1992. Single mothers and fathers in the U.S. military. *Journal of Employee Assistance Research* 1(2): 380-390.

This study found that work and family roles in the military present challenges for both single mothers and fathers. Indeed, in terms of work-related stress, there was no significant difference found between single mothers and single fathers.

177   Bowen, G. L., D. K. Orthner, and L. I. Zimmerman. 1993. Family adaptation of single parents in the United States Army: An empirical analysis of work stressors and adaptive resources. *Family Relations* 42: 293-304.

A secondary analysis of the 1989 Army Soldier and Family Survey focused on family adaptation of single parents (n = 94 single fathers, 144 single mothers). Specifically, the researchers examined work stressors (e.g., work predictability) and two types of adaptive resources: (1) family and community resources; and (2) Army support resources. The results suggest family, community, and Army resources contribute to family adaptation. Policy recommendations are offered.

178   Burden, D. S. 1986. **Single parents and the work setting: The impact of multiple job and homelife responsibilities.** *Family Relations* **35: 37-43.**

In this analysis of single parents and the workplace, survey data were gathered from employees (n = 293) of a large corporation in New England. Although single parents experienced more strain than their married counterparts, single parents did not miss more days of work.

179   Campbell, M. L., and P. Moen. 1992. **Job-Family role strain among employed single mothers of preschoolers.** *Family Relations* **41: 205-211.**

Focus group data with 30 employed single mothers provided the basis for the survey study. In the second phase of the study, employed mothers with preschoolers (n = 160) were surveyed concerning work-family role strain. The findings suggest that certain factors were related to increased strain (e.g., number of hours worked, number of children, and ages of children).

180   Goldberg, W. A., E. Greenberger, S. Hamill, and R. O'Neil. 1992. **Role demands in the lives of employed single mothers with preschoolers.** *Journal of Family Issues* **13(3): 312-333.**

Single, employed women with a preschool child (n = 76) were surveyed. Analyses revealed that work-family interface variables were important for women's well-being (e.g., perceived quality of child care).

181   Jackson, A. P. 1993. **Black, single, working mothers in poverty: Preferences for employment, well-being and perceptions of preschool age children.** *Social Work* **38(1): 26-34.**

This study focuses on employment preferences and well-being. Interview and questionnaire data were gathered from

111 black, single, employed mothers (with a child 3-4 years old). Mothers who wanted to work reported lower role strain and scored high on measures of life satisfaction.

182   Jones, L. E., and E. Wattenberg. 1991. **Working, still poor: A loan program's role in the lives of low-income single parents.** *Social Work* **36(2): 146-153.**

Jones and Wattenberg present and discuss an interest-free loan program that targets working poor single-parent families.

183   Mahler, S. R. 1989. **How working single parents manage their two major roles.** *Journal of Employment Counseling* **26: 178-185.**

Mahler explores the issue of working single parents. Topics discussed include: (1) the psychological benefits of work; (2) work attitudes and performance; and (3) strain and coping strategies. Organizational support is discussed briefly.

184   Marlow, C. 1993. **Coping with multiple roles: Family configuration and the need for workplace services.** *Affilia: Journal of Women and Social Work* **8(1): 40-55.**

This study explores the relationships between work and family issues and family structure. A stratified random sample of 338 women clerical workers were surveyed. Although women with children reported more problems coping with work and family responsibilities than women without children; overall there were few differences between married and single mothers. Explanations for the somewhat surprising results are discussed.

185   Mulroy, E. A., and M. Pitt-Catsouphes. 1994. *Single Parents at the Workplace.* **Work-Family Policy Paper Series. Boston, MA: Center on Work and Family at Boston University.**

This paper examines the work-family implications of the dramatic increase in the numbers of single parents. The challenges faced by single parents are outlined. Also included is a discussion of the public and private sector policies that affect the experiences of these employees. The results of survey and focus group research are presented.

186   Parker, L. 1994. **The role of workplace support in facilitating self-sufficiency among single mothers on welfare.** *Family Relations* **43: 168-173.**

Using data from the longitudinal study, the Family Income Study, the researchers tested a model that examined factors affecting the transition of single mothers to economic independence. The study found that workplace support was the most significant factor in that transition.

187   Quinn, P., and K. R. Allen. 1989. **Facing Challenges and Making Compromises: How single mothers endure.** *Family Relations* **38: 390-395.**

Interview data from 30 employed single parents reveal their concerns about handling limited resources (i.e., time, money, and energy).

188   Schorr, A. L. and P. Moen. 1979. **The single parent and public policy.** *Social Policy* **9(5): 15-20.**

The authors place this discussion of single parenthood in a societal context. For example, the image of single parenthood, or rather the misrepresentations, contribute to the complexity of policy issues addressing the needs of single parents.

189   Sorensen, A. 1994. **Women's economic risk and the economic position of single mothers.** *European Sociological Review* **10(2): 173-188.**

This paper examines the economic position of single-mother households. Drawing on data from the Luxembourg Income Study, Sorensen compares rates of poverty in the U. S. and West Germany with Sweden's.

CHAPTER 6

Dual-Earner Families

190   Aldous, J., ed. 1982. *Two Paychecks: Life in Dual-Earner Families*. Beverly Hills, CA: Sage Publications.

191   Anderson, E. A., and J. W. Spruill. 1993. The dual-career commuter family: A lifestyle on the move. *Marriage and Family Review* 19(1/2): 131-147.

This study examines role strain, division of family work, and decision-making for 39 dual-career commuter couples. Analyses found that family work was unevenly divided, with women doing more.

192   Anderson, E. A., and L. A. Leslie. 1991. Coping with employment and family stress: Employment arrangement and gender differences. *Sex Roles* 24(3/4): 223-237.

This study investigates employment status and family structure in relation to stress, coping strategies, and marital satisfaction. The sample consists of 82 couples (26 dual-career, 12 mixed working status, 22 dual-job, and 22 traditional status, i.e., husband working, wife at home).

193   Barnett, R. C., N. L. Marshall, S. W. Raudenbush, and R. T. Brennan. 1993. Gender and relationship between job experiences and psychological distress: A study of men and women in dual-earner couples. *Journal of Personality and Social Psychology* 64: 794-806.

The association between job role quality and psychological distress is examined in this study using a sample of full-time employed dual-earner couples (n = 300). The analyses show that for both men and women, job role quality is negatively associated with psychological distress.

194   Barnett, R. C., R. T. Brennan, and N. L. Marshall. 1994. Gender and the relationship between parent role quality and psychological distress. *Journal of Family Issues* 15(2): 229-252.

The association between parent role quality and psychological distress is examined in this study. A random sample of full-time employed dual-earner couples with children (n = 180) filled out questionnaires and were interviewed. The major finding was the absence of gender differences.

195   Barnett, R. C., R. T. Brennan, S. W. Raudenbush, and N. L. Marshall. 1994. Gender and the relationship between marital-role quality and psychological distress: A study of women and men in dual-earner couples. *Psychology of Women Quarterly* 18: 105-127.

This study found that marital-role quality and psychological distress are negatively associated for both men and women in a sample of 300 dual-earner full-time employed couples. Using identity theory as a framework, the findings are discussed.

196   Benin, M. H., and B. C. Nienstedt. 1985. Happiness in single- and dual-earner families: The effects of marital happiness, job satisfaction, and life cycle. *Journal of Marriage and the Family* 47(4): 975-984.

This study examines causes of happiness and unhappiness. Drawing from NORC GSS data (1978, 1980, 1982, and 1983 combined), the researchers' analysis indicates a best-fit model for happiness depends on the family structure by earner status (i.e., dual-earner husbands and wives, single-earner husbands and wives).

197   Bielby, W. T., and D. D. Bielby. 1992. I will follow him: Family ties, gender-role beliefs, and reluctance to relocate for a better job. *American Journal of Sociology* 97(5): 1241-1267.

This article examines the issue of job relocations and dual-earner couples. Drawing on data from the 1977 Quality of Employment Survey, a probit model is developed. Based on the results, the authors conclude that the way couples view the provider role may determine how they respond.

198   Brett, J. M. and S. Yogev. 1988. **Restructuring work for family: How dual-earner couples with children manage.** In *Journal of Social Behavior and Personality: Work and Family: Theory, Research, and Applications,* edited by E. B. Goldsmith. Corte Madera, CA: Select Press. 159-174.

This study addresses the question of how men and women restructure work to handle family responsibilities. The sample consists of 76 dual-career professional couples with children. Presents factors associated with restructuring, for example, gender (women restructure more than men) and opportunity (professionals restructure more when they work in occupations that provide the opportunity).

199   Granrose, C. S., S. Parasuraman, and J. H. Greenhaus. 1992. **A proposed model of support provided by two-earner couples.** *Human Relations* 45(12): 1367-1391.

This paper examines a model of social support and the dual-earner couple. Using data from 238 dual-earner couples, the researchers analyze factors of spousal support (e.g., type of support, factors prompting support, and resources to provide support).

200   Hall, F. S., and D. T. Hall. 1979. *The Two-Career Couple.* Reading, MA: Addison-Wesley.

201   Hertz, R. 1986. *More Equal Than Others: Women and Men in Dual-Career Marriages.* Berkeley, CA: University of California Press.

202   Hiller, D. V., and J. Dyehouse. 1987. **A case for banishing "dual-career marriages" from the research literature.** *Journal of Marriage and the Family* 49: 787-795.

The authors use a review of the literature to support their argument that career and dual-career marriages lack clear operational definitions. In support of this critique, the researchers present their own research findings. Recommendations are made for dual-career research.

203   Karambayya, R., and A. H. Reilly. 1992. Dual earner couples: Attitudes and actions in restructuring work for family. *Journal of Organizational Behavior* 13: 585-601.

Survey data from men and women in 39 dual-earner couples were used to examine work restructuring for family. Overall, wives restructured more than husbands. Qualitative data from open-ended questions are discussed.

204   Kingston, P. W., and S. L. Nock. 1987. Time together among dual-earner couples. *American Sociological Review* 52: 391-400.

This study analyzes time spent together among dual-earner couples. Daily time diaries from the 1981 Study of Time Use show that time couples spend together is contingent on the combined hours couples work and the way they schedule those hours.

205   Lewis, S., D. N. Izraeli, and H. Hootsmans, eds. 1992. *Dual-Earner Families: International Perspectives.* London: Sage Publications.

206   Marshall, N. L., and R. C. Barnett. 1993. Work-family strains and gains among two-earner couples. *Journal of Community Psychology* 21: 64-78.

Marshall and Barnett examined the work-family strains and "gains" that dual-earner couples experience, addressing questions of gender-differences and the factors associated with these stresses and gains. The sample of 300 two-earner couples were administered the Work-Family Gains Scale (Marshall and Barnett, 1991); the Work-Family Strains Scale (Barnett and Baruch, 1985); Work-Parenting Gains Scale; and Work-Parenting Strains Scale. The researchers found that major predictors of work-family strain were workload and quality of experiences in the work and family domains.

207   Nock, S. L., and P. W. Kingston. 1984. The family work day. *Journal of Marriage and the Family* 46(2): 333-343.

The researchers suggest using family patterns of work-time as a unit of analysis. For example, researchers might use specific dimensions: (1) total work time; (2) time one spouse is at work; and (3) time only one spouse is at work. The effect of children on the "family work day" is discussed.

208   **Parasuraman, S., J. H. Greenhaus, and C. S. Granrose. 1992. Role stressors, social support, and well-being among two-career couples.** *Journal of Organizational Behavior* **13: 339-356.**

The researchers assess the effects of work and family role stressors on well-being, which is operationalized as job satisfaction, family satisfaction, and life stress. In addition, the study tests a model of social support and the dual-earner couple. The results indicate that relationship of stressors and well-being are stronger within domains.

209   **Perry-Jenkins, M. 1988. Future directions for research on dual-earner families: A young professional's perspective.** *Family Relations* **37: 226-228.**

The author proposes directions for future research on issues confronting dual-career families: (1) the unit of analysis should examine the impact of both spouses' jobs on family; and (2) researchers should differentiate between role responsibility and role enactment. Policy and practice implications are discussed.

210   **Peterson, R. R., and K. Gerson. 1992. Determinants of responsibility for child care arrangements among dual-earner couples.** *Journal of Marriage and the Family* **54: 527-536.**

This study examines child care responsibilities among dual-earner couples. The researchers employ a structural explanation.

211   **Pleck, J. H., and G. L. Staines. 1985. Work schedules and family life in two-earner couples.** *Journal of Family Issues* **6(1): 61-82.**

This study explores the issue of work schedules and the impact of schedules on dual-earner couples and draws on data from the 1977 Quality of Employment Survey. The study found differences by sex in job demands, but not in family responsiveness.

212   Rapoport, R., and R. Rapoport. 1977. *Dual-Career Families Reexamined.* **New York: Harper and Row.**

213   Schneer, J. A., and Reitman, F. 1993. **Effects of alternate family structures on managerial career paths.** *Academy of Management Journal* **6(4): 830-843.**

In this study, the authors expand and employ a family structure typology to account for current diversity (e.g., single, no children; married, children, employed spouse). Using survey data from MBA degree holders, the authors found that family structure was related to income and career satisfaction for both men and women. For example, married males in dual-earner families with children earn less than married males in traditional families with children (non-working wife).

214   Schwartzberg, N. S., and R. S. Dytell. 1996. **Dual-earner families: The importance of work stress and family stress for psychological well-being.** *Journal of Occupational Health Psychology* **1(2): 211-223.**

This study examines the importance of work, family, and interference stress in relation to the variables of self-esteem and depression in dual-earner families, in particular the differences between working mothers' and fathers' well-being. Both dual-earner fathers' and mothers' self-esteem and depression were affected by job and family stress. Other significant findings are reported and discussed.

215   Sekaran, U. 1989. **Understanding the dynamics of self-concept of members in dual-career families.** *Human Relations* **42(2): 97-116.**

Investigates the gender differences in dual-career couples. Specifically, the analysis tested self-esteem and competence as intermediary variables between work variables and job satisfaction.

216   Sekaran, U. 1983. How husbands and wives in dual-career families perceive their family and work worlds. *Journal of Vocational Behavior* **22: 288-302.**

This study found that husbands and wives in dual-career families share a view of their work and family worlds. Sekaran discusses four specific dimensions of those views.

217   Young, M., and P. Wilmott. 1973. *The Symmetrical Family: A Study of Work and Leisure in the London Region.* **Boston, MA: Routledge and Kegan-Paul.**

CHAPTER 7

Life Course/Family Stage/Career Stage

218   Baruch, G. K., and R. C. Barnett. 1986. Role quality, multiple role involvement, and psychological well-being in midlife women. *Journal of Personality and Social Psychology* 51(3): 578-585.

This study examines the quality of women's roles in mid-life and the number of roles women occupy (i.e., paid worker, wife, and mother) in relation to well-being. Psychological well-being was operationalized and measured by three scales: self-esteem, depression, and pleasure. An index to measure quality of role was formulated from focus group data collected in a pilot study. The findings underscore the importance of the quality of roles.

219   Brannen, J., and P. Moss. 1992. British households after maternity leave. In *Dual-Earner Families: International Perspectives*, edited by S. Lewis, D. N. Izraeli, and H. Hootsmans. London: Sage Publications. 109-126.

In the context of the early to mid 1980s, the authors examine the early family formation stage of dual-earner couples. Drawing upon data from a longitudinal study, the authors consider: (1) the decision to return to work after the first child is born; (2) the division of roles within the family; and (3) the effects of support, both formal and informal.

220   Chi-Ching, Y. 1995. The effects of career salience and life-cycle variables on perceptions of work-family interfaces. *Human Relations* 48(3): 265-284.

This paper places the life-cycle variables in the context of the work-family interface. A stratified sample of 429 business administration graduates from a local university in Singapore were administered The Life-Role Salience scale. Findings suggest an interaction between career salience and life-cycle variables with gender differences.

221   Greller, M. M., and L. K. Stroh. 1995. **Careers in midlife and beyond: A fallow field in need of substance. Careers from Midlife.** *Journal of Vocational Behavior* **47(3): 232-247.**

The authors explore the midlife career stage by reviewing some of the empirical data. Issues considered include: effects of physiological and psychological factors on the aging process, the turbulent workforce, restructuring, and the effects of technological change. Also considered is the need for work-family researchers and policy planners to address midlife workers.

222   Hayghe, H. V. 1990. **Family members in the work force.** *Monthly Labor Review* **113(3): 14-19.**

Hayge examines the trends in family structure and labor force patterns from pre-World War II to the current decade. The analysis concludes with Hayge's observation that today there is no dominant family type, such as the traditional family was a few decades ago; rather, there are numerous work-family patterns.

223   Higgins, C., L. Duxbury, and C. Lee. 1994. **Impact of life-cycle stage and gender on the ability to balance work and family responsibilities.** *Family Relations* **43: 144-150.**

This study examines the effects of gender and life-cycle stage on three dimensions of work-family conflict: (1) role overload; (2) interference from family to work; and (3) interference from work to family. Based on an analysis of time spent in work and family, the findings suggest that men are doing more child care and family work. Dual-earner mothers' time spent in family work is lower; whereas, dual-earner fathers' time spent is higher. The study also finds gender differences among the dimensions of work-family conflict and life-cycle stage.

224   Howard, A. 1992. **Work and family crossroads spanning the career.** In *Work, Families, and Organizations,* **edited by S. Zedeck. San Francisco, CA: Jossey-Bass Publishers. 70-137.**

Howard proposes a model that explores the "crossroads" of the work and family domains. Work and family involvement is tested overtime by career stage and family stage using longitudinal data from 422 managers in six Bell telephone companies (The Management Progress Study).

225   Joshi, H., and P. R. A. Hinde. 1993. Employment after childbearing in post-war Britain: Cohort-Study evidence on contrasts within and across generations. *European Sociological Review* 9(3): 203-227.

This study examines the trend in post-war Britain of mothers returning to work after having a baby. Using longitudinal data from the National Survey of the 1946 cohort study, the authors analyze change between cohorts.

226   Krishnan, V. 1992. Family life cycle and labour force behaviour of married women. *International Journal of Sociology of the Family* 22: 119-136.

Using a life cycle perspective, this paper focuses on women's labor force participation. Based on pregnancy histories of women of varying marital status aged 18 to 49 years, Krishnan classifies three life stages and uses them as life cycle variables in the study. The study found that selected demographic, socioeconomic, and attitudinal variables predict labor force participation relative to the life cycle stages. For example, husband's attitude towards wife's employment appears important for the group who expect no more children. Another determinate of labor force participation was number of children for those who expect no more children.

227   Lewis, S., and C. L. Cooper. 1987. Stress in two-earner couples and stage in the life-cycle. *Journal of Occupational Psychology* 60: 289-303.

Different life-stages provided the backdrop for this examination of sources and manifestations of stress in dual-earner couples. The sample consisted of 152 couples classified by parental status: (1) non parents; (2) parents; or (3) transitional between the two stages. The study found that parents experienced more pressures than those who were not parents, especially mothers. However, fathers scored higher on negative impact of parenthood. All couples, especially parents, experienced stress from organizational factors.

228 MacDermid, S. M., and A. C. Crouter. 1995. Midlife, adolescence, and parental employment in family systems. *Journal of Youth and Adolescence* 24(1): 29-54.

229 Moen, P. 1994. Women, work, and family: A sociological perspective on changing roles. In *Age and Structural Lag*, edited by M. W. Riley, R. L. Kahn, and A. Foner. New York: John Wiley and Sons. 151-170.

This sociological analysis clarifies the links between women's changing roles of combining work and family and broad social institutions. Moen underscores the slow structural lag in responding to rapid changes in work-family life. Further, Moen calls for a "redesign in the configuration of the life course and the surrounding social structures." One example is to reexamine the "traditional lockstep pattern of education, employment, and retirement."

230 Moen, P., and K. R. Smith. 1986. Women at work: Commitment and behavior over the life course. *Sociological Forum* 1(3): 450-475.

This study evaluates women's subjective commitment to work and labor force participation over the life course. Women's patterns of employment and subjective commitment to work were examined over a five-year period using data from six waves of the Michigan Panel Study of Income Dynamics. Differences in family cycle changes and subjective commitment to work were reported. The study also found subjective commitment predicted women's work pattern over the past five years.

231 Moen, P., G. Downey, and N. Bolger. 1990. Labor-force reentry among U.S. homemakers in midlife: A life-course analysis. *Gender and Society* 4(2): 230-243.

This study considers the life-stage and the historical period of women homemakers' midlife decision to reenter the workforce.

The authors examine two time periods, 1970-1975 and 1975-1980. Likelihood of reentry to the labor force was associated with time period, age, education, and marital status.

232   Pavalko, E. K., G. H. Elder and E. C. Clipp. 1993. **Worklives and longevity: Insights from a life course perspective.** *Journal of Health and Social Behavior* 34: 363-380.

This study examines the relationship between career mobility among middle-class men and the effects on longevity. Life history data from the Stanford-Terman study were used to predict mortality risks. Results of the study indicate that work-life patterns impact on mortality, for example men were more at risk when they progressed early in careers and then remained stable, than men who progressed in both time periods.

233   Saraceno, C. 1991. **Changes in life-course patterns and behavior of three cohorts of Italian women.** *Journal of Women in Culture and Society* 16(3): 502-521.

234   Schlesinger, B., and D. Raphael. 1993. **The woman in the middle: The sandwich generation revised.** *International Journal of Sociology of the Family* 23: 77-87.

Personal interview data were gathered from 66 women who had young adult children living at home and were responsible, for at least some care, for elders.

235   Shaw, L. B., and R. Shaw. 1987. **From midlife to retirement: The middle-aged woman worker.** In *Working Women: Past, Present, Future,* edited by K. S. Koziara, M. H. Moskow, and L. D. Tanner. Washington, DC: The Bureau of National Affairs. 299-331.

This chapter presents an overview of research midlife women's working lives from a life stage perspective. Implications and limitations for research are addressed.

236   Smith, K. R., and P. Moen. 1988. **Passage through midlife: Women's changing family roles and economic well-being.** *Sociological Quarterly* 29(4): 503-524.

Smith and Moen consider women's transition to the midlife stage as a major career determinate. They explore various hypotheses concerning changes in family composition at midlife, such as divorce, widowhood, and/or an empty nest, using data from thirteen waves of the University of Michigan Panel Study of Income Dynamics. Implications of the analysis are discussed in terms of economic and labor supply outcomes.

237   Ward, C., and A. Dale. 1992. **The impact of early life-course transitions on equality at work and home.** *Sociological Review* 40(3): 509-532.

Ward and Dale examine equality at work and home from the perspective of early life-course transitions. Longitudinal data from men and women living in Britain, aged 23, were drawn from the fourth sweep (1981) National Child Development Study. Findings are discussed within the context of power and equality.

238   Young, M. B. 1996. **Career issues for single adults without children. In *The Career Is Dead. Long Live the Career*, edited by D. T. Hall. San Francisco, CA: Jossey-Bass. 196-219.**

This chapter explores the career impacts of being a single employee without kids. Young operationalizes "single" as never married, widowed, divorced, or separated; and "without kids" as having none under the age of 18 living at home. Also discussed are the cultural, organizational, and individual-level factors impacting work and life issues.

239   Young, M. B. Forthcoming 1997. *Life Status, Work Time, and the Meaning of a Day's Work.* **Unpublished doctoral dissertation. Boston University, Boston, MA.**

In this doctoral dissertation, Young explores the impact of life status (e.g., being a partner and/or parent) on work time and organizational commitment. In addition, life status similarity between employee and supervisor is examined. Includes recommendations for organizational practice.

PART 3

WORK AND FAMILY ROLES

CHAPTER 8

Work-Family Interface

240   Barnett, R. C. 1996. *Toward a Review of the Work/Family Literature: Work in Progress.* Funded by Alfred P. Sloan Foundation. Special Report CRW #16. Wellesley, MA: Center for Research on Women at Wellesley College.

In this review of the work-family research literature, Barnett identifies theoretical limitations and methodological biases that shape and constrain the current research. To address these biases, Barnett proposes a conceptual model that is inclusive and contextual. For example, the model integrates the work-family sphere and is centered in a work/social system framework.

241   Belsky, J., M. Perry-Jenkins, and A. C. Crouter. 1985. The work-family interface and marital change across the transition to parenthood. *Journal of Family Issues* 6(2): 205-220.

Interview and questionnaire data were gathered from sixty-seven white families (recruited from local obstetrical practices) at three points in time: last trimester of pregnancy and at three and nine months post-partum. Overall, the findings suggest that marital conflict increases when work-family interference is high. Different scores from the three to nine-month period are discussed.

242   Bielby, D. D. 1992. Commitment to work and family. *Annual Review Sociology* 18: 281-302.

Provides a definitional and relational overview of the issue of commitment to work and family.

243   Bowen, G. L., and J. F. Pittman, eds. 1995. *The Work and Family Interface: Toward a Contextual Effects Perspective.* Minneapolis, MN: National Council on Family Relations.

244   Burden, D. S., and B. K. Googins. 1987. *Balancing Job and Homelife Study: Managing Work and Family Stress in Corporations.* Boston, MA: Center on Work and Family at Boston University.

This study is one of the first to examine work-family stress within the corporation. Employees in a Fortune 100 company responded to a survey.

245   Burke, R. J. 1986. Occupational and life stress and the family: Conceptual frameworks and research findings. *International Review of Applied Psychology* 35: 347-369.

Discusses the work-family interface and considers the context of the work-family research. Burke, then, presents preliminary findings from an on-going study that examines how work experiences affect individual and family well-being.

246   Cappelli, P., J. Constantine, and C. Chadwick. 1995. *It Pays to Value Family: Work and Family Trade-Offs Reconsidered.* Working Paper. Center for Human Resources at the Wharton School, University of Pennsylvania, Philadelphia, PA.

The researchers draw on data from the National Longitudinal Survey of the Class of 1972. The analysis reveals that respondents who earned more were the respondents who placed a greater importance on marriage and family prior to entering the labor market.

247   Chow, E. N., and C. W. Berheide. 1988. The interdependence of family and work: A framework for family life education, policy, and practice. *Family Relations* 37: 23-28.

After reviewing and critiquing three work-family conceptual models, the researchers propose an "interactive model of interdependence."

248   Crouter, A. C. 1994. Processes linking families and work:
         Implications for behavior and development in both settings. In
         Exploring Family Relationships with other Social Contexts,
         edited by R. D. Parke and S. G. Kellam. Hillsdale, NJ:
         Lawrence Erlbaum Associates. 9-28.

While emphasizing the complex and reciprocal nature of the
linkages between work and family, Crouter examines the
processes linking both domains. She identifies and explores
three areas of research that link domains: (1) processes of work
or family status; (2) influences of mood; and (3) the effects on
adult development.

249   Edwards, J. R., and N. P. Rothbard. 1996. An Integrative Model
         of Stress, Coping, and Well-Being Within and Between Work
         and Family Domains. Working Paper. School of Business
         Administration, University of Michigan, Ann Arbor, MI.

Following a review of the stress literature relating to the work
and family domains, the authors present a model that
integrates and expands current applications. The analysis
considers theoretical perspectives, such as spillover,
compensation, segmentation, and work-family conflict.

250   Ford Foundation. 1989. *Work and Family Responsibilities:
         Achieving a Balance.* New York: Ford Foundation.

251   Frone, M. R., M. Russell, and M. L. Cooper. 1992. Antecedents
         and outcomes of work-family conflict: Testing a model of the
         work-family interface. *Journal of Applied Psychology* 77(1)
         65-78.

Frone and colleagues develop and test a model of the work-
family interface that examines antecedents and outcomes of
work-family conflict. The model was tested on a three-stage
probability sample designed to approximate equal
representation of blacks and non-blacks and equal
representation of three education levels (some college, high
school graduate, not a high school graduate). Analyses from
structural equation modeling techniques support the model.
Class differences are reported.

252   Galinsky, E., and P. H. Bragonier, D. Hughes, M. Love. 1987. *The Family Study.* New York, NY: Bank Street College, Division of Research, Demonstration, and Policy.

This study explores the negative impacts of work on blue collar workers (at two pharmaceutical factory sites) and their families using survey and interview data. In addition, this action-based research addresses potential avenues for reducing work-family stress. For example, the project protocol included the observation and evaluation of a "work-family life committee" established by workers at one of the sites.

253   Greenhaus, J. H. 1988. The intersection of work and family roles: Individual, interpersonal and organizational issues. In *Journal of Social Behavior and Personality: Work and Family: Theory, Research, and Applications,* edited by E. B. Goldsmith. Corte Madera, CA: Select Press. 23-44.

Greenhaus identifies and reviews areas of work-family research. The article focuses on the work-family interface, dual-career relationships, and organizational response to work-family issues.

254   Hughes, D., E. Galinsky, and A. Morris. 1995. The effects of job characteristics on marital quality: Specifying linking mechanisms. In *The Work and Family Interface: Toward a Contextual Effects Perspective,* edited by G. L. Bowen and J. F. Pittman. Minneapolis, MN: National Council on Family Relations. 74-83.

Presents and evaluates a conceptual model linking work-family interference to both the work domain (job characteristics, such as, work hours) and the marital domain (tension and companionship). Questionnaire data were gathered from 188 female and 334 male married workers. Analyses suggest that job characteristics predict dimensions of work-family interference (i.e., negative mood spillover, family role difficulty, and job role difficulty). Work-family interference, then predicts marital quality.

255   Ishii-Kuntz, M. 1994. Work and family life: Findings from international research and suggestions for future study. *Journal of Family Issues* 15(3): 490-506.

This paper examines conceptual perspectives of the work and family interface in the United States, and then examines comparative research conducted in other countries. Alternative frameworks and conceptualizations used in the international research are discussed.

256   Kanter, R. M. 1977. Work and Family in the United States: A Critical Review and Agenda for Research and Policy. New York: Russell Sage Foundation.

This classic, ground-breaking study exposed the "myth of separate worlds."

257   Kline, M. L., and P. A. Cowan. 1988. Re-thinking the connections among "work" and "family" and well-being: A model for investigating employment and family work contexts. In *Journal of Social Behavior and Personality: Work and Family: Theory, Research, and Applications*, edited by E. B. Goldsmith. Corte Madera, CA: Select Press. 61-90.

In this paper, Kline and Cowan propose a heuristic model to research the combined impact of work in both the organization and family domains on indices of well-being.

258   Marshall, N. L., and R. C. Barnett. 1994. Family-friendly workplaces, work-family interface, and worker health. In *Job Stress in a Changing Workforce: Investigating Gender, Diversity and Family Issues*, edited by G. P. Keita and J. J. Hurrell. Washington, DC: American Psychological Association. 253-264.

In this chapter, the authors examine the linkages in the work-family interface between family-friendly workplaces and job satisfaction, work interference, and worker mental health. Based on interview data with 300 dual-earner couples employed full-time, the findings suggest an indirect effect of job flexibility on psychological distress via work interference and job satisfaction (Fig. 1, Path diagram, p. 261).

259   Near, J. P., R. W. Rice, and R. G. Hunt. 1980. The relationship between work and nonwork domains: A review of empirical research. *Academy of Management Review* 5(3): 415-429.

Reviews studies relating the conditions of worklife and the worker's behaviors and attitudes in his or her non-worklife. In particular, the authors examine the question of how structural variables in one domain affect behaviors in the other domain. Policy issues and research strategies are addressed.

260   Pittman, J. F. 1994. Work/family fit as a mediator of work factors on marital tension: Evidence from the interface of greedy institutions. *Human Relations* 47(2): 183-209.

Data were analyzed from 407 male U. S. Army members and their wives. Pitmann concludes that work-family balance mediates work factors and marital tension.

261   Rapoport, R., and R. N. Rapoport. 1965. Work-Family in contemporary society. *American Sociological Review* 30: 381-394.

Pioneering study in the work-family field drawing attention to the interdependence of the work and family spheres.

262   Renshaw, J. R. 1976. An exploration of the dynamics of the overlapping worlds of work and family. *Family Process* 15(1): 143-165.

Qualitative data were gathered at a multinational corporation from managers and families who were experiencing stress from three organizational events: international transfer, extensive travel, and job change. Renshaw uses both a grounded theory approach and a systems theory approach, thereby integrating the work-family interface.   The study indicates that the individual's perceived sense of influence over stressful events is significant for effectiveness in both the organizational and family context.

263   Rossi, A. S. 1993. The future in the making: Recent trends in the work-family interface. *American Journal of Orthopsychiatry* 63(2) 166-176.

Reviews demographic trends in family life and emerging trends in the work-family interface.

264   Staines, G. L., and J. H. Pleck. 1983. *The Impact of Work Schedules on the Family.* Survey Research Center and Institute for Social Research. Michigan: Institute of Social Research.

This seminal work investigates the work-family interface, specifically the effects of work schedules on family life, moderating effects of schedule control, and the patterns of joint schedules in dual-earner couples.

265   Stephens, G. K., and D. C. Feldman. Forthcoming 1997. A motivational approach for understanding career versus personal life investments. In *Research in Personnel and Human Resources Management,* edited by G. R. Ferris. Greenwich, CT: JAI Press. Vol. 15.

Examines the question of how and when individuals choose to focus their energies on either the work or family domain. Using the motivational perspective of the individual, the authors explore available strategies from various academic fields for handling work-family conflict.

266   Swiss, D. J., and J. P. Walker. 1993. *Women and the Work/Family Dilemma: How Today's Professional Women Are Finding Solutions.* New York: John Wiley and Sons.

This book is based on interviews with women graduates (classes of 1971–1981) of Harvard Business School, Harvard Law School, and Harvard Medical School concerning the effects of children on careers.

267   Tenbrunsel, A. E., J. M. Brett, E. Maoz, L. K. Stroh, and A. H. Reilly. 1995. Dynamic and static work-family relationships. *Organizational Behavior and Human Decision Processes* 63(3): 233-246.

This study examines the work-family linkages between dual-earner couples in which the male's career was dominant (n = 281). After classifying social and psychological mechanisms explaining directions of the work-family interface, the researchers develop a model for a specific homogeneous sample. Structural equations modeling (LISREL 7) reveals that for this sample the relationship between work and family for men was reciprocal (or dynamic). On the other hand, for women there was a unidirectional (or static) relationship from family to work. The organizational role in helping employees reduce role demand is discussed.

268   Thomas, L. T., and D. C. Ganster. 1995. Impact of family-supportive work variables on work-family conflict and strain: A control perspective. *Journal of Applied Psychology* 80(1): 6-15.

This study examines the relationship between employer-supported policies and practices aimed at reducing work-family conflict and measures of strain including psychological, from 398 health professionals with children who worked at 45 acute-care facilities. In light of the findings, the researchers conclude that supportive practices—in particular flexible scheduling and supportive supervisors—directly influenced worker's sense of control and mastery. This sense of mastery was related to lower scores on the measures of strain.

269   Voydanoff, P. 1992. Work role characteristics, family structure demands and work-family conflict. *Journal of Marriage and the Family* 50: 749-761.

This study focuses on sources of conflict emanating from the work-family interface. Interview data from the 1977 Quality of Employment survey are analyzed using the following independent variables: family structure demands, perceived control, and work role characteristics (e.g., amount and scheduling of work time). The analysis indicates that work role characteristics and family structure contribute to work-family conflict, while perceived control over the work situation appears to serve as a buffer.

270   Voydanoff, P. 1988. Work and family: A review and expanded conceptualization. In *Journal of Social Behavior and Personality: Work and Family: Theory, Research, and Applications,* edited by E. B. Goldsmith. Corte Madera, CA: Select Press. 1-22.

Voydanoff reviews the work-family research including, among others, sections on the "structural and psychological characteristics of work, effects of work on family, effects of family on work, and combined effects of husbands' and wives' work role characteristics." In addition, Voydanoff suggests an expansion of the theoretical and research models (e.g., incorporate broad economic trends).

CHAPTER 9

Spillover and Crossover Models

271   Barnett, R. C. 1994. Home-to-work spillover revisited: A study of full-time employed women in dual-earner couples. *Journal of Marriage and the Family* 56: 647-656.

Interview data were gathered from a random sample of full-time working women in dual-earner families (n = 300) and used in this analysis of spillover from home to work. Findings suggest that family relationships moderate negative work experiences. For example, when marital or parental relationships are good, there is no relationship between negative work experiences and distress.

272   Barnett, R. C., and N. L. Marshall. 1992. Men's job and partner roles: Spillover effects and psychological distress. *Sex Roles* 27(9/10): 455-472.

Using data from a random sample of 300 men in dual-earner couples, the study examines the relationship between men's work and partnership roles and their mental health. Results indicate spillover effects are additive. For example, troubled relationships with partners appeared to heighten work stress and mental distress for men (home-to-work-negative-spillover). Analysis provides some support to role stress model.

273   Barnett, R. C., and N. L. Marshall. 1992. Worker and mother roles, spillover effects, and psychological distress. *Women and Health* 18(2): 9-40.

Examines the negative- and positive- spillover effects from job to parenting and parenting to job in a sample of 403 employed women (social workers and licensed practical nurses). The study found that there were no negative-spillover effects in either direction. However, there was a main effect for positive-spillover from job to home: a rewarding job appears to weaken the negative mental health effects of troubled relationships with children.

274 Barnett, R. C., N. L. Marshall, and A. Sayer. 1992. **Positive-spillover effects from job to home: A closer look.** *Women and Health* **19(2/3: 13-41.**

Prior research found that a rewarding job appears to weaken the negative mental health effects of troubled relationships with children. The researchers re-examine the sample of 228 employed women and address the specific dimensions of rewarding jobs that contribute to positive-spillover. Findings suggest that it is not a rewarding job in itself that contributes to positive-spillover; rather, specific dimensions appear to lessen stress. For example, "challenge" buffers distress associated with certain aspects of troubled parental relationships.

275 **Bolger, N., A. DeLongis, R. C. Kessler, and E. Wethington. 1990. The microstructure of daily role-related stress in married couples. In *Stress Between Work and Family*, edited by J. Eckenrode and S. Gore. New York: Plenum Press. 95-115.**

276 **Bolger, N., A. DeLongis, R. C. Kessler, and E. Wethington. 1989. The contagion of stress across multiple roles.** *Journal of Marriage and the Family* **51: 175-183.**

This quantitative study examines daily variation in stress contagion across work and family domains. Daily diaries for six weeks were completed by men and women in 166 married couples. The results reveal that husbands are more likely than wives to bring home stresses into the workplace. Both wives and husbands brought stress from work to home.

277 **Campbell, D. J., K. M. Campbell, and D. Kennard. 1994. The effects of family responsibilities on the work commitment and job performance of non-professional women.** *Journal of Occupational and Organizational Psychology* **67: 283-296.**

This study examined the effects of family life on women's work attitudes and job performance. Respondents included 94 non-professional women who completed work and family questionnaires. The women's managers completed job performance ratings. Findings suggest women without children were more committed to work.

278   **Crouter, A. C. 1984. Spillover from family to work: The neglected side of the work-family interface.** *Human Relations* **37(6): 425-441.**

Explores home-to-work spillover based upon data from a field study in a large manufacturing plant. A "theoretical sampling" approach was used to select comparison groups reflecting variations in family and work situations. Interview data were gathered from the sample (38 men and 17 women). Field study results indicate that employees are aware of family spillover into workplace. The researchers examine and discuss spillover and the family life cycle.

279   **Crouter, A. C., M. Perry-Jenkins, T. L. Huston, and D. W. Crawford. 1989. The influence of work-induced psychological states on behavior at home.** *Basic and Applied Social Psychology* **10(3): 273-292.**

This pilot study examines the work-to-home spillover, specifically, the employee's emotional state at the end of the work day (stress, fatigue, arousal, and depression) and his or her subsequent behavior at home. Drawing on data from a subsample (n = 29 men) of the Processes of Adaptation in Intimate Relationships (PAIR) project, the researchers compared groups on the basis of scores. This report includes a discussion of methodological issues in measuring spillover.

280   **Delong, T. J., and C. C. Delong. 1992. Managers as fathers: Hope on the homefront.** *Human Resource Management* **31(3): 171-181.**

Interview data with more than 300 male managers over a four-year period produced several themes relating the way work roles spillover into family, for example, the difficulty of switching roles from manager to father. Strategies for change are presented.

281   Doby, V. J., and R. D. Caplan. 1995. **Organizational stress as threat to reputation: Effects on anxiety at work and at home.** *Academy of Management Journal* 38(4): 1105-1123.

Doby and Caplan hypothesize that anxiety symptoms caused by job stressors will carry over from work to home. Thirty-six accountants rated job stressors as high (lack of feedback, training inadequacy, role overload, role ambiguity) or low (lack of control, lack of meaningfulness, high interdependency, and role conflict). In the second phase of the study, an independent sample of 102 accountants responded to a questionnaire. The analyses indicate that the job stressors rated high were more likely to carry over to the home.

282   Jones, F., and B. C. Fletcher. 1993. **An empirical study of occupational stress transmission in working couples.** *Human Relations* 46(7): 881-903.

Based on the demands, constraint and support model, this study examines occupational stress transmission. Survey data of 60 employed couples (54% response rate) were analyzed. The researchers conclude that occupations stress is transmitted; however, the direction is primarily from men to women.

283   Kinnunen, U., J. Gerris, and A. Vermulst. 1996. **Work experiences and family functioning among employed fathers with children of school age.** *Family Relations* 45: 449-455.

Data gathered in a national survey, "Child-rearing and the Family in the Netherlands" (n = 657, employed men) were used to examine the effects of work on family functioning. Informed by spillover theory, the analysis revealed that all four family domains (individual, father-child, marital, and child) were affected by the job.

284   Kirchmeyer, C. 1993. **Nonwork-to-work spillover: A more balanced view of the experiences and coping of professional women and men.** *Sex Roles* 28(9/10): 531-552.

A sample of 78 female and 143 male managers (including 39 members of ethnic minorities) responded to a questionnaire. Overall, the managers agreed with statements about positive aspects of nonwork-to-work spillover than with negative aspects. The questionnaire was designed to tap community work and recreation as well as parenting and use of coping strategies.

285 **Lambert, S. J. 1990. Processes linking work and family: A critical review and research agenda.** *Human Relations* **43(3): 239-257.**

Reviews the theoretical frameworks linking work and family—segmentation, compensation, and spillover. Lambert presents and discusses a model for future research, particularly in terms of understanding the processes linking the work and family domains to effectively evaluate policies and programs supporting families.

286 **Liou, K., R. D. Sylvia, and G. Brunk. 1990. Non-work factors and job satisfaction revisited.** *Human Relations* **43:(1) 77-86.**

This study tests Wilensky's theory of nonwork variables and job satisfaction. Survey responses of 1,473 subjects were examined, and support was found for Wilensky's spillover theory.

287 **Piotrkowski, C. S. 1979.** *Work and the Family System: A Naturalistic Study of Working-Class and Lower Middle-Class Families.* **New York: Free Press.**

288 **Rook, K., D. Dooley, and R. Catalano. 1991. Stress transmission: The effects of husbands' job stressors on the emotional health of their wives.** *Journal of Marriage and the Family* **53: 165-177.**

This study examines the stress-transmission phenomenon by focusing on the marital relationship. Data were drawn from the Los Angeles Stressor Project, including panel data from a subset (n = 92). The study found that husbands' job stressors were related to wives psychological distress (e.g., nervousness, outbursts).

289 **Sears, H. A., and N. L. Galambos. 1992. Women's work conditions and marital adjustment in two-earner couples: A structural model.** *Journal of Marriage and the Family* **54: 789-797.**

Questionnaires were completed by 86 dual-earner couples with adolescents. The validity of a structural model was tested using LISREL VII. Results from this study supports a spillover model but do not support a crossover model. Women's work stress mediated a link between their work conditions (e.g., work overload, low rewards, work status) and their perceptions of marital adjustment (cohesion, consensus, and satisfaction). This effect did not "crossover" to their husbands.

290   **Small, S. A., and D. Riley. 1990. Toward a multidimensional assessment of work spillover into family life.** *Journal of Marriage and the Family* **52: 51-61.**

A sample of 130 male executives and wives were surveyed. The Work Spillover Scale, which consists of 20 items for worker's self-report (Table 1, p. 53) and for spouse (Table 2, p. 52), are presented. Evidence of construct validity and internal reliability is presented and discussed.

291   **Staines, G. L. 1980. Spillover versus compensation: A review of the literature on the relationship between work and nonwork.** *Human Relations* **33(2): 111-129.**

Staines frames a discussion of the relationship between work and nonwork with an extensive review of the literature. The review focuses on two competing models: spillover theory and compensation theory. Staines supports his analysis with empirical data.

292   **Westman, M., and D. Etzion. 1995. Crossover of stress, strain and resources from one spouse to another.** *Organizational Behavior* **16: 169-181.**

Questionnaire data were gathered from 101 couples (male Israeli military officers and wives). Structural equation analysis demonstrated a crossover effect. A crossover of burnout was exhibited from wives to husbands and husbands to wives.

293   **Williams, K. J., and G. M. Alliger. 1994. Role stressors, mood spillover, and perceptions of work-family conflict in employed parents.** *Academy of Management Journal* **37(4): 837-868.**

Daily diary reports of 41 employed parents were analyzed. The study found that unpleasant moods spilled over from work to family and from family to work. However, there was only weak evidence for positive spillover.

CHAPTER 10

Role Conflict/Strain/Stress and Well-Being

294   Beehr, T. A., and J. E. Newman. 1978. Job stress, employee health, and organizational effectiveness: A facet analysis, model, and literature review. *Personnel Psychology* 31: 665-699.

The authors review the empirical research conducted by industrial/organizational psychologists on job stress and employee health from several approaches (e.g., environmental, organizational consequences, personal). Methodological problems are identified and discussed.

295   Bhagat, R. S. 1983. Effects of stressful life events on individual performance effectiveness and work adjustment processes within organizational settings: A research model. *Academy of Management Review* 8(4): 660-671.

This paper proposes a conceptual model that integrates stressful life events in the personal domain with stresses in the organizational domain. The implications of the findings are discussed.

296   Bhagat, R. S., S. J. McQuaid, H. Lindholm, and J. Segovis. 1985. Total life stress: A multimethod validation of the construct and its effects on organizationally valued outcomes and withdrawal behaviors. *Journal of Applied Psychology* 70(1): 202-214.

This study's stated purpose was to validate a construct—"total life stress." Bhagat and colleagues suggest that researchers use a holistic perspective by combining effects of job stress, personal life stress and total life stress with employee well-being. The authors make suggestions for future organizational research and discuss the implications for human resource management.

297   Billings, A., and R. Moos. 1982. Work stress and the stress-buffering roles of work and family resources. *Journal of Occupational Behaviour* 3: 215-232.

The authors assess work and family environments. This study measures an individual's perception of his or her work setting (Work Environment Scale [WES]); measures family resources (Family Environment Scale [FES]; and assesses personal functioning (Health and Daily Living Form [HDL]). Billings and Moos suggest that the WES is a useful assessment technique. Results indicate that characteristics of the work environment not only affect the individuals' personal functioning, but also their family members.

298   Burke, R. J. 1988. Some antecedents and consequences of work-family conflict. In *Journal of Social Behavior and Personality: Work and Family: Theory, Research, and Applications*, edited by E. B. Goldsmith. Corte Madera, CA: Select Press. 287-302.

In this model, work-family conflict is an intervening variable. Using questionnaire data from 828 men and women police officers, the study found work-family conflict significantly related to outcome measures, and weakly correlated with demographic antecedents.

299   Burke, R. J., and E. R. Greenglass. Work and family. In *International Review of Industrial and Organizational Psychology*, edited by C. L. Cooper and I. T. Robertson. New York: John Wiley. 273-320.

300   Burley, K. A. 1994. Gender differences and similarities in coping responses to anticipated work-family conflict. *Psychological Reports* 74(1): 115-123.

Burley addresses the issue of how men and women differ in their future expectations of work-family conflict and the coping strategies that they use to handle work-family conflict. A sample of university students (n = 256) were measured on the Interrole Conflict Scale and the Dual Employed Coping Scales. Findings suggest a gender difference in expected work-family conflict and use of coping strategies.

301   Cooke, R. A., and D. M. Rousseau. 1984. **Stress and strain from family roles and work-role expectations.** *Journal of Applied Psychology* **69(2): 252-260.**

In this classic study, Cooke and Rousseau examined the effects of work role expectations and family roles on employed men and women (n = 200 teachers). The study showed that work-nonwork conflict is negatively related to life satisfaction.

302   Crosby, F. J., ed. 1987. *Spouse, Parent, Worker: On Gender and Multiple Roles.* **New Haven, CT: Yale University Press.**

This book provides an overview of the empirical research on balancing work and family. Also included is an analysis of Gilligan's research and data.

303   Duxbury, L., C. Higgins, and C. Lee. 1994. **Work-Family conflict: A comparison by gender, family type, and perceived control.** *Journal of Family Issues* **15(3): 449-466.**

Two perspectives guide this research on work-family conflict: the rational model of work-family conflict (time, role overload) and the two-dimensional model of work strain (perceived control). Drawing on survey data, the researchers examined the impact of gender, family structure (i.e., dual-career, single-parent), and perceived control on work-family conflict. The results support the job strain model.

304   Eckenrode, J., and S. Gore. 1990. *Stress between Work and Family.* **New York: Plenum Press.**

305   Edwards, J. R. 1988. **The determinants and consequences of coping with stress.** In *Causes, Coping and Consequences of Stress at Work,* **edited by C. L. Cooper and R. Payne. Chichester, U. K.: John Wiley and Sons. 233-263.**

A review and analysis of the literature on theoretical perspectives of coping serves as a framework for the introduction of an integrated model of coping. Suggestions for future research are made.

306   Frame, M. W., and C. L. Shehan. 1994. Work and well-being in the two-person career: Relocation stress and coping among clergy husbands and wives. *Family Relations* 43: 196-205.

This paper focused on stress and involuntary and frequent relocation of clergy families— a family structure referred to as a "two-person career." Themes gleaned from the qualitative data are discussed. Among the concepts receiving support in this study was the "pile-up of demands" that basically is a cumulative effect of stressors occurring during a major life crisis.

307   Frone, M. R., M. Russell, and M. L. Cooper. 1992. Prevalence of work-family conflict: Are work and family boundaries asymmetrically permeable? *Journal of Organizational Behavior* 13: 723-729.

Interview data from 631 employed adults (with approximate equal representation of race and class) are examined in terms of the permeability of work and family boundaries. The findings suggest that both work and family boundaries are permeable. However, work appears to interfere with family life more often than family life interferes with work.

308   Googins, B. K. 1991. *Work/Family Conflicts: Private Lives-Public Responses.* New York: Auburn House Publishing.

309   Googins, B. K., M. L. Griffin, and J. C. Casey. 1994. *Balancing Job and Homelife: Changes over Time in a Corporation.* Boston, MA: Center on Work and Family at Boston University.

This is one of the first longitudinal, work-family workplace-based studies. The data were collected at an electronics corporation during 1985 (n = 849) and 1992 (n = 724). Between the two data collection periods, the company established a series of work-family supports. In 1992, concerns about managing personal and family time were reported by an increased percentage of respondents. Data about job-family role strain, job satisfaction, family environment, work environment, and job/family management are presented.

310   Greenglass, E. R., K. Pantony, and R. J. Burke. 1988. A gender-role perspective on role conflict, work stress and social support.

Chapter 10/ Role Conflict/Strain/Stress and Well-Being

In *Journal of Social Behavior and Personality: Work and Family: Theory, Research, and Applications,* edited by E. B. Goldsmith. Corte Madera, CA: Select Press. 317-328.

This study tests gender role differences on role conflict scales developed by Holahan and Gilbert, 1979. The scales assess role conflict in the work and non-work domains (e.g., Professional vs. Self, Professional vs. Spouse, Spouse vs. Parent). Survey data were gathered from school teachers and administrators (n = 556). The study found that women experience more role conflict than men (e.g., between work and family roles and between wife and mother).

311   Greenhaus, J. H., and N. J. Beutell. 1985. Sources of conflict between work and family roles. *Academy of Management Review* 10(1): 76-88.

This analysis and review of the literature on conflict focuses on the sources of conflict between work and family roles. Greenhaus and Beutell present a number of research propositions on work-family conflict. The paper concludes with a discussion of research issues (e.g., psychometric limitations).

312   Greenhaus, J. H., and S. Parasuraman. 1987. A work-nonwork interactive perspective of stress and its consequences. *Journal of Organizational Behavior Management* 8(2): 37-60.

Proposes an integrative model designed to illuminate the relationships between stress in the work and non-work domains. The researchers identify organizational strategies and make suggestions for future research.

313   Guelzow, M. G., G. W. Bird, and E. H. Koball. 1995. An exploratory path analysis of the stress process for dual-career men and women. In *Work and Family Interface: Toward a Contextual Effects Perspective,* edited by G. L. Bowen and J. F. Pittman. Minneapolis, MN: National Council on Family Relations. 62-73.

This study presents and tests a "job demands model" of the stress process. The underlying premise is that work-family stress is a result of job characteristics or attributes. Data from women and men (n = 309) were analyzed and support for the model was found.

314   Gutek, B. A., S. Searle, and L. Klepa. 1991. Rational versus gender role explanations for work-family conflict. *Journal of Applied Psychology* 76(4): 560-568.

Examines two competing perspectives that might explain work-family conflict: the rational view perspective and the gender role perspective. The results of the study support elements of each perspective.

315   Hibbard, J. H., and C. R. Pope. 1987. Employment characteristics and health status among men and women. *Women and Health* 12(2): 85-102.

Using survey data from 1,490 employed women and men in 1970-71 and seven years of medical record data, the researchers analyze work and job characteristics of men and women, and then determine if a relationship exists with health status.

316   Holm, J. E., and K. A. Holroyd. 1992. The Daily Hassles Scale (revised): Does it measure stress or symptoms? *Behavioral Assessment* 14(3/4): 465-482.

Examines a revised Daily Hassles Scale (DHS-R). This study explores and evaluates the underlying structure and framework for conceptualizing the DHS-R.

317   Izraeli, D. N. 1993. Work/family conflict among women and men managers in dual-career couples in Israel. *Journal of Social Behavior and Personality* 8(3): 371-385.

In this study of managers in dual-career couples in Israel (n = 237 women, 211 men), the findings indicate little differences for gender. The implications are that women and men of similar occupational status are affected by similar sources of conflict.

318   Kahn, R. L., D. M. Wolfe, R. Quinn, J. D. Snoek, and R. A. Rosenthal. 1964. *Organizational Stress.* New York: Wiley.

319 Kelloway, E. K., and J. Barling. 1991. Job characteristics, role stress and mental health. *Journal of Occupational Psychology* 64 : 291-304.

Proposes and evaluates a process model linking job and role characteristics to mental health. The model identifies job and role characteristics that predict mental health.

320 Kelly, R. F., and P.Voydanoff. 1985. Work/family role strain among employed parents. *Family Relations* 34: 367-374.

Examined the sources of work-family role strain using questionnaire data from 468 employed parents in the Southeast. A multiple regression analysis was performed on an inductive model of work-family role strain containing sources at three levels: (1) individual; (2) family-related; and (3) work-related. Results indicated that the work-related variables impacted the dependent variable (job tension) the most.

321 Kopelman, R. E., J. H. Greenhaus, and T. F. Connolly. 1983. A model of work, family, and interrole conflict: A construct validation study. *Organizational Behavior and Human Performance* 32: 198-215.

The authors define the concepts of work-family conflict, and then examine the construct validity of three scales (Likert-Type) measuring work conflict, family conflict, and interrole conflict.

322 Larson, R. W., M. H. Richards, and M. Perry-Jenkins. 1994. Divergent worlds: The daily emotional experience of mothers and fathers in the domestic and public spheres. *Journal of Personality and Social Psychology* 67(6): 1034-1046.

This study compares the emotional states of mothers and fathers in the private and public spheres. Self-reports of emotional states were recorded for one week at the time of a beeping pager. Results differ by gender: (1) mothers reported more positive emotional states away from home; and (2) fathers reported more positive emotional states at home.

323   Lobel, S. A. 1991. Allocation of investment in work and family roles: Alternative theories and implications for research. *Academy of Management Review* 16(3): 507-521.

Lobel reviews and compares two theoretical approaches —utilitarian and social identity—to career and family role investment. The perspectives attribute different factors to work-family conflict and offer differing pathways to work-family balance. Lobel suggests that researchers might focus on gender, life course, and culture, and move towards an integrated model.

324   Marshall, N. L., and R. C. Barnett. 1993. Variations in job strain across nursing and social work specialties. *Journal of Community and Applied Social Psychology* 3: 261-271.

This study examines job strain variation across different nursing and social work specialties (n = 285). Analyses indicate that the specialties that reported the best job conditions reported better physical and mental health. For example, school social workers reported good job conditions and reported better mental and psychological health.

325   Moen, P., and D. Dempster-McClain. 1987. Employed parents: Role strain, work time, and preferences for working less. *Journal of Marriage and the Family* 49: 579-590.

This study examines the work-time preferences for dual-career couples, both the amount of time they would like to work and the amount of time they prefer their spouse would work. A subsample of dual-earner couples with young children drawn from the 1977 Quality of Employment Survey is analyzed. The results reveal that gender, actual work hours, work-family interference are important factors in preferring reduced hours a t work.

326   O'Driscoll, M. P., D. R. Ilgen, and K. Hildreth. 1992. Time devoted to job and off-job activities, interrole conflict, and affective experiences. *Journal of Applied Psychology* 77(3): 272-279.

This study focuses on time demands in work and non-work

domains and the resulting conflicts and affective experiences. Path Analyses were conducted on three theoretical models linking job and off-job conflict (interference).

327   O'Neil, R., and E. Greenberger. 1994. **Patterns of commitment to work and parenting: Implications for role strain.** *Journal of Marriage and the Family* **56: 101-118.**

This study examined commitments to roles and the effect on strain. Self-report measures were administered to middle-class parents (n = 296) concerning their perceptions of role strain, role commitment, role quality, social support, and occupation.

328   Perry-Jenkins, M., and K. Folk. 1994. **Class, couples, and conflict: Effects of the division of labor on assessments of marriage in dual-earner families.** *Journal of Marriage and the Family* **56: 165-180.**

Drawing on data from the 1988 National Survey of Families and Households, dual-earner couples were categorized by class. The study found differences by class (e.g., sharing housework unequally created more conflict for middle-class wives).

329   Pleck, J. H. 1995. **Work roles, family roles, and well-being: Current conceptual perspectives.** In *The Work and Family Interface: Toward a Contextual Effects Perspective,* edited by G. L. Bowen and J. F. Pittman. **Minneapolis, MN: National Council on Family Relations. 17-22.**

This introduction examines three work-family models: multiple roles, job demands model, and spillover/crossover models.

330   Pleck, J. H., and G. L. Staines. 1983. **Work schedules and work-family conflict in two-earner couples.** In *Two Paychecks: Life in Dual-Earner Families,* edited by J. Aldous. **Beverly Hills, CA: Sage Publications. 63-87.**

Prior research approaches to work-family conflict used a "between groups" approach. This study examines dual career couples from within-individual schedule conflict and between-spouse schedule conflict.

331   Pleck, J. H., G. L. Staines, and L. Lang. 1980. Conflicts between work and family life. *Monthly Labor Review* 103(3): 29-32.

Examines prevalence and types of work-family conflict. Job characteristics contributing to work family conflict are discussed (e.g., hours worked, frequent overtime). The paper concludes with data and remarks correlating work-family conflict and job satisfaction.

332   Stephens, G. K., and S. H. Sommer. 1995. Linking work-family conflict, work-based social support, and work group climate with job involvement and organizational citizenship behavior: Testing a path analytic model. *Journal of Health and Human Services Administration* Summer: 44-67.

Stephens investigates the direct and indirect impact of work-family conflict on job involvement and organizational citizenship. The results of a path analysis show no direct impact. However, results indicate that both behavior-based and strain-based conflict affect job involvement and organizational citizenship indirectly through social support and work group climate.

333   Stephens, G. K., and S. M. Sommer. 1996. The measurement of work to family conflict. *Educational and Psychological Measurement* 56(3): 475-486.

The authors developed a measure designed to assess conflict originating in the work domain and affecting the family domain. Data from a larger survey were used for both the exploratory and confirmatory analysis. Results indicate the three-factor solution (i.e., time based, strain based, and behavior based) was superior.

334   Voydanoff, P. 1980. Work roles as stressors in corporate families. *Family Relations* 29(4): 489-494.

This paper addresses the issue of executive work roles and their impact on families. Voydanoff considers specific work role stressors that impact corporate families, such as employment insecurity, career mobility, geographic mobility, work time, and the corporate wife role.

335 Wharton, A. S., and R. J. Erickson. 1993. Managing emotions on the job and at home: Understanding the consequences of multiple emotional roles. *Academy of Management Review* 18(3): 457-486.

This organizational research focuses on work-family relations from an emotion management perspective. The variation in types and degree of emotion management required in the work and family domains is considered.

CHAPTER 11

Role Experiences and Work/Life/ Marital Satisfaction

336   Andrews, A., and L. Bailyn. 1993. Segmentation and synergy: Two models of linking work and family. In *Men, Work, and Family*, edited by J. C. Hood. Newbury Park, CA: Sage Publications. 262-275.

Andrews and Bailyn present two models for handling the tension between work and family spheres: the segmented model and the synergistic model. The basic thesis is that the majority of men employ a segmented model, which is a way of viewing work and family roles as distinct and of viewing one sphere as a drain on the other. Women, on the other hand, are more apt to utilize a synergistic model, or a way of bridging the two spheres. Interview data from a longitudinal study of MBAs are analyzed and discussed in terms of the two models. In the long term, women adapted better because of their synergistic outlook, whereas men, after 10 years experienced more work-family stress than women.

337   Barling, J., and K. E. MacEwen. 1992. Linking work experiences to facets of marital functioning. *Journal of Organizational Behavior* 13: 573-583.

This study examines the effects of the nature of work (i.e., role ambiguity, conflict, job insecurity, and job satisfaction) on marital functioning. Rather than proposing a direct model (e.g., spillover), Barling and MacEwen propose an indirect model involving the mediational variables of depression and concentration. It is hypothesized that stressors (e.g., role conflict) will affect attention and concentration; whereas job satisfaction will affect depression. Results of path analysis indicate mediating effects of work on marital functioning. The researchers underscore the importance of understanding the nature of the stressor.

338   Barnett, R. C., N. L. Marshall, and J. H. Pleck. 1995. Men's multiple roles and their relationship to men's psychological distress. In *The Work and Family Interface: Toward a Contextual Effects Perspective, edited by G. L. Bowen and J. F. Pittman.* Minneapolis, MN: National Council on Family Relations. 33-41.

This paper examines the quality of men's family roles and work roles and their relationship to psychological distress in a sample of 300 employed, married men in dual-earner relationships. In particular, the researchers assess the moderating effects of the marital role between job-role quality and psychological distress. Results indicate general support for the moderating effects of the quality of marital role and parental role. In other words, when men have rewarding experiences in the marital roles and parental roles, poor experiences on the job will have less effect on their mental health.

339   Bedeian, A. G., B. G. Burke, and R. G. Moffett. 1988. Outcomes of work-family conflict among married male and female professionals. *Journal of Management* 14(3): 475-491.

Examines the processes involved in the interrelationships between work-role stress and parental demands, and how they influence work and family outcomes (i.e., job, marital, and life satisfaction). A hypothesized model is tested on a sample of accounting professionals (n = 423 male, 335 female). Overall, the results support the model. The researchers note the absence of significant gender differences.

340   Blair, S. L., and M. P. Johnson. 1992. Wives' perceptions of the fairness of the division of household labor: The intersection of housework and ideology. *Journal of Marriage and the Family* 54: 570-581.

Set within an ideological framework, this analysis draws upon data from the 1988 National Survey of Families and Households. Using a subsample of 778 married white women, the study examines wives' reports regarding the division of housework. Wives' perception of fairness is related to two primary factors: (1) husbands' share of work traditionally considered women's work; and (2) husbands' appreciation of wives' work. The authors note that ideological factors are not central to women's perceptions of fairness.

341   Burke, R. J., and C. A. McKeen. 1994. **Work, career, and life experiences associated with different career patterns among managerial and professional women.** In *Job Stress in a Changing Workforce: Investigating Gender, Diversity, and Family Issues,* edited by G. P. Keita and J. J. Hurrell. Washington, DC: American Psychological Association. 301-310.

In this study, 792 managerial and professional female graduates in Canada were asked to respond to scenarios and place themselves on a work-family continuum. The researchers characterized their involvement in the work-family domains from career-primary to career-family, thus representing the ends of the continuum. The study examined both antecedent and outcome variables. More respondents placed themselves in the career-family end of the continuum. The researchers briefly consider the implications both to women and organizations.

342   Forthofer, M. S., H. J. Markman, M. Cox, S. Stanley, and R. C. Kessler. 1996. **Associations between marital distress and work loss in a national sample.** *Journal of Marriage and the Family* **58: 597-605.**

Examines the association between marital problems and work loss. Data are drawn from the National Comorbidity Survey and analyzed. Results indicate that marriage does spill over to produce work loss among males, particularly in the first 10 years of marriage. Discusses gender differences, developmental issues, and social policy implications.

343   Grimm-Thomas, K., and M. Perry-Jenkins. 1994. **All in a day's work: Job experiences, self-esteem, and fathering in working-class families.** *Family Relations* **43: 174-181.**

This study examines linkages between working-class fathers' job experiences, self-esteem, and their parenting styles. Interview data were collected from 59 working-class, dual-earner families (mother, father, and a target child). Results indicate that the fathers' positive work experiences, such as autonomy, involvement, and supervisor support, were positively related to fathers' self-esteem. High self-esteem, in turn, predicts a more accepting parental style. The authors discuss results from the perspective of employers and family practitioners.

344   Hanson, S. L., and D. M. Sloane. 1992. **Young children and job satisfaction.** *Journal of Marriage and the Family* **54: 799-811.**

Performs a secondary analysis of the General Social Surveys (GSS) family and work data to examine the effects of young children on both men and women's job satisfaction. In particular, the authors were interested in comparative effects of different work and marital status at different points in time. The analysis using logistic regression models reveal no effects of young children on job satisfaction, regardless of gender, work status (e.g., full-time or part-time), marital status, and for workers in the 1970s and the 1980s.

345   Hood, J. C., ed. 1993. *Men, Work, and Family.* **Newbury Park, CA: Sage Publications.**

346   Iris, B., and G. V. Barrett. 1972. **Some relations between job and life satisfaction and job importance.** *Journal of Applied Psychology* **56(4): 301-304.**

Examined the relationships between job satisfaction, job importance, and life satisfaction. Iris and Barret studied two samples of foreman who had varying levels of job satisfaction, and concluded that the results support the role spillover theory. The researchers also underscored the utility of the concept of "job importance" in understanding the relationship between job and life satisfaction.

347   Ladewig, B. H., and G. W. McGee. 1986. **Occupational commitment, a supportive family environment, and marital adjustment: Development and estimation of a model.** *Journal of Marriage and the Family* **48: 821-829.**

The researchers examine marital adjustment among men and women in dual-earner marriages using a structural equation analysis to test the model separately for men and women. The sample consisted of 92 married couples. The results suggest that higher levels of job commitment for women negatively affected marital adjustment. For men, however, higher levels of job commitment did not affect marital adjustment.

348   McHale, S. M., and A. C. Crouter. 1992. You can't always get what you want: Incongruence between sex-role attitudes and family work roles and its implications for marriage. *Journal of Marriage and the Family*   54: 537-547.

Data drawn from a short-term longitudinal Penn State Family Relations project were used to examine sex-role attitudes (e.g., traditional, nontraditional), division of family work, and marital evaluations in a sample of 153 couples with firstborn school-age children. Group comparisons supported the researchers' hypothesis that couples with incongruent attitudes and roles would be at risk for lower marital evaluations. Follow-up revealed that for men, negative marital evaluation persisted across a one-year period, and for women, across a two-year period.

349   Menaghan, E. G. 1991.   Work experiences and family interaction processes: The long reach of the job? *Annual Review Sociology*   17: 419-444.

350   Parasuraman, S., J. H. Greenhaus, S. Rabinowitz, A. G. Bedeian, and K. W. Mossholder. 1989. Work and family variables as mediators of the relationship between wives' employment and husbands' well-being.   *Academy of Management Journal*   32(1): 185-201.

This study compares the well-being (i.e., job satisfaction, marital adjustment, and quality of life) of husbands of housewives and husbands of employed women. Drawing upon a database of accountants, the sample consisted of 413 employed, married men. The researchers report a small negative relationship between wives' employment status and two measures of husbands' well-being (i.e., job satisfaction and quality of life).

351   Rice, R. W., D. B. McFarlin, R. G. Hunt, and J. P. Near. 1985. Organizational work and the perceived quality of life: Toward a conceptual model. *Academy of Management Review* 10(2): 296-310.

Presents a conceptual model designed to examine the effects of organizational work and the perceived quality of life. The perceived quality of life is defined in psychological terms, such as "affect," or one's present level of pleasure, happiness, well-being, or satisfaction. In this model, perceived quality of life is related and mediated by various domains, for example the work domain. The researchers posit that the way work may influence the perceived quality of life emphasizes the psychosocial aspects of work and the importance of linkages to human health and well-being.

352   Rice, R. W., M. R. Frone, and D. B. McFarlin. 1992. Work-nonwork conflict and the perceived quality of life. *Journal of Organizational Behavior* 13: 155-168.

Examines mediating variables that might moderate the relationship between work-nonwork conflict and overall perceived quality of life. Drawing on data from the 1977 Quality of Employment Survey, the reports of 823 employed respondents were analyzed. Results showed that job satisfaction and nonwork satisfaction mediated work-nonwork conflict and perceived quality of life.

353   Rogers, S. J. 1996. Mothers' work hours and marital quality: Variations by family structure and family size. *Journal of Marriage and the Family* 58: 606-617.

This study examined the relationship between married mothers' employment and marital conflict and marital happiness. Panel data were drawn from the 1988 wave of the National Longitudinal Survey of Youth, Merged Child-Mother. Two types of family structure were examined: (1) continuously married families with children; and (2) mother-stepfather families with children. The results indicated that for mother-stepfather families, mothers' full-time employment was associated with more positive reports of marital quality when there were more children in the household.

354   **Staines, G. L., J. H. Pleck, L. J. Shepard, and P. O'Connor. 1978. Wives' employment status and marital adjustment: Yet another look.** *Psychology of Women Quarterly* **3(1): 90-120.**

This study focuses on wives' employment status and the marital adjustment evaluations of wives' and husbands'. This study uses data from two national surveys: the 1971 Quality of Life Survey and the 1973 Omnibus Survey. Analyses indicate that wives' employment status does not affect husbands' reports of marital adjustment. However, reports of negative marital adjustment were linked to employment status for two groups of women: (1) mothers of preschool children; and (2) wives with less than a high school diploma.

355   **Staines, G. L, K. J. Pottick, and D. A. Fudge. 1985. The effects of wives' employment on husbands' job and life satisfaction.** *Psychology of Women Quarterly* **9(3): 419-423.**

This study examines the effects of wives' employment on husbands' mental health. Survey data from the 1977 Quality of Employment Survey were used in this analysis of two groups of employed husbands: (1) one group whose wives worked more than 20 hours a week; and (2) one group whose wives were housewives. Results showed that husbands whose wives worked reported lower levels of job satisfaction and life satisfaction.

356   **Zedeck, S., C. Maslach, K. Mosier, and L. Skitka. 1988. Affective response to work and quality of family life: Employee and spouse perspectives.** In *Journal of Social Behavior and Personality: Work and Family: Theory, Research, and Applications,* **edited by E. B. Goldsmith. Corte Madera, CA: Select Press. 135-157.**

The researchers focused on link between affective responses to work and the impairment of family life. Two samples were studied: an employee and a spouse sample. The employee sample consisted of 818 females and 257 males, with spouse sample being reversed. Affective responses of employees were measured by three satisfaction measures and three burnout measures. Spouses were questioned concerning happiness with own and spouses' job, and the effects of spouses' job on family life. Employees' affective responses (i.e., burnout and job satisfaction) were related to spousal reports of problems in family life.

357   Zvonkovic, A. M., C. J. Schmiege, and L. D. Hall. 1994. Influence strategies used when couples make work-family decisions and their importance for marital satisfaction. *Family Relations* 43: 182-188.

This study investigated the research question of how husbands and wives influence each other in the decision-making process concerning work-family issues. Further, the study connected the influence strategies to marital satisfaction. The volunteer sample consisted of 61 married couples who recently faced a work-family decision. An analysis of the questionnaire data indicated that indirect strategies are related to marital satisfaction. The study also found that men and women did not differ in the influence strategies they used.

CHAPTER 12

Changing Roles (Mother as Breadwinner, Father as Caregiver)

358   Cohen, T. F. 1993. What do fathers provide? Reconsidering the economic and nurturant dimensions of men as parents. In *Men, Work, and Family*, edited by J. C. Hood. Newbury Park, CA: Sage Publications. 1-22.

Cohen provides a descriptive profile of father as a nurturer using interview data from a purposive sample of working- and middle-class men. Cohen makes the point that "traditional work-centered definitions of fathering are inadequate" (p. 19). The need for researchers to separate the two dimensions (provider and nurturer) of parenting to fully understand them is emphasized.

359   Cohen, T. F. 1989. Becoming and being husbands and fathers: Work and family conflict for men. In *Gender in Intimate Relationships*, edited by B. J. Risman and P. Schwartz. Belmont, CA: Wadsworth. 220-234.

In this grounded theory analysis, Cohen operationalizes "opportunities" that men have and "role conceptualizations" as continuous variables rather than dichotomous variables. Themes and patterns are presented and discussed.

360   Coltrane, S. 1989. Household labor and the routine production of gender. *Social Problems* 36(5): 473-490.

Data were gathered on a sample (snowball) of 20 moderate to middle income families by interview and observation in their homes. The interview data is woven throughout Coltrane's exploration of how families share child care and housework responsibilities.

361   Crouter, A. C., and M. S. Crowley. 1990. School-age children's time alone with fathers in single- and dual-earner families: Implications for the father-child relationship. *Journal of Early Adolescence* 10(3): 296-312.

Focuses on fathers' involvement with school age children. Data on time and "quality time" were gathered by interviews, home visits, and follow-up phone calls. The study found that dual-earner fathers spent equal time alone with sons and daughters, whereas single-earner dads spent more time with sons. The greater time spent alone with father, the closer girls felt to their fathers.

362   Crouter, A. C., M. Perry-Jenkins, T. L. Huston, and S. M. McHale. 1987. Processes underlying father involvement in dual-earner and single-earner families. *Developmental Psychology* 23(3): 431-440.

Father involvement was compared between dual-earner and single-earner families. Using data from the Processes of Adaptation in Intimate Relationships (PAIR) project, this study uses a subsample of data (n = 40) gathered from interviews and followed by nine phone calls through the next few weeks. Findings suggest fathers in dual-earner families were more involved with child care; however, involvement in leisure activities did not differ.

363   Dennehy, K., and J. T. Mortimer. 1993. Role allocation and role change: Work and family orientations of contemporary adolescent boys and girls. In *Men, Work, and Family*, edited by J. C. Hood. Newbury Park, CA: Sage Publications. 87-107.

Survey data from a panel study of Minnesota high school students is analyzed. The study examines adolescent boys' and girls' attitudes toward work and family.

364   Downey, G., and P. Moen. 1987. Personal efficacy, income, and family transitions: A longitudinal study of women heading households. *Journal of Health and Social Behavior* 28: 320-333.

This study examines women's sense of personal efficacy in

relation to their earnings using data from the Panel Study of Income Dynamics (PSID). The subsample used includes women who headed households for whom data was gathered on the following measures: personal efficacy, income, work transitions, parenting transitions, and marital transitions. Regression analyses indicate that an increase in income is associated with personal efficacy supporting the theoretical perspective of role enhancement.

365   Families and Work Institute. 1995. *Women: The New Providers.* New York: Families and Work Institute. Whirlpool Foundation Study, Part One.

The findings in this report underscore women's role as provider. Data comes from two sources: a nationally representative sample of 1,502 women and focus groups.

366   Gerson, K. Forthcoming. The social construction of fatherhood: The decline of primary breadwinning and the rise of new fathering patterns. In *Parenting: Contemporary Issues and Challenges,* edited by T. Arendell. Newbury Park, CA: Sage. 170-173.

Based on patterns of fatherhood culled from interview data with 138 men, Gerson, identifies three general types of fathers: (1) the breadwinners (36%); (2) the avoidant father (no children, estranged from children, 30%); and (3) the involved father (33%). The analysis links patterns of fatherhood to social change.

367   Gerson, K. Forthcoming. An institutional perspective on generative fathering: Creating social supports for parenting equality. In *Generative Fathering: Beyond Deficit Perspectives,* edited by A. J. Hawkins and D. C. Dollahite. Newbury Park, CA: Sage.

This chapter focuses on how institutional processes shape the degree and type of father involvement. The institutional approach underscores the social context and identifies social arrangements that support or block the pathway to generative fathering.

368   Gerson, K. 1994. A few good men: Overcoming the barriers to involved fatherhood. *American Prospect* 16: 78-90.

Examines the issue of involved fatherhood from several perspectives using interview data. Social and ideological obstacles are explored.

369   Gerson, K. 1993. *No Man's Land: Men's Changing Commitments to Family and Work.* New York: Basic Books.

370   Gerson, K. 1991. Coping with commitment: Dilemmas and conflicts of family life. In *America at Century's End,* edited by A. Wolfe. Berkeley, CA: University of California Press. 35-57.

Gerson posits that the conflict between work and family responsibilities results primarily from "incomplete and unequal social change." The analysis uses interview data from two studies to illustrate both women's and men's family responses. Social implications are discussed.

371   Gerson, K. 1988. Reluctant mothers: Employed women in the '80s. In *Gender in Intimate Relationships: A Microstructural Approach,* edited by B. J. Risman and P. Schwartz. Belmont, CA: Wadsworth. 205-219.

Gerson examines the processes by which a group of work-committed women are making choices about motherhood and work. Because of the changing trends in our society, women face different forms of "structural ambiguity" and choose divergent pathways even when they begin from the same baseline (fig. 1, p. 207).

372   Gerson, K. 1988. Briefcase, baby, or both? In *Feminist Frontiers: Rethinking Sex, Gender, and Society,* edited by B.J. Risman and P. Schwartz. New York: Wadsworth. 170-173.

Using life history data, Gerson illustrates the "powerful, interactive link between women's work and family decisions." Conflict between work and family responsibilities often force "hard choices" (p. 172). The point is made that women have progressed from few choices to "hard choices" because gender equity still does not exist.

373   Gerson, K. 1987. **How women choose between employment and family: A developmental perspective.** In *Families and Work,* edited by N. Gerstel and H. E. Gross. Philadelphia, PA: Temple University Press. 270-288.

This analysis links the choices women make between work and family commitments and the structural arrangements that shape those choices. Based on 60 in-depth life history interviews with women who became adults in the 1970s, the analysis compares the processes involved in making differing family commitments. Implications of structural and individual change are discussed.

374   Gerson, K. 1985. *Hard Choices: How Women Decide about Work, Career, and Motherhood.* Berkeley, CA: University of California Press.

375   Gerson, K. 1983. **Changing family structure and the position of women: A review of the trends.** *Journal of the American Planning Association* 4: 138-148.

Provides an overview of two major societal trends—changing family structure and patterns of female labor participation. Gerson underscores two points: (1) the trends are interrelated; and (2) the trends are deeply rooted. The analysis notes the growing challenges for social policy planners and makes suggestions.

376   Glass, J. 1992. **Housewives and employed wives: Demographic and attitudinal changes, 1972-1986.** *Journal of Marriage and the Family* 54: 559-569.

Attitudinal differences between employed women and housewives are explored. Using data from the General Social Survey, both demographic and attitudinal differences between housewives and wives employed full-time and part-time in 1972 and 1986. For the purposes of this study, the researchers divided attitudes into the following three groups: (1) political; (2) marital and work roles; and (3) sexual (and fertility control). The analysis revealed differences between housewives and full-time employed women. Women employed part-time were more likely to share "traditional" attitudes with housewives.

377 **Hood, J. C. 1986. The provider role: Its meaning and measurement.** *Journal of Marriage and the Family* **48: 349-359.**

This articles examines and critiques the way researchers have measured the provider role, that is, using measures that are underconceptualized. Hood argues that researchers need to use direct measures of the provider role. Qualitative data from a study of dual-earner couples and CPS statistics are used to support the argument.

378 **LaRossa, R. 1988. Fatherhood and social change.** *Family Relations* **37: 451-457.**

LaRossa distinguishes between the actual behavior of fathers and the culture of fatherhood which is defined as the "ideologies surrounding men's parenting." The basic thesis is that the behavior or conduct of fathers in the role of fatherhood is actually behind the culture, in other words, behavior lags ideology. Suggestions for researchers and practitioners are made.

379 **Manke, B., B. L. Seery, A. C. Crouter, and S. M. McHale. 1994. The three corners of domestic labor: Mothers', fathers', and children's weekday and weekend housework.** *Journal of Marriage and the Family* **56: 657-668.**

Examines how families (n = 153) divide housework between mothers, fathers, and children. Variables included in the analysis were earner status, child gender, and weekend or weekday housework. The study found fathers in single-earner families were less involved in housework during the week than their dual-earner counterparts.

380 **Moen, P. 1989.** *Working Parents: Transformations in Gender Roles and Public Policies in Sweden.* **Madison, WI: The University of Wisconsin Press.**

381   Perry-Jenkins, M., B. Seery, and A. C. Crouter. 1992. Linkages between women's provider-role attitudes, psychological well-being, and family relationships. *Psychology of Women Quarterly* 16: 311-329.

This study examines the meanings women attach to their provider-role responsibilities. Drawing from a longitudinal study, interview data from a subsample of 43 dual-earner and 50 single earner families (including children) were analyzed. Based on discriminant function analyses, the researchers created four provider groups: main/secondary providers, ambivalent coproviders, coproviders, and homemakers. Ambivalent providers were the most depressed.

382   Pleck, J. H. 1992. Families and work: Small changes with big implications. *Qualitative Sociology* 15(4): 427-432.

Pleck reviews three feminist sociological qualitative studies concerned with work-family issues: "The Second Shift," by A. Hochschild; "Feeding the Family," by M. DeVault; and "Brave New Families," by J. Stacey.

383   Pleck, J. H. 1986. Employment and fatherhood: Issues and innovative policies. In *The Father's Role: Applied Perspectives*, edited by M. E. Lamb. New York: Wiley. 385-412.

Based on the premise that fathers' employment affects their parental role, Pleck identifies institutional barriers and social policies that affect that parental role. Policies and practices reviewed include alternative work schedules and parental leave.

384   Pleck, J. H. 1985. *Working Wives/Working Husbands.* Beverly Hills, CA: Sage Publications.

385   Pleck, J. H. 1979. Men's family work: Three perspectives and some new data. *The Family Coordinator* 28: 481-488.

Pleck provides an overview of three value perspectives underpinning research on men's family work (i.e., housework, child care). Of the three perspectives—traditional, exploitative and changing roles—changing roles is an emerging perspective grounded in five areas of research. Pleck's discussion then centers on the changing roles perspective within the context of research.

386   Pleck, J. H., M. E. Lamb, and J. A. Levine. 1985/86. Epilog: Facilitating future change in men's family roles. *Marriage and Family Review* 9(3/4): 11-16.

Pleck identifies and discusses social factors that contribute to men's involvement in family roles: motivation, skills, social supports, and institutional barriers.

387   Potuchek, J. L. 1992. Employed wives' orientations to breadwinning: A gender theory analysis. *Journal of Marriage and the Family* 54: 548-558.

Using interview data from 153 dual-earner wives, Potuchek explores the meanings women attach to breadwinning. Potucheck posits that gender theory provides a useful framework because it raises the visibility of breadwinning, whereas early feminist theory obscured breadwinning. Regression analysis of the data supports the use of gender theory.

388   Russell, G. 1989. Work/Family patterns and couple relationships in shared caregiving families. *Social Behavior* 4(4): 265-283.

Russell provides a review of the research on shared caregiving families in various countries with child care as a major role of the father. Using the Dyadic Adjustment Scale, the investigation looks at (1) sharing of traditional male/female domains; (2) fathers' satisfaction as the instigator of shared caregiving; and (3) couple interactions among shared caregiving couples compared to traditional couples.

389   Russell, G., D. James, and J. Watson. 1988. Work/Family policies, the changing role of fathers and the presumption of shared responsibility for parenting. *Australian Journal of Social Issues* 23(4): 249-267.

390   Willinger, B. 1993. **Resistance and change: College men's attitudes toward family and work in the 1980s. In** *Men, Work, and Family,* **edited by J. C. Hood. Newbury Park, CA: Sage Publications. 108-130.**

Time series data were collected from 1,120 male college seniors from two southern universities (spring 1980, 1985, 1990). The study found that ascribed characteristics influence men's attitudes toward men's work and family roles. However, men's attitudes towards women's work and family roles is primarily influenced by family experiences and involvement in organizations that support sex segregation.

391   Woodhouse, L. 1988. **The new dependencies of women.** *Family Relations* **37: 379-384.**

Provides a description of the daily transition from family responsibilities to work responsibilities for mothers with children in daycare. Data for this ethnographic study of the culture of the day-care setting were gathered through participant observation and interviews with mothers, children, and staff. For Woodhouse, the "new dependencies of women can be defined as the gap between what the culture provides and what the individual needs."

CHAPTER 13

Impact of Parental Roles on Children
(annotated by Irene Fassler)

392   Bird, G. W., and L. N. Kemerait. 1990. Stress among early
        adolescents in two-earner families. *Journal of Early
        Adolescence* 10(3): 344-365.

        A sample of 173 eighth-grade adolescents (79 males and 94
        females) and their working parents were surveyed regarding
        adolescent role strain, coping strategies, psychological
        resources and parental work habits. Parental work habits did
        not have a negative effect on the level of emotional stress for
        adolescents.

393   Brayfield, A. 1995. Juggling jobs and kids: The impact of
        employment schedules on fathers' caring for children. *Journal
        of Marriage and the Family* 57: 321-332.

        Data on 1,452 families (National Child Care Survey 1990)
        indicate that fathers are more likely to be responsible for child
        care when they work different hours than their wives.
        Temporal features of maternal employment are more important
        than those of paternal employment when determining the level
        of father's involvement in child care.

394   Bronfenbrenner, U., and A. C. Crouter. 1982. Work and family
        through time and space. In *Families that Work: Children in a
        Changing World,* edited by S. B. Kamerman and C. D. Hayes.
        Washington, DC: The National Academy Press. 39-83.

        The authors analyze research on work-family issues prior to
        1960, as well as discuss scientific developments in the field
        during the next twenty years (1960-1980). This analysis
        examines two primary areas: (1) continuity and changes in
        questions posed for investigation; and (2) theoretical and

research models used. Implications for future research and public policy are offered.

395   Curtner-Smith, M. E., T. L. Bennett, and M. R. O'Rear. 1995. **Fathers' occupational conditions, values of self-direction and conformity, and perceptions of nurturant and restrictive parenting in relation to young children's depression and aggression.** *Family Relations* **44: 299-305.**

This study examines the relationship between employment and father's values and beliefs of his child's self-direction and conformity. Fifty-one mother-father dyads with older pre-school aged children participated in the study. Fathers who value self direction over conformity view themselves as less restrictive parents than fathers who value conformity over self-direction. A discussion of the implications for practitioners is included.

396   Demo, D. H. 1992. **Parent-child relations: Assessing recent changes.** *Journal of Marriage and the Family* **54 104-117.**

A review of research regarding parent-child relations demonstrates that while parents and children spend less time together than in the past, there is a general satisfaction regarding their relationship, due in part to a pattern of consistent parental support. The author encourages researchers to spend less time focusing on the consequences of maternal employment, divorce and the single parent family structure and more time investigating economic hardship and marital and family conflict.

397   Galambos, N. L., and J. L. Maggs. 1990. **Putting mothers' work-related stress in perspective: Mothers and adolescents in dual-earner families.** *Journal of Early Adolescence* **10(3): 313-328.**

This short term longitudinal study sampled 96 sixth graders (54 girls and 42 boys) and their employed mothers. A mother's work related stress, unlike her global stress, had little impact on the nature of the mother-adolescent relationship.

398   Gilbert, L. A., and L. S. Dancer. 1992. **Dual-earner families in the United States and adolescent development.** In *Dual-Earner*

Families: International Perspectives, edited by S. Lewis, D. N. Izraeli, and H. Hootsmans. London: Sage Publications. 151-171.

This chapter reviews literature on the dual-earner family and its influences on adolescents' expectations and choices.

399   Kamerman, S. B., and C. D. Hayes, eds. 1982. *Families that Work: Children in a Changing World.* Washington, DC: National Academy Press.

400   Keith, J. G., C. S. Nelson, J. H. Schlabach, and C. J. Thompson. 1990. The relationship between parental employment and three measures of early adolescent responsibility: Family-related, personal, and social. *Journal of Early Adolescence* 10(3): 399-415.

A sample of 174 early adolescents and their parents (1987 Michigan Early Adolescent Survey II) were surveyed. The survey was designed to measure four areas of responsibility for early adolescents: family related, personal and two forms of social responsibility. Parental work habits were found to have no significant effect on early adolescents' personal or family-related responsibility.

401   Menaghan, E. G., and T. L. Parcel. 1990. **Parental employment and family life: Research in the 1980s.** *Journal of Marriage and the Family* 52: 1079-1098.

The author reviews research on the effect of parental employment on: (1) parental well-being; (2) marital relationships; and (3) interaction patterns in families and the consequences for children. Suggestions for future research are made.

402   Mortimer, J. T., and M. J. Shanahan. 1994. **Adolescent work experience and family relationships.** *Work and Occupations* 21(4): 369-384.

Data were obtained from a randomly selected sample (n = 1000) of 9th grade students. This longitudinal study indicates that adolescent work has no significant effect on child-parent relationships.

403   Nock, S. L., and P. W. Kingston. 1988. **Time with children: The impact of couples' work-time commitments.** *Social Forces* 67(1): 59-85.

Detailed time diaries of 226 mother-father dyads demonstrate strong connections between couples' time in paid labor and time of parent-child contact. The data primarily reflect negative differences in maternal time allocation for activities in which children are peripherally involved, but not for child-oriented activities.

404   Orthner, D. K. 1990. **Parental work and early adolescence: Issues for research and practice.** *Journal of Early Adolescence* 10(3): 246-259.

The author reviews the literature on parental work and its effect on early adolescents. A discussion of maternal and adolescent adaptations to maternal work is developed. Suggestions for future research are offered.

405   Parcel, T. L., and E. G. Menaghan. 1994. *Parents' Jobs and Children's Lives.* New York: Aldine De Gruyter.

406   Quay, L. C. 1992. **Personal and family effects on loneliness.** *Journal of Applied Developmental Psychology* 13: 97-110.

A questionnaire to assess third through sixth grade children's feelings of loneliness and social dissatisfaction was modified for administration to kindergarten through fourth-grade students. The author found that children living in both two parent and single-parent families were less lonely than children in other arrangements. Further, maternal employment did not affect children's feelings of loneliness.

407   Repetti, R. L. 1994. **Employment and women's health: Short-term and long-term processes linking job stressors to father-child interaction.** *Social Development* 3 1-15.

Fifteen male air traffic controllers with a child between 4-10 years old contributed 41 days of data. Findings include presence of emotional withdrawal from parenting in response to high workload. Further, negative mood spillover increased negative interactions (immediately following negative mood) between parent and child.

408   Spade, J. Z. 1991. Occupational structure and men's and women's parental values. *Journal of Family Issues* 12(3): 343-360.

The author reviews research literature on parental values. Data collected in a 1981 survey of 186 dual-worker families demonstrates a similar relationship for men and women between educational and occupational histories, and parental values.

409   Stroh, L. K. 1990. Parents Perceptions on adjustment. *Children's Environmental Quarterly* 7(2): 26-34.

Data from 309 children, 6 - 18 years of age, who were involved in a family corporate move were gathered at two time points over an 18 month period. The analysis revealed no short-term effects and no cumulative effects from corporate moves.

PART 4

WORK-FAMILY EXPERIENCES AMONG POPULATION GROUPS

CHAPTER 14

Ethnic and Cultural Groups
(annotated by Irene Fassler)

410   Benin, M. H., and V. M. Keith. 1995. The social support of employed African American and Anglo mothers. *Journal of Family Issues* 16(3): 275-297.

Data from the 1988 National Survey of Families and Households of Non-Hispanic White and African American mothers employed 20 or more hours per week and who have children age 11 and under (n = 1,711) were analyzed. The authors conclude that African American working mothers are not obtaining the needed level of social support from family, friends, or neighbors.

411   Berger, P. S., A. S. Cook, R. L. DelCampo, R. S. Herrera, and R. R. Weigel. 1994. Family/work roles' relation to perceived stress: Do gender and ethnicity matter? *Journal of Family and Economic Issues* 15(3): 223-241.

A sample of 199 Anglo females, 115 Anglo males, 85 Mexican-American females and 35 Mexican-American males were surveyed. The authors found that regardless of ethnicity or gender, individuals experience less stress if it is believed that they maintain control over family matters; rather than if it is believed that outside forces control family matters.

412   Boyd, R. L. 1991. A contextual analysis of black self-employment in large metropolitan areas, 1970-1980. *Social Forces* 70(2): 409-429.

Data collected from the Public Use Samples, census volumes, and other sources indicate a rise in black self-employment from 1970 to 1980. The effects of family relationships and the demographic, ecological, and labor market characteristics on black entrepreneurship are studied. Suggestions for future research are made.

413   Boyd, R. L. 1990. **Black and Asian self-employment in large metropolitan areas: A comparative analysis.** *Social Problems* **37(2): 258-274.**

A history of self-employment for Asians and blacks is presented. Data were collected from the 1980 Public Use Microdata Samples, U.S. Bureaus of the Census, and other published sources. Findings include, a higher rate of support from social networks (e.g., family members), and therefore a higher rate of self-employment for Asians than blacks. Suggestions for future research are made.

414   Broman, C. L. 1995. **Gender, work-family roles, and psychological well-being of blacks.** In *The Work and Family Interface: Toward a Contextual Perspective,* edited by G. L. Bowen and J. F. Pittman. Minneapolis, MN: National Council on Family Relations. 171-181.

A sample (n = 2,107) from the National Survey of Black Americans (1979-1980) were interviewed regarding work and family roles. Married employed women were found to have lower levels of family life satisfaction than married unemployed women. Further, the presence of gender specific social roles has a significant effect on the psychological well-being among blacks.

415   Broman, C. L. 1988. **Household work and family life satisfaction of blacks.** *Journal of Marriage and the Family* 50: 743-748.

This study draws on data from the National Survey of Black Americans (1979-1980). Employed individuals who do most of the household chores, whether male or female, were found to have lower levels of family life satisfaction. Suggestions for further research are made.

416   Clark-Nicolas, P., and B. Gray-Little. 1995. **Effect of economic resources on marital quality in black married couples.** In *The Work and Family Interface: Toward a Contextual Effects*

Perspective, edited by G. L. Bowen and J. F. Pittman. Minneapolis, MN: National Council on Family Relations. 182-190.

417   Coltrane, S., and E. O. Valdez. 1993. Reluctant compliance: Work-family role allocation in dual-earner Chicano families. In *Men, Work, and Family,* edited by J. C. Hood. Newbury Park, CA: Sage Publications. 151-175.

A semistructured interview was utilized for a sample (n = 20) of Chicano couples. Findings included: husbands of white collar-working-class families shared more household chores than husbands of upper-middle-class families.

418   Crohan, S. E., T. C. Antonucci, P. K. Adelmann, and L. M. Coleman. 1989. Job characteristics and well-being at midlife: Ethnic and gender comparisons. *Psychology of Women Quarterly* 13: 223-235.

Data collected from two national surveys, Americans View Their Mental Health (AVTMH) and the National Survey of Black Americans (NSBA, 1979) were analyzed using multiple regressions. Occupational status was found to have a positive effect on perceived control for both black and white women. In addition, higher personal earnings was also found to have a positive effect on perceived control for black women. For white men, role conflict was found to have a negative effect on life satisfaction. The authors suggest that white men may experience higher incidence of conflict when attempting to integrate work and family at midlife.

419   Fulbright, K. 1987. The myth of the double-advantage: Black female managers. In *"Slipping through the Cracks: The Status of Black Women,"* edited by M. C. Simms and J. Malveaux. New Brunswick, NJ: Transaction Books. 33-45.

Reporting on the data from interviews with 25 black female managers, the author found that racial and/or gender discrimination, as well as other, more typical constraints that non-minority women managers may experience, act as barriers for black female managers.

420   Gutierres, S. E., D. S. Saenz, and B. L. Green. 1994. Job stress and health outcomes among white and Hispanic employees: A test of the person-environment fit model. In *Job Stress in a Changing Workforce: Investigating Gender, Diversity and Family Issues,* edited by G. P. Keita and J. J. Hurrell. Washington, DC: American Psychological Association. 107-125.

The results of surveys (n = 687) regarding employee stress in the workplace were reported. Higher levels of job-related stress were found to negatively impact employee health. Social supports at work minimized to a degree the negative impact that job related stress had on employee health.

421   Harrison, A. O. 1989. Black working women: Introduction to a life span perspective. In *Black Adult Development and Aging,* edited by R. L. Jones. Berkeley, CA: Cobb and Henry. 91-115.

422   Hossain, Z., and J. L. Roopnarine. 1994. African-American fathers' involvement with infants: Relationship to their functioning style, support, education, and income. *Infant Behavior and Development* 17: 175-184.

A sample of 40 full-time dual earner African-American families and 23 African-American families in which the wife worked part-time were surveyed regarding father's involvement in the care of their infant. Paternal involvement was not impacted by the amount of maternal work (e.g., full-time vs. part-time).

423   Jayakody, R., L. M. Chatters, and R. J. Taylor. 1993. Family support to single and married African American mothers: The provision of financial, emotional, and child care assistance. *Journal of Marriage and the Family* 55: 261-276.

Analyses of a subsample from The National Survey of Black Americans (NSBA, 1979-1980) (n = 620) demonstrate that networks of relatives supported (e.g., emotional, child care and/or financial) single and married African-American mothers.

424   Johnson, L. B. 1989. The employed Black: The dynamics of
        work-family tension. *Review of Black Political Ecomony*
        17(3): 69-85.

The author offers three conceptual models for balancing work
and family: Spillover/Generalization model, Compensatory-
Nonwork model, and segmentation model. This study analyzed
data (n=86) regarding job stressors, job strain, and couple strain
of married black police officers. The findings support the
presence of a spillover/generalization model.

425   Katz, M. H., and C. S. Piotrkowski. 1983. Correlates of family
        role strain among employed black women. *Family Relations*
        32: 331-339.

Data from 51 black, employed women concerning family role
strain were collected and analyzed. The level of autonomy
within the workplace was found to have a negative effect on
family role strain.

426   Lichter, D. T., and N. S. Landale. 1995. Parental work, family
        structure, and poverty among Latino children. *Journal of
        Marriage and the Family* 57: 346-354.

The 5% 1990 Public Use Microdata Sample (PUMS) was used to
examine the connection between family structure and child
poverty as well as the connection between parental work
patterns and child poverty. The authors assert that policies
advancing maternal employment for Latino women are not
sufficient to address child poverty in the minority population.
Rather, policies that address the minority population's
limited human capitial, racial discrimination and gender wage
inequality are needed.

427   Malson, M. R., and B. Woody. 1985. *The Work and Family
        Responsibilities of Black Women Single Parents.* Working
        Paper #148. Wellesley, MA: Center for Research on Women a t
        Wellesley College.

The authors discuss the general trends and sociodemographic
characteristics of single parent black families and guide this
conversation toward labor force patterns, wages and work

patterns as well as occupations. Program implications are briefly mentioned.

428   Malveaux, J., and P. A. Wallace. 1987. **Minority women in the workplace.** In *Working Women: Past, Present, Future,* edited by K. S. Koziara, M. H. Moskow, and L. D. Tanner. Washington, DC: The Bureau of National Affairs. 265-298.

The literature on the labor force participation and earnings of minority women is reviewed. The question of whether there is a convergence of occupational status of all women or whether black women are in significantly different employment than white women is raised. Implications for policy initiatives as well as research projects are discussed.

429   Marlow, C. 1990. **Management of family and employment responsibilities by Mexican American and Anglo American women.** *Social Work* 35: 259-265.

Data from a stratified random sampling of female clerical workers (n=142) were analyzed. Findings indicated that Mexican American women were more likely to request formal services than their Anglo American counterparts. Both groups of women, however, stated a preference for informal supports (e.g., friends, family) rather than formal ones (e.g., professional counselors, physicians, supervisors).

430   McLoyd, V. C. 1993. **Employment among African-American mothers in dual-earner families: Antecedents and consequences for family life and child development.** In *The Employed Mother and the Family Context,* edited by J. Frankel. New York: Springer Publishing. 180-226.

The author explored the historical context of maternal employment for African and African-American women. Causes of the high rate of working married mothers are outlined and include: economic need, role modeling, direct training, and spousal approval. Further, the effects of maternal employment on family relations, role strain and children are discussed.

431   Orbuch, T. L., and L. Custer. 1995. **The social context of married women's work and its impact on black husbands and white**

husbands. *Journal of Marriage and the Family* 57: 333-345.

A sample of 143 white couples and 124 black couples were interviewed in the third year of their marriage. White couples reported a higher participation in houshold chores by the husband in dual-earner couples than in couples with a homemaker. However, women's work status did not predict husband's particpation rate in household chores for black couples.

432   Rexroat, C. 1990. Race and marital status differences in the labor force behavior of female family heads: The effect of household structure. *Journal of Marriage and the Family* 52: 591-601.

The author used data from the March 1985 Current Population Survey (CPS) tape. The presence of extended family members has an effect on labor force behavior; however, the effect it has is dependent on one's race and/or marital status. For instance, the employment practices of previously married white female heads of household are not effected by the presence of related adults. In comparison however, the employment practices of previously married black female heads of household with children under age 5 are more likely to be employed if there is an extended family present than if extended family is not present.

433   Shelton, B. A., and D. John. 1993. Ethnicity, race, and difference: A comparison of white, black, and Hispanic men's household labor time. In *Men, Work, and Family,* edited by J. C. Hood. Newbury Park, CA: Sage Publications. 131-150.

Data from the 1987 National Survey of Families and Households (NSFH) were analyzed. The authors found that the relationship between men's employment and level of involvement with household chores is variable according to race/ehtnicity. For example, black and Hispanic men spend significantly more time than white men on household work.

434   Shukla, A. 1987. Decision making in single- and dual-career families in India. *Journal of Marriage and the Family* 49: 621-629.

A sample of 47 single-income and 54 dual-income families were surveyed regarding the decision making power of the husband and wife. Dual-income families were found to be more egalitarian than single-income families.

435   Simms, M. C. 1987. **Black women who head families: An economic struggle.** In *Slipping through the Cracks: The Status of Black Women,* edited by M. C. Simms and J. Malveaux. New Brunswick, NJ: Transaction Books. 140-151.

The author discusses the economic impact of government programs on black female headed households. Suggestions for policy initiatives are offered.

436   Simms, M. C. and J. Malveaux. 1987. *Slipping through the Cracks: The Status of Black Women.* New Brunswick, NJ: Transaction Books.

437   Stier, H., and M. Tienda. 1993. **Are men marginal to the family? Insights from Chicago's inner city.** In *Men, Work, and Family,* edited by J. C. Hood. Newbury Park, CA: Sage Publications. 23-44.

Data from the Urban Poverty and Family Life Survey of Chicago (UPFLS) and the National Survey of Families and Households (NSFH) were analyzed. Perceived economic potential and employment status of fathers, regardless of ethnicity were found to be predictors of economic support of children.

438   Thomas, V. G. 1990. **Problems of dual-career black couples: Identification and implications for family interventions.** *Journal of Multicultural Counseling and Development* 18: 58-67.

A sample of 41 dual-career black couples were interviewed regarding perceived issues of dual-career families. Difficulties cited included: (1) inadequate family time; (2) competing work and family obligations; and (3) difficulty in locating affordable high-quality child-care. Additional issues relating to the couples race and ethnicity were also cited: (1) job related racial discrimination spillover; (2) competition and resentment stemming from the perceived notion that black women are able to advance faster than black men; (3) a "cognitive dissonance" from having economic security not shared with relatives; and (4) difficulty in relaying black values to their children while living and working in the dominant culture.

439   Toliver, S. D. 1993. **Movers and shakers: Black families and corporate relocation.** *Marriage and Family Review* 19(1/2): 113-130.

The author analyzed data from interviews with 187 black managers and their families. Specific issues relevant to relocation for blacks were identified: a high level of social isolation and, separation from relative supports. Suggestions for easing difficult relocations are offered.

440   Valdez, E. O., and S. Coltrane. 1993. **Work, family, and the Chicana: Power perception, and equity.** In *The Employed Mother and the Family*, edited by J. Frankel. New York: Springer Publishing Company. 153-179.

Multiple in-depth interviews were held with 20 Chicano dual-income couples. The families were placed into one of four categories: traditional, semi-traditional, transitional and nontraditional. Egalitarian marriages were significantly more likely to be found between couples who were "income-balanced."

441   Waldinger, R., and T. Bailey. 1991. **The continuing significance of race: Racial conflict and racial discrimination in construction.** *Politics and Society* 19(3): 291-323.

The authors discuss past and present employment and ownership practices and their impact on black men in the field of construction. Barriers to employment in construction for black men (e.g. nepotism) are explored.

442   Wallace, P. A. 1987. **A research agenda on the economic status of black women.** In *Slipping Through the Cracks: The Status of Black Women*, edited by M. C. Simms and J. Malveaux. New Brunswick, NJ: Transaction Books. 293-295.

443   Wilkinson, D. Y. 1990. Afro-Americans in the corporation: An assessment of the impact on the family. *Marriage and Family Review*   15(3/4): 115-129.

The author discusses the opportunities available to both black men and women in industrial corporations. Influences of the corporate environment on the typically traditional Afro-American household are briefly explored. Suggestions for further research in the field are offered

444   Williams, N. 1993. Elderly Mexican American men: Work and family patterns. In *Men, Work, and Family*, edited by J. C. Hood. Newbury Park, CA: Sage Publications. 68-85.

Data collected through in-depth interviews with older Mexican American men (n=23) illustrated two distinct roles played by this population: provider or neglected elder. The work histories (low-paying unstable employment) of the sample were found to be connected to their current family patterns. Suggestions for further research are made.

445   Woody, B. 1992. *Black Women in the Workplace: Impacts of Structural Change in the Economy.* New York: Greenwood Press.

446   Ybarra, L. 1982. When wives work: The impact on the Chicano family. *Journal of Marriage and the Family*   44: 169-178.

In-depth interviews of 100 Chicano men and women were conducted in 1977. Data collected indicated that men in dual-income families do significantly more household chores and child care than men in single-income families.

447   Zambrana, R. E., and S. Frith.   1988.   Mexican-American professional women: Role satisfaction differences in single and multiple role lifestyles.   In *Journal of Social Behavior and Personality: Work and Family: Theory, Research, and Applications*, edited by E. B. Goldsmith. Corte Madera, CA: Select Press. 347-361.

A survey was distributed (1985) to Hispanic managerial and entrpreneurial women (n=170, response rate 45.1%). Data collected indicated that the level of autonomy in the workplace experienced by women has a significant positive effect on role satisfaction. Further, single mothers place a heavy emphasis on economic support when choosing employment. Suggestions for futher research are offered.

448   Zavella, P. 1987. *Women's Work and Chicano Families: Cannery Workers of the Santa Clara Valley.* Ithaca, NY: Cornell University Press.

CHAPTER 15

Income Groups
(annotated by Irene Fassler)

449 **Albelda, R., and C. Tilly. 1992. All in the family: Family types, access to income, and family income policies.** *Policy Studies Journal* **20(3): 388-404.**

Data were collected from the March Current Population Survey (CPS) in 1973, 1979, and 1987. Families were categorized into one of seven groups and then further grouped according to family income. Large differences in income among family types were noted. The authors urge policy initiatives which remove the burden of responsibility from the individual and apply it to the family and society.

450 **Blackburn, M. L., D. E. Bloom, and R. B. Freeman. 1990. The declining economic position of less skilled American men.** In *A Future of Lousy Jobs: The Changing Structure of U. S. Wages,* edited by G. Burtless. **Washington, DC: The Brookings Institution. 31-76.**

The discussion regarding less skilled American men is placed within a historical context (1900-1960). In addition, the authors offer alternative arguments for the decline of this population's economic situation, including: changes in labor quality, changes in sources of labor supply, and deunionization.

451 **Bromet, E. J., M. A. Dew, and D. K. Parkinson. 1990. Spillover between work and family: A study of blue-collar working wives.** In *Stress between Work and Family,* edited by J. Eckenrode and S. Gore. **New York: Plenum Press. 133-151.**

This study examines domestic stress and occupational stress among a sample of 389 married female assembly-line employees in a large electronics plant. Interview data were gathered on the following measures: health, job strain,

strain, spillover, and social support. The researchers conclude that spillover is a risk factor for poor mental health, especially among a specific group of younger, more 'distressed' blue-collar working women.

452   Burris, B. H. 1991. **Employed mothers: The impact of class and marital status on the prioritizing of family and work.** *Social Science Quarterly* 72(1): 50-66.

A sample of 164 employed mothers were surveyed and a sub-sample of 32 were interviewed regarding how they balance work and family. Professional/managerial women were found to prioritize their work role over their family role while working class women prioritized their family role over work role. Working class women were found to have more structural barriers (e.g. inadequate child care; inflexible jobs) to work roles than did the professional/managerial women.

453   Elder, G. H., J. S. Eccles, M. Ardelt, and S. Lord. 1995. **Inner-city parents under economic pressure: Perspectives on the strategies of parenting.** *Journal of Marriage and the Family* 57: 771-784.

Data from 429 inner-city families were collected through interviews and questionnaires. Economic pressure through its effect on depressed mood was found to diminish parental efficacy in both black and white inner city parents.

454   Ferree, M. M. 1987. **Family and job for working-class women: Gender and class system seen from below.** In *Families and Work,* edited by N. Gerstel and H. E. Gross. Philadelphia, PA: Temple University Press. 289-301.

455   Herring, C., and K. R. Wilson-Sadberry. 1993. **Preference or necessity? Changing work roles of black and white women, 1973-1990.** *Journal of Marriage and the Family* 55: 314-325.

Data were collected from black and white female respondents in the 1973, 1974, 1976, 1977, 1980, 1982, 1984, 1985, 1988, 1989, and 1990 General Social Surveys (n = 6,483). Black women were found more likely to be employed outside of the family home due to economic necessity than white women. White women were more likely to work due to personal preference. Overall, black women were less likely to stay at home than white women.

456   Kelly, R. F. 1988. The urban underclass and the future of work-family relations research. In *Journal of Social Behavior and Personality: Work and Family: Theory, Research, and Applications,* edited by E. B. Goldsmith. Corte Madera, CA: Select Press. 45-54.

The author proposes that work-family research be integrated with research on populations that are economically disadvantaged. Specific suggestions for future research are offered.

457   Lichter, D. T., and D. J. Eggebeen. 1994. The effect of parental employment on child poverty. *Journal of Marriage and the Family* 56: 633-645.

A sample of 41,996 children living with at least one parent was drawn from the 1990 March annual demographic supplement of the Current Population Survey (CPS). The authors found that parental employment has an effect on child poverty. Two income households have fewer children in poverty than households with either one wage earner or no wage earners. Policy initiatives promoting parental work and creating higher wage jobs are encouraged.

458   Marshall, N. L., and R. C. Barnett. 1991. Race, class and multiple role strains and gains among women employed in the service sector. *Women and Health* 17(4): 1-19.

Data were collected from the first year of a three year long study of 403 women employed as licensed practical nurses or social workers. Class differences were found in regard to parenting. For instance, LPNs children's health and safety were of greater concern to the LPNs than the social workers. The authors conclude that the work and family balance is most difficult for women in the lower socio-economic class primarily due to limited resources.

459   Moen, P. 1980. **Measuring unemployment: Family considerations.** *Human Relations* 33(3): 183-192.

The connection between the unemployment of a family member
and its effect on the family system is explored. Available
family resources, community supports and methods of
distributing the financial hardship (e.g. presence of a
secondary income producer, unemployment benefits) are
discussed. Policy implications are briefly mentioned.

460   Moen, P. 1979. **Family impacts of the 1975 recession: Duration
of unemployment.** *Journal of Marriage and the Family* 41: 561-
567.

A sub-sample of the Michigan Panel Study of Income Dynamics
(n=532) was used to analyze family responses to unemployment.
Two forms of responses were found: adaptiveness and coping.
Furthermore, it was found that two parent families with
children under the age of six have longer periods of
unemployment than households with children older than six
years.

461   Morgan, L. A., G. C. Kitson, and J. T. Kitson. 1992. **The economic
fallout from divorce: Issues for the 1990s.** *Journal of Family and
Economic Issues* 13(4): 435-443.

The authors place the issues of economic consequences of divorce
within a global context. Trends for the 1990s are discussed.
Suggestions for future research are offered.

462   Mueller, E. J. 1994. **Running hard to stay in one place: Low-
wage poverty among immigrant women in Los Angeles.**
Economic Development Quarterly 8(2): 158-170.

This study was conducted at a cooperative of domestic workers
over a 13 month period. Nineteen women from the cooperative
were interviewed about the work-family balance in their lives.
In addition, a survey of all cooperative members (n=120) was
completed. Household form and relationships among
household members were found to be areas which impede this
population's efforts toward obtaining higher wage work. A

shift of attention from the "problems" of the lower socio-
economic class to that of "low wage poverty" is suggested.

463   Osterman, P. 1993. Why don't "they" work? Employment
       patterns in a high pressure economy. *Social Science Research*
       22: 115-130.

A phone and door-to-door survey was conducted of all Boston
residents in 1989. It was found that poor women were not well
represented in the labor market. Day care issues and language
differences were identified as two of the barriers to
employment for this population.

464   Osterman, P. 1991. Welfare participation in a full employment
       economy: The impact of neighborhood. *Social Problems* 38(4):
       475-491.

Data collected from a representative sample of 1,065 poor
households and 903 non-poor households in 1988-1989, indicate
the presence of neighborhood effects such as: neighborhoods
which have fewer households with employed adults also
contain more households on welfare and a higher crime rate
than neighborhoods with more households with employed
adults.

465   Poulton, E. C. 1978. Blue collar stressors. In *Stress at Work*,
       edited by C. L. Cooper and R. Payne. Chichester, U. K.: John
       Wiley and Sons. 51-79.

The author outlines subjective and objective measures of
stressors found in blue collar work. Among other stressors, work
overload and underload, as well as night shifts and loss of
sleep, are identified.

466   Rosen, E, I. 1987. *Bitter Choices: Blue Collar Women in and out
       of Work.* Chicago: The University of Chicago Press.

467   Stegelin, D. A., and J. Frankel. 1993. Families of lower-income
       employed mothers. In *The Employed Mother and the Family
       Context*, edited by J. Frankel. New York: Springer Publisher.
       115-131.

Maternal employment in the lower socio-economic classes is discussed in terms of available coping mechanisms and life styles. Stressors such as financial limitations, child care issues and time as a resource are outlined. Role strain, shift work, unemployment, and the effects of maternal employment on family systems in the lower socio-economic class, are also discussed.

468   Sutherland, V. J., and C. L. Cooper. 1995. Out of the frying pan into the fire: Managing blue-collar stress at work. In *Changing Employment Relations,* edited by L. E. Tetrick and J. Barling. Washington, DC: American Psychological Association. 109-132.

Work stressors for blue collar employees are identified and discussed. Positive changes in both work conditions (e.g., technological advancements, automation, stricter legislation) and employer-employee relations (e.g., empowerment, culture change) are outlined as possible ameliorating factors for blue collar stress at work.

469   Swanberg, J. E. 1996. *Job-Family Role Strain: Understanding the Experience of Lower Wage Service Employees.* Unpublished doctoral dissertation, Brandeis University, Waltham, MA.

Qualitative and quantitative data were gathered from hourly wage workers employed at a Fortune 100 urban hotel concerning strain experienced while balancing work and family responsibilities. While the data revealed single parents experience the most strain, parents whose partners did not help with child care also reported high levels of strain. The study's findings emphasize the stressful effects of lack of autonomy and participation in work schedules for all workers irrespective of race, gender, and ethnicity.

470   Voydanoff, P., B. W. Donnelly, and M. A. Fine. 1988. Economic distress, social integration, and family satisfaction. *Journal of Family Issues* 9(4): 545-564.

The question of whether, and to what degree, social integration minimizes the effect of economic hardship on family life is addressed in this study. A sample of 1,561 married individuals from the 1983 and 1986 General Social Surveys by the National Opinion Research Center was interviewed. Satisfaction with social integration was found to have an effect on the relationship between economic strain and family satisfaction.

PART 5

DEPENDENT CARE

CHAPTER 16

Dependent Care Experiences/Corporate Strategies/Public Policies

471 Arthur Emlen and Associates. 1996. *Oregon Child Care Research Partnership: Project Description.* Grant from Child Care Bureau, Administration for Children, Youth and Families, U. S. Department of Health and Human Services.

Presents the current survey questionnaire—Quality of Care From a Parent's Point of View. The survey is designed to elicit parents' opinions of quality child care. Parental assessment of quality will be part of a larger project collecting detailed data on child care and establishing quality indicators of child care.

472 Auerbach, J. D. 1990. Employer-supported child care as a women-responsive policy. *Journal of Family Issues* 11(4): 384-400.

Auerbach examines employer-supported child care using survey data (n = 99) and qualitative data from telephone interviews (n = 25). Two groups of employers are compared: employers who are "offering" (or "investigating") child-care policies and employers who are not. Findings indicate that organizational self-interest motivates employers to offer child care policies. Regardless of motivation, Auerbach makes the point that women's chances for advancement increase with women-responsive policies, not via a "mommy track."

473 Barr, J. K., K. W. Johnson, and L. J. Warshaw. 1992. Supporting the elderly: Workplace programs for employed caregivers. *The Milbank Quarterly* 70(3): 509-533.

Prior research studies facilitate an examination of workplace programs for employed caregivers. The focus is on employer-sponsored programs, however, government polices are discussed briefly. The article concludes with suggestions for future research.

474   Berkeley Planning Associates. 1989. *Employer-Supported Childcare: Measuring and Understanding Its Impacts on the Workplace.* A final report to the U.S. Department of Labor, Office of Strategic Planning and Policy Development. Berkeley, CA: Berkeley Planning Associates.

475   Burud, S. L., P. R. Aschbacher, and J. McCroskey. 1984. *Employer Supported Child Care: Investing in Human Resources.* Boston, MA: Auburn House Publishing.

476   Chapman, N. J., B. Ingersoll-Dayton, and M. B. Neal. 1994. Balancing the multiple roles of work and caregiving for children, adults, and elders. In *Job Stress in a Changing Workforce: Investigating Gender, Diversity, and Family Issues,* edited by G. P. Keita and J. J. Hurrell. Washington, DC: American Psychological Association. 283-300.

This study focuses on balancing employment and different kinds of caregiving responsibilities (child, elder, adult) at the same time. Survey data from employees in 33 businesses and agencies (38% response rate), were gathered on absenteeism rates and stress levels related to caregiving responsibilities. In general terms, the study found that the number of caregiving roles and the specific combination of roles make a difference in the level of stress and the number of days absent.

477   Coberly, S., and G. G. Hunt. 1995. *The Metlife Study of Employer Costs for Working Caregivers.* Prepared for Senior Services Division, Metropolitan Life Insurance Company, by the Washington Business Group on Health, Washington, DC.

This study focuses on employer eldercare costs resulting from employees who provide personal assistance with the Activities of Daily Living (ADLs). The authors developed prevalence estimates and cost estimates (e.g., absenteeism, reduced productivity). An explication of assumptions underpinning the estimates and the formulae are presented in detail. It was "conservatively" estimated that 2% are providing personal assistance at a cost of $5.5 million dollars per year.

478   Creedon, M. 1990. **The dependent elder and workplace support for the family caregiver: Some public policy considerations.** In *Sharing the Caring: Options for the 90s and Beyond: A Policy Forum.* U.S. Congress, House of Representatives. Select Committee on Aging, Subcommittee on Human Services. Committee Pub. No. 101-750. 111-117.

479   Creedon, M., and M. Tiven. 1989. **Eldercare in the Workplace.** Washington, DC: National Council on the Aging.

480   Denton, K., L. T. Love, and R. Slate. 1990. **Eldercare in the '90s: Employee responsibility, employer challenge.** *Families in Society: The Journal of Contemporary Human Services* 71(6): 349-359.

This exploratory, qualitative study identifies trends in employer responses to employed elder caregivers. Interviews were conducted with employers (n = 20) from profit and nonprofit companies varying in size from 1,000 to more than 10,000. Survey and interview data are used to develop a taxonomy of eldercare benefits. The authors conclude that the employers need to systematically examine employee problems to address needs and develop policies.

481   Eichman, C. 1992/93. **Surveys reveal needs for work/family benefit—by both employees and employers.** *Employment Relations Today* 19(4): 389-395.

Eichman reviews two surveys to assess needs by employees: National Child Care Survey 1990 (NCCS) and The Society for Human Resource Management (SHRM) Survey. Employer response to employee needs is analyzed using two case studies as examples—The Los Angeles Department of Water and Power and America West's Child Care Programs.

482   Emlen, A. C. 1995. *Market Rate, 1994: Sampling the Price of Child Care in Oregon.* Arthur Emlen and Associates, Inc. **In cooperation with the Regional Research Institute for Human Services at Portland State University: Portland, OR.**

Federal-State policy legislates subsidized child care for
families during the transition from welfare to work. The State
reimburses families up to the price of the 75th percentile of all
prices by child care providers. This study reports the 1994
market rate study findings, or in other words, reports the 75th
percentile rate charged for child care throughout Oregon. In
addition, the report addresses methodological issues of
market-rate data (e.g., sampling representativeness, measurement validity).

483   Emlen, A. C. 1991. *Rural Child Care Policy: Does Oregon Have
One? 1991 Legislative Discussion Series.* **Rural Policy Research
Group, Oregon State University and University of Oregon,
Oregon Economic Development Department.**

Compares rural and urban child care for the purpose of
developing policy. Among the findings, differences were found
in availability, cost, usage of out-of-home child care, and
distances traveled. Policy implications of the findings are
discussed.

484   Emlen, A. C., and P. E. Koren. 1993. *Estimating child-care
demand for statewide planning.* **1993 Proceedings of the
Government Statistics Section of the American Statistical
Association. 77-82.**

This report focuses on availability, accessibility, and afford-
ability of child care. The researchers detail the population-
based analysis of the demand (or current usage) and assessment
of supply of child care.

485   Emlen, A. C., and P. E. Koren. 1984. *Hard To Find and Difficult
to Manage: The Effects of Child Care on the Workplace.* **A
report to employers for distribution at a forum on Child Care
and Employee Productivity: The Workplace Partnership.
Portland, OR: Regional Research Institute for Human Services
at Portland State University.**

In 1983 a survey of 20,000 employees from 33 diverse companies
elicited a response rate of 40%. The questionnaire focused on
child care arrangements and resulting work-family difficulties.
Three types of child care are distinguished: (1) home care by

adult; (2) out-of-home care; and (3) care by child. Difficulties with child care arrangements and the effect on the workplace are analyzed.

486   **Emlen, A. C., P. E. Koren, and D. Louise. 1988.** *1987 Dependent Care Survey: Sisters of Providence.* **Final Report, Vol. 1 and 2. Regional Research Institute for Human Services at Portland State University: Portland, OR.**

This case study uses survey data collected from employees (n = 6,143, a response rate of 36%) at 20 work sites of the Sisters of Providence. (Of the workforce employed at Sisters, 82% are women and 42% have children under 18.) A Child and Elder Care Survey was developed and designed to assess relationships between stress and work-family responsibilities and the relationship between work interruptions and productivity. Based on the analysis, the researchers conclude that there is a significant impact on productivity resulting from work interruptions due to dependent care responsibilities (e.g., days missed, shortened work hours). Profiles of employees are included with the final report.

487   **Emlen, A. C., P. E. Koren, and K. H. Schultze. 1995.** *Work and Family Issues at DHR: Report of a 1994-95 Employee Survey at the Oregon Department of Human Resources.* **Arthur Emlen and Associates, Inc.**

In cooperation with the Regional Research Institute for Human Services at Portland, OR: Portland State University. This study surveyed the employees of the Oregon Department of Human Resources (DHR) concerning work and family demands. Men and women employees with or without children (n = 5390, 56% response rate) were surveyed in December 1994 and January 1995. The report findings cover a broad range of work-family issues, among them: (1) the impact of caregiving for elders and/or disabled adults; (2) employees who do not have dependent care issues; and (3) company policies, including flexibility, management, and supervision. The report also contains a selected compilation of employee comments.

488   **Emlen, A. C., P. E. Koren, and K. S. Yoakum. 1990.** *1990 Dependent Care Survey: 15 Employers of Lane County, Oregon.*

Portland, OR: **Regional Research Institute for Human Services at Portland State University.**

This study assessed the extent and characteristics of child care and adult care needs for employees in 15 companies and agencies in Lane County, Oregon. The summary report highlights the findings and conclusions, including: (1) the similarities and differences between adult care and child care; (2) the impact of dependent care responsibilities on careers; and (3) employee perceptions of companies policies. In addition, the report's findings and conclusions draw attention to linkages between community resources and child care (e.g., availability, accessibility, and quality).

489   **Fortune Magazine and John Hancock Financial Services. 1989.** *Corporate and Employee Response to Caring for the Elderly: A National Survey of U. S. Companies and the Workforce.* **New York: Fortune Magazine.**

The researchers surveyed two groups: heads of households and the CEOs of companies in the Fortune 500 registry. Both groups' responses to eldercare are highlighted in the study's executive summary. Overall, company executives believe that individuals should be responsible for costs for long-term care of elderly. Survey data profiling the nature of elder caregiving responsibilities are presented (e.g., 41% of working elder caregivers report that they are the primary caregiver).

490   **Friedman, D. E. 1986. Child care for employees' kids.** *Harvard Business Review* **64: 28-34.**

Friedman extrapolates findings from research studies to document the competitive advantages companies gain from responding to employees' child care needs. The findings from three national surveys of employers providing child care are presented in a summary chart. In addition, Friedman discusses the various options companies provide for employees and gives specific examples.

491   **Friedman, D. E. 1983.** *State and Local Strategies Promoting Employer Supported Child Care.* **New York: Center for Public Advocacy Research.**

492   Friedman, D. E. Impact of Childcare on the Bottom Line. Vol. 2: 1427-1475. Commission on Workforce Quality and Labor Market Efficiency, U.S. Department of Labor, Washington, DC.

493   Galinsky, E., and A. Morris. 1991. *Employers and Child Care.* Paper presented at The Symposium on Day Care for Children, Washington, DC. New York: Families and Work Institute.

Using data from two studies—The State Parental Leave Study and the Fortune 1000 Study—the authors investigate the prevalence of employer involvement in child care and other work-family initiatives. The analyses show that size is the most important predictor of employer involvement (i.e., the larger the size, the more involvement). Companies experiencing business changes (e.g., downsizing, merger) were also more likely to be more involved ("survivor benefits"). Policy implications are discussed.

494   Hayes, C. D., J. Palmer, and M. Zaslow. 1990. *Who Cares for America's Children? Child Care Policy for the 1990's.* Report of the Panel on Child Care Policy, Committee on Child Development Research and Public Policy, Commission on Behavioral and Social Sciences and Education, National Research Council. Washington, DC: National Academy Press.

495   Hayghe, H. V. 1988. Employers and child care: What roles do they play? *Monthly Labor Review* 111(9): 38-44.

Hayghe uses data from "Child Care: A Workforce Issue" (U. S. Department of Labor) to examine the scope of the child care issue. Additional data from employers are presented in tables (e.g., child care benefits).

496   Heck, R. K. Z., N. C. Saltford, B. Rowe, and A. J. Owen. 1992. The utilization of child care by households engaged in home-based employment. *Journal of Family and Economic Issues* 13(2): 213-237.

This study focuses on the likelihood that home-based workers will use child care services. Using a subsample (n = 373) households with children needing care) from a nine-state project on households where one individual was a home-based worker, a logit analysis was run. Home-based working households do use child care. A profile of those more likely to use it is offered.

497   **Hofferth, S. L., and D. Phillips. 1987. Child care in the United States, 1970 to 1995.** *Journal of Marriage and the Family* **49: 559-571.**

Examines trends in the demand and supply of child care for the past two decades. Hofferth and Phillips conclude that projected increases in demand can only be met by center-based care which has the potential for expansion. Implications are discussed.

498   **Howes, C., E. Smith, and E. Galinsky. 1995.** *The Florida Child Care Quality Improvement Study.* **New York: Families and Work Institute.**

Florida's recent legislated quality improvement efforts in child care provided an opportunity for the researchers to evaluate the impact of new ratios and requirements impact on quality. This interim report includes background, methodology, and key findings.

499   **Ingersoll-Dayton, B., N. Chapman, and M. B. Neal. 1990. A program for caregivers in the workplace.** *Gerontologist* **30(1): 126-130.**

This study evaluates a program for employed caregivers of the elderly in four demonstration sites. The program included an education seminar and a choice of service options: careplanning, a support group, and a buddy system. Careplanning and participation in the support group were chosen by the employees. Following the program, a decrease in negative affect was found; however, absenteeism increased.

500   **Joseph, G., and P. Ward. 1991.** *Options for the 90s: Employer Support for Child Care.* **New York: National Council of Jewish Women.**

This paper provides employer options for meeting employee child care needs. Advantages and disadvantages are discussed.

501   Kisker, E. E., R. Maynard, A. Gordon, and M. Strain. 1989. *The Child Care Challenge: What Parents Need and What is Available in Three Metropolitan Areas.* Princeton, NJ: Mathematica Policy Research.

502   Kisker, E. E., S. L. Hofferth, D. Phillips, and E. Farquhar. 1991. *A Profile of Child Care Settings: Early Education and Care in 1990.* Volume 1. Washington, DC: U.S. Department of Education.

Information on the extent and characteristics of early education and care programs was obtained through computer assisted telephone interviews with a national sample of center directors and regulated home providers. The report described the supply of programs, key characteristics of programs, and indicators of quality of care.

503   Kossek, E. E. 1990. **Diversity in child care assistance needs: Employee problems, preferences, and work-related outcomes.** *Personnel Psychology* 43: 769-791.

Dependent care needs were assessed using survey data from employees with a dependent under the age of 12 (n = 198) at a public utility in the Midwest. The relationship between employee's demographic variables, problems with child care arrangements, and work/care attitudes and behaviors is examined. The study found that background variables do influence child care preferences.

504   Kossek, E. E., and V. Nichol. 1992. **The effects of on-site child care on employee attitudes and performance.** *Personnel Psychology* 45: 485-509.

Data were collected from two mid-western hospitals (same corporation) that have provided on-site child care. A quasi-experimental posttest design was used. On-site child care positively influenced management of work-family conflict as well as employee views of company.

505   Kossek E. E., B. J. DeMarr, K. Backman, and M. Kollar. 1993. **Assessing employees' emerging elder care needs and reactions to**

dependent care benefits. *Public Personnel Management* 22(4): 617-638.

This study focuses on two employer responses to elder care needs: the dependent care spending account and the leave of absence program. Survey data from three Midwest firms were collected and analyzed. Employees felt that spending accounts and unpaid leaves were somewhat helpful. Managers used the spending accounts more than nonmanagers. Various employee benefits are discussed.

506   Krauskopf, M. S., and S. H. Akabas. 1988. Children with disabilities: A family/workplace partnership in problem resolution. *Social Work Papers* 21: 28-35.

Following a review of the literature, the authors suggest ways that management can assist families with disabled infants to maintain and balance work and caregiving responsibilities. Various options are discussed (e.g., "time banks," greater flexibility, employee assistant programs (EAP) involvement).

507   Landis, S. E., and J. A. Earp. 1987. Sick child care options: What do working mothers prefer? *Women and Health* 12(1): 61-77.

The authors review available sick child care options in the United States. Data from a survey of 134 working mothers of children who attend day care—state preferences in care and are compared with available options in communities. Authors suggest that out of home sick child care be offered through communities, day care centers, employers and women's resource centers.

508   Lechner, V. M., and M. Creedon. 1994. *Managing Work and Family Life.* New York: Springer Press.

509   Liazos, A. 1991. Childcare and time to be parents: Parenting, childcare, and work. *Humanity and Society* 15(3): 291-303.

The author explores options for traditional daycare. The Swedish system's parental leave policies are offered as suggestions. Four related issues are also discussed: how children experience daycare, the difficult work of daycare providers, the effects of daycare on parents, and the cost of daycare.

510   Liebig, P. S. 1993. Factors affecting the development of employer-sponsored eldercare programs: Implications for employed caregivers. *Journal of Women and Aging* 5(1): 59-78.

A sample of 66 employers identified as leaders in dependent care was selected from "industry clusters," namely insurance, finance, communications and consumer products. With a response rate of 50%, the sample consisted of 13 employers with an eldercare program, 19 without, and 1 respondent who did not know. Employers with designated eldercare programs were more aware of work-family conflicts, offered more work-family benefits, and were more knowledgeable about which benefits were used for eldercare purposes (e.g., flexhours or vacation time). Both employer groups predicted the growth of generic benefits rather than specific eldercare policies.

511   Magid, R. L. 1983. *Child-Care Initiatives for Working Parents: Why Employers Get Involved.* New York: American Management Association.

Magid studied 204 companies with child care programs and concluded that employers felt the programs reduced absenteeism, improved morale, and helped recruit employees.

512   Marshall, N. L. 1991. *The Bottom Line: Impact of Employer Child Care Subsidies.* Working Paper Series, No. 225. Wellesley, MA: Center for Research on Women at Wellesley College.

This study matches 14 companies which offer subsidies with 16 companies that do not have this benefit. The article describes the subsidy programs in regard to eligibility, usage, and cost. It is concluded that subsidy programs do not have a company-wide effect on recruitment costs, turnover rates or retention.

513   Miller, J. J., B. A. Stead, and A. Pereira. 1991. Dependent care and the workplace: An analysis of management and employee perceptions. *Journal of Business Ethics* 10: 863-869.

This exploratory study compares the perceptions of top management (CEOs, presidents) and middle management (supervisory) on two dimensions of dependent care: (1) the effects of dependent care on work performance; and (2) the extent of the company's responsibility on work/family issues (e.g., eldercare). Discriminate analyses reveal different perceptions between the two groups. Overall, the middle managers (predominately women) thought dependent care impacted work performance to a greater extent; and saw the need for more company responsibility.

514   Miller, T. I. 1984. **The effects of employer-sponsored child care on employee absenteeism, turnover, productivity, recruitment or job satisfaction: What is claimed and what is known.** *Personnel Psychology* **37: 277-289.**

Miller evaluates and disputes claims that employer-sponsored child care programs positively impact employee work behaviors (e.g., absenteeism, productivity). The claims rest on "poorly designed research studies" without proper controls that offer conflicting evidence. Suggestions for better research designs to illuminate the benefits of employer-sponsored child care programs are included.

515   Neal, M. B., N. J. Chapman, B. Ingersoll-Dayton, A. C. Emlen, **and L. Boise. 1990. Absenteeism and stress among employed caregivers of the elderly, disabled adults, and children. In** *Aging and Caregiving: Theory, Research and Practice,* **edited by D. E. Biegel and A. Blum. Newbury Park, CA: Sage Publications. 160-183.**

Four groups experiencing different types of caregiving responsibilities (i.e., adult, elder, child, or none) were compared on measures of stress and absenteeism. Also analyzed were background variables and job characteristics of each group. The authors conclude that caregivers do experience more work interruptions and stress. In addition, different types of caregivers find different company responses helpful.

516   Neal, M. B., N. J. Chapman, B. Ingersoll-Dayton, and A. C. **Emlen. 1993.** *Dependent Care as a Corporate, Family, and Community Concern.* **Newbury Park, CA: Sage Publications.**

517   Neal, M. B., N. J. Chapman, B. Ingersoll-Dayton, and A. C. Emlen. 1993. Employees who care for adults with disabilities. In *Balancing Work and Caregiving for Children, Adults, and Elders.* Newbury Park, CA: Sage Publications. 90-113.

This chapter reviews the literature on caregivers for adults and includes a discussion of caregiving within the context of work. The authors perform a hierarchical multiple regression analysis on survey data (n = 357) using the dependent variables of absenteeism and stress. Women adult-caregivers had higher stress and more absences and were more likely to be interrupted at work than men. Caregivers with informal support and flexible work schedules combined work-family roles with less difficulty.

518   Neal, M. B., N. J. Chapman, B. Ingersoll-Dayton, and A. C. Emlen. 1993. *Balancing Work and Caregiving for Children, Adults, and Elders.* Newbury Park, CA: Sage Publications.

519   Perry, K. S. 1982. *Employers and Child Care: Establishing Services through the Workplace.* Washington, DC: Women's Bureau, U. S. Department of Labor.

This study focuses on the employer perceptions of the benefits of corporate on-site child care programs. The majority of employers reported that child care programs increased recruitment, lowered absenteeism, and improved morale.

520   *RMC Research Corporation, School-Age Child Care Project at Wellesley College, and Mathematica Policy Research.* 1993. National Study of Before- and After-School Programs. Portsmouth, NH: RMC .

This study provides a descriptive profile of public schools providing before- and after-school programs. The authors analyze the findings from a thematic perspective. Policy implications are discussed.

521   Scharlach, A. E. 1993. *Survey of Dependent Care Responsibilities for the Lawrence Berkeley Laboratory.* Berkeley, CA: Personnel Department, Lawrence Berkeley Laboratory.

522   Scharlach, A. E., and K. I. Fredriksen. 1994. **Elder care versus adult care: Does care recipient age make a difference?** *Research on Aging* 16(1): 43-68.

Using a stratified random sample of 4,256 university employers, the study compares employed caregivers of elders with employed caregivers of disabled adults. The caregivers of disabled adults provided more extensive care and experienced more strain. Policy implications are discussed.

523   Scharlach, A. E., B. F. Lowe, and E. L. Schneider. 1991. *Elder Care and the Work Force: Blueprint for Action.* Lexington, MA: Lexington Books.

524   Seligson, M., E. Fersh, N. L. Marshall, F. Marx, and R. K. Baden. 1990. **School-age child care: The challenge facing families.** *Families in Society: The Journal of Contemporary Human Services* 71(6): 324-331.

This Boston area survey attempts to determine the level of parent demand for child care services for school-age children. The survey addressed issues such as: where children spent their time before and after school, impediments to the use of existing programs and how the lack of adequate and affordable child care affected parents education training as well as employment opportunities. The study confirms that low- and moderate-income families have the greatest challenge in providing a stable after school environment for their children while achieving economic self-sufficiency.

525   Svirsky, A. J., M. Y. Abolafia, and P. Moen. 1996. *Whose Business is Child Care? Managers' Support for Family Support Policies.* Unpublished draft. Albany, New York: State University of New York, Center for Women in Government.

This paper reports on a survey of a national sample of managers to aid in the identification and explanation of variance among managers' orientations. Managers' family characteristics have little impact on their dispositions regarding child care.

526   Tetrick, L. E., R. L. Miles, L. Marcil, and C. M. Van Dosen. 1994. **Child-care difficulties and the impact on concentration, stress,**

and productivity among single and non-single mothers and fathers. In *Job Stress in a Changing Workforce: Investigating Gender, Diversity, and Family Issues,* edited by G. P. Keita and J. J. Hurrell. Washington, DC: American Psychological Association. 229-239.

This study examines child care difficulties using a needs assessment sample that includes men (54%) and single parents. Single parents represented 25% of the sample, of whom 47% were single fathers. This study also examines the impact of child-care problems on co-workers. Overall, 15% of the men (without children living with them) reported their jobs were more difficult to do because of co-workers child care problems.

527   **The Conference Board. 1992. Elder care. Work-Family Roundtable. New York, NY: The Conference Board. 3(1): 1-11.**

Employers' opinions and experiences on elder care issues and initiatives were tapped in a 1992 survey given to 159 members of The Conference Boards' Work-Family Roundtable who have had experience administering work-family programs. Respondents overwhelmingly (94%) agreed with the survey statement: "Elder care responsibilities affect employee productivity to a greater degree than generally acknowledged." Charts profiling respondents motivations for establishing elder care policies, barriers to establishing policies, as well as prevalence rates of elder care policies are presented in the report.

528   **United States General Accounting Office (GAO). 1994. *Long-Term Care: Support for Elder Care Could Benefit the Government Workplace and the Elderly.* GAO/HEHS-94-64.**

Report to the Chairman, Subcommittee on Employment, Housing and Aviation Committee on Government Operations, House of Representatives. This study focuses on the extent and nature of elder care practices in all levels of government, federal, state and local. A survey of "the 50 states and 100 city governments with the largest workforces" was conducted. Further information was gathered from interviews with federal, state, and local officials and elder care experts. The report suggests that the federal government should improve elder care initiatives in particular and work/family benefits in general. Currently, flexible schedules or elder care information options are offered by almost all governments. However, the report cautions that many managers and supervisors do not encourage usage.

529   United States General Accounting Office (GAO). 1994. *Child Care: Child Care Subsidies Increase Likelihood That Low-Income Mothers Will Work.* **GAO/HEHS-95-20.**

Report to the Congressional Caucus for Women's Issues, House of Representatives. Data from a nationally representative sample of households with children (The Urban Institute's 1990 National Child Care Survey) is analyzed. The findings indicate that reducing child care costs raises the probability that poor and near-poor mothers will work. The paper briefly reviews policy implications.

530   United States General Accounting Office (GAO). 1994. *Long-Term Care: Private Sector Elder Care Could Yield Multiple Benefits.* **GAO/HEHS-94-60. Report to the Honorable Olympia Snowe, House of Representatives.**

A national survey of a representative sample of companies (with 100 or more employees) was conducted. interviews were conducted with benefits and human resource managers and elder care experts. The report identifies the most useful and common forms of assistance available for caregivers (e.g., flexibility in scheduling) noting that they are not specifically designated as eldercare policies. A sample of the survey is included.

531   Wagner, D. L., and G. G. Hunt. 1994. The use of workplace eldercare programs by employed caregivers. *Research on Aging* 16(1): 69-84.

This pilot study used a phone survey (n = 115) to examine the correlates of employee use of eldercare programs. Lack of knowledge of programs was not a barrier for use. What did influence employee use of programs was the type of caregiving situation (e.g., "hands-on") and the perception of work interference.

532   Wagner, D. L., M. Creedon, J. M. Sasala, and M. B. Neal. 1989.
        Helping employees balance work and family responsibilities.
        In *Employees and Eldercare: Designing Effective Responses for
        the Workplace.* Bridgeport, CT: Center for the Study of Aging
        at University of Bridgeport. 9-18.

        Presents a review of company responses to eldercare issues. The
        authors   discuss   specific   eldercare   programs,   namely,
        Information Models, Referral and Linkage Models, Direct
        Provision of Services, Reimbursement Models, and Consortia
        Models. Additionally, the authors review the components of
        corporate policies that frequently serve eldercare needs: work
        scheduling, benefits, EAPs, corporate social responsibility,
        health   promotion and wellness, and management training
        programs. Specific responses from leading corporations are
        included.

533   Wagner, D. L., M. Creedon, J. M. Sasala, and M. B. Neal. 1989.
        The needs of employees who provide eldercare. In *Employees
        and Eldercare: Designing Effective Responses for the
        Workplace.* Bridgeport, CT: Center for the Study of Aging at
        University of Bridgeport. 19-27.

        This chapter considers various employee approaches to
        caregiving and offers suggestions for companies interested in
        responding to employees caregiving needs. Several tables
        illustrate comparative data culled from six studies on working
        caregivers.

534   White-Means, S. I., and M. C. Thornton. 1990. Labor market
        choices and home health care provision among employed
        ethnic caregivers. *Gerontologist* 30(6): 769-775.

        This exploratory paper contributes a racially and ethnically
        differentiated analysis on the determinants of caregiving.

535   Whitebrook, M., C. Howes, and D. Phillips. 1989. *Who Cares?
        Child Care Teachers and the Quality of Care in America:
        Executive Summary of the National Child Care Staffing
        Study.* New York: Child Care Employee Project.

536   Whitebrook, M., D. Phillips, and C. Howes. 1993. *National Child Care Staffing Study Revisited: Four Years in the Life of Center-Based Child Care.* Oakland, CA: Child Care Employee Project.

This updated study reassesses child-care centers from the original (1988) sample. Thus, the current study sampled 193 centers still in operation. The authors suggest that the quality of center-based care is questionable in light of the findings: (1) exceptionally low wages with no or limited health insurance for teaching staff; and (2) high turnover of teaching staff.

537   Wolf, D. A., and F. L. Sonenstein. 1991. Child-care use among welfare mothers: A dynamic analysis. *Journal of Family Issues* 12(4): 519-536.

This study investigates factors related to the turnover in the child-care arrangements of AFDC mothers. A sample of mothers who received AFDC from three cities (Boston, Charlotte, and Denver) were interviewed on two occasions, six months apart. The study concludes that the lower cost of care will probably lead to more stable child-care arrangements. In addition, mothers' perceptions of the quality of the child-care arrangement is positively related to the pattern of continued child-care use.

538   Zigler, E. F. and M. E. Lang. 1991. *Child Care Choices: Balancing the Needs of Children, Families and Society.* New York: Free Press.

CHAPTER 17

Child Care

539 Atkinson, A. M. 1994. **Rural and urban families' use of child care.** *Family Relations* 43: 16-22.

A randomly selected sample of 982 mothers from rural and urban areas were interviewed regarding their selection and use of child care. Analyses indicate that rural mothers were significantly more likely than urban to use child care by relatives. Atkinson suggests that economic concerns and the limited availability of child care may contribute to rural mothers' reliance on relatives. Program implications are discussed.

540 Belsky, J. 1990. **Parental and nonparental child care and children's socioemotional development: A decade in review.** *Journal of Marriage and the Family* 52: 885-903.

Belsky identifies and reviews three themes in the literature concerning the socioemotional development of the child and child care. Following an assessment of prior research on nonparental care, Belsky considers future research agendas.

541 Belsky, J. 1988. **The "effects" of infant day care reconsidered.** *Early Childhood Research Quarterly* 3(1): 235-272.

Using the theoretical constructs of attachment theory, Belsky analyzes infant day care and concludes that risks seem to be associated with extensive (defined as more than twenty hours a week) nonmaternal care in a child's first year.

542 Belsky, J., and L. D. Steinberg. 1978. **The effects of day care: A critical review.** *Child Development* 49: 929-949.

Belsky reviews the research findings on the effects of day care and identifies the limitations. In particular, he notes researchers' tendency to study high-quality settings; hence, Belsky's qualifying conclusion, " ... in high-quality day care centers there were no detrimental effects."

543   Benin, M. H., and Y. Chong. 1993. **Child care concerns of employed mothers.** In *The Employed Mother and the Family Context,* edited by J. Frankel. New York: Springer. 229-244.

This chapter addresses the child care concerns of employed mothers, including usage, preferences, quality, employer assistance, care of sick children, and before and after school care. The policy implications of these concerns are discussed.

544   Brayfield, A. 1992. *Child Care Costs as a Barrier to Women's Employment.* **Prepared by the Urban Institute for The Women's Bureau. Washington, DC: U. S. Department of Labor.**

Brayfield uses data from two sources: the National Child Care Survey 1990 and A Profile of Child Care Settings study. Analyses reveal that child care costs affect not only the likelihood of women's employment, but the number of hours worked. When child care costs increase, initially, hours worked increase; but when a "maximum cost" is reached, hours decrease. Moreover, what women "perceive" about the price of child care determines likelihood of employment and number of hours worked (e.g., if women think that the market price is higher, they may not work). Availability of "free" child care from relatives/friends increases likelihood of employment.

545   Breslau, N., D. Salkever, and K. S. Staruch. 1982. **Women's labor force activity and responsibilities for disabled dependents: A study of families with disabled children.** *Journal of Health and Social Behavior* 23: 169-183.

This study compares families with children with disabilities (n = 369) to a random sample of families with children without disabilities (n = 456). Child disability interacted with race and income for two-parent black families. Mothers in black and low-income families were less likely to work; whereas mothers in white and higher income families were more likely to work (although they work fewer hours than their white counterparts with children without disabilities).

546   Clarke-Stewart, K. A. 1988. "The 'effects' of infant day care reconsidered": Risks for parents, children, and researchers. *Early Childhood Research Quarterly* 3: 293-318.

After reviewing Belsky's (1988) article "The 'Effects' of Infant Day Care Reconsidered," as well as other research in the field, Clarke-Stewart concludes that there is no clear evidence that day care places infants at risk. Suggestions are made for further research to assess and investigate mediating factors, such as mother's attitude toward the infant, and her emotional accessibility, behavioral sensitivity, and desire for independence.

547   Freedman, R. I., L. C. Litchfield, and M. E. Warfield. 1995. Balancing work and family: Perspectives of parents of children with developmental disabilities. *Families in Society: The Journal of Contemporary Human Services* 76(8): 507-514.

Focus-group data inform this exploratory study on balancing work and family responsibilities among working parents of children with developmental disabilities. The authors present the key themes (e.g., having a child with special needs influences the decision to work part-time). Implications for work and family policies are discussed.

548   Friedman, D. E. 1985. *Corporate Financial Assistance for Child Care.* Research Bulletin No. 177. New York: The Conference Board.

This report reviews corporate programs for the provision of financial assistance to employees with child care. The author describes four corporate initiatives that aid employees to pay for work related child care expenses: vouchers, discounts, comprehensive cafeteria plans and flexible spending accounts with salary reduction. Financing solutions for corporations, with specific case studies, are presented.

549   Galinsky, E., and D. Hughes. 1987. *Fortune Magazine Child Care Study.* New York: Bank Street College of Education.

This summary report analyzes interview data gathered from employed parents (n = 405) in dual-earner families. Overall, employed parents cite child care problems as a critical issue in balancing work-family responsibilities. The authors conclude that parents are more likely to be absent from work, experience higher degrees of stress, and experience more health problems when they have difficulties in finding and keeping child care.

550   Goldberg, W. A., E. Greenberger, J. Koch-Jones, R. O'Neil, and S. Hamill. 1989. **Attractiveness of child care and related employer-supported benefits and policies to married and single parents.** *Child and Youth Care Quarterly* **18(1): 23-37.**

Employed parents (n = 321) recruited from 68 preschools in Southern California were surveyed on the attractiveness of child care and related employer benefits. The survey was designed to tap recruitment and retention potentials of employer offered child care benefits. Fathers, single mothers, and married mothers reported that the policies were appealing. Indeed, significant percentages of employees would change jobs for more benefits.

551   Hofferth, S. L., A. Brayfield, S. G. Deich, and P. Holcomb. 1991. *National Child Care Survey, 1990.* **Urban Institute Report 91-95. Washington, DC: Urban Institute Press.**

Telephone interviews were conducted with a nationally representative sample of parents (who were then asked for the telephone numbers of their children's day-care providers). These providers then were contacted and surveyed. This report provides extensive information on choices parents make for day-care arrangements, parental satisfaction with arrangements, impact of arrangements on work, and parental views on policies and programs addressing child care needs.

552   Kahn, A. J., and S. B. Kamerman. 1987. *Child Care: Facing the Hard Choices.* **Dover, MA: Auburn House Publishing.**

553   Kisker, E. E., and M. Silverberg. 1991. **Child care utilization by disadvantaged teenage mothers.** *Journal of Social Issues* **47(2): 159-177.**

This study evaluated the impact of the Teenage Parent Demonstration program on welfare-dependent, teenage mothers' use of child care. The program provided on-site child care, referrals and financial support for child care. A sample of participants and control group members was selected from three areas: Chicago, Camden, and Newark. The study found that teenagers in the programs were more likely to remain in school, work, or job training. Findings discussed include the need for child care, the cost of child care, types of child care, and mothers' perceptions of child care.

554   **Kossek, E. E., and P. Grace. 1990. Taking a strategic view of employee child care assistance: A cost-benefit model.** *Human Resource Planning* **13(3): 189-202.**

The authors encourage human resource managers to adopt a business planning approach and explore alternatives when initiating child care programs. The article presents a model, based on utility theory, to estimate the costs and benefits of offering child care assistance.

555   **Lamb, M. E., and K. J. Sternberg. 1990. Do we really know how day care affects children?** *Journal of Applied Developmental Psychology* **11: 351-379.**

The authors review and critique the literature on day care research. The controversy concerning parent attachment is explored in depth. The authors conclude that the available evidence needs to be used to implement quality care for children.

556   **Lobel, S. A. 1990. Managing attitudes in the workplace: Working parents get what they deserve. In** *Child Care Challenges for Employers,* **edited by E. E. Kossek.**

557   **Maume, D. J. 1991. Child-care expenditures and women's employment turnover.** *Social Forces* **70(2): 495-508.**

This survey of a nationally representative sample of women (n = 1,814) uses a longitudinal design and explores the impact of child care expenditures on employment turnover. The author concludes that child care expenses are a primary determinant of quitting work for mothers of preschoolers, regardless of mother's wage.

558   Maume, D. J., and K. R. Mullin. 1993. **Men's participation in child care and women's work attachment.** *Social Problems* **40(4): 533-546.**

This study draws on the Survey of Income and Program Participation (SIPP) 1985 data using a subsample of 1,814 employed women with children younger than 13 years old. The study examines the issue of cost of child care and continued employment. The results indicate that costs of child care are a major factor in women quitting work, especially among women with pre-school children.

559   **National Council of Jewish Women (NCJW).   August 1988.** *Employer Supports for Child Care.* **New York: NCJW Center for the Child.**

This report addresses employer responses to child care needs of the workforce. In particular, the report focuses on the concerns that prompt employers to respond, such as recruitment, retention, and productivity. The analysis draws on data from the Mothers in the Workplace study.

560   **Neal, M. B., N. J. Chapman, B. Ingersoll-Dayton, and A. C. Emlen. 1993. Employees who have children.** In *Balancing Work and Caregiving for Children, Adults, and Elders.* **Newbury Park, CA: Sage Publications. 59-89.**

A review of the literature serves as a backdrop for this exploration of the work and family demands on employees concerned with child care arrangements. Demands from the workplace (e.g., shift worked, hours worked) or the families' caregiving situation impact on the ability to balance work and family responsibilities. To assess how demands and resources affect absenteeism and stress, the researchers analyze survey data (n = 4,422). Resources from both work and family mitigate stress from demands.

561   Robinson, B. E., B. H. Rowland, and M. Coleman.   1986.
       Latchkey Kids: Unlocking Doors for Children and Their
       Families. Lexington, MA: Lexington Books.

562   Sonenstein, F. L. 1991.   The child care preferences of parents
       with young children: How little is known. In *Parental Leave
       and Childcare: Setting a Research and Policy Agenda,* edited
       by J. S. Hyde and M. J. Essex. Philadelphia, PA: Temple
       University Press. 337-353.

       This chapter reviews the child care preferences of parents, in
       particular (1) parental versus nonparental care; and (2) types
       of child care arrangements. The child care preferences of
       mother's who receive welfare are also addressed.

563   Stith, S. M., and A. J. Davis.   1984.   Employed mothers and
       family day-care substitute caregivers: A comparative analysis
       of infant care. *Child Development*   55: 1340-1348.

       Unlike previous studies, this study of maternal care (own
       home) and nonmaternal care (unregulated) examined the same
       infants in the care of their mother and the substitute caregiver.
       The sample consisted of 10 infants and their employed mothers;
       the same infants and their 10 caregivers; and 10 other infants
       and their unemployed mothers. Observation data were
       gathered during home and day-care visits. Although no
       differences were found between the infants, it was found that
       mothers provide a more responsive environment than the
       substitute caregivers.

564   Vertulli, S., and S. Stubbs. *Metropolitan Child Care Project:
       Final Report.* Eric Document Reproduction Service No, ED 277
       450. Kansas City, MO: School of Education at Missouri
       University.

565   Willer, B., S. L. Hofferth, E. E. Kisker, P. Divine-Hawkins, E.
       Farquhar, and F. B. Glantz. 1991. *The Demand and Supply of
       Child Care in 1990.*

       This report presents findings from "The National Child Care
       Survey 1990" and "A Profile of Child Care Settings."

CHAPTER 18

Elder Care

566   **American Association of Retired Persons (AARP) and The Travelers' Foundation. 1989. A National Survey of Caregivers: Working Caregivers Report. Washington, DC: AARP.**

Data from 754 telephone interviews conducted nationwide were analyzed to examine the effects of caregiving on work. Key findings included: (1) 55% of caregivers are employed; (2) working caregivers spend about 10 hours weekly providing care; (3) one-third of employed caregivers report lost time or late arrivals due to caregiving; and (4) employed caregivers are more likely to be male, younger, and college-educated than non-employed caregivers.

567   **Anastas, J. W., J. L. Gibeau, and P. J. Larson. 1990. Working families and eldercare: A national perspective in an aging America.** *Social Work*   35(5): 405-411.

Based on data from one of the first national survey of 436 full-time working caregivers from nine states and the District of Columbia, the authors provide a demographic profile of caregivers and an analysis of work and caregiving conflict. Overall, 39% of respondents providing eldercare reported conflict and 8% considered quitting. Women reported higher degrees of work and caregiving conflict than men. Workplace supports are discussed.

568   **Anastas, J. W., J. L. Gibeau, and P. J. Larson. 1987.** *Breadwinners and Caregivers: Supporting Workers Who Care for Elderly Family Members.* **Grant #90AM158, Final report submitted by the National Association of Area Agencies on Aging. Washington, DC: Administration on Aging.**

569   Barling, J., K. E. MacEwen, E. K. Kelloway, and S. F. Higginbottom. 1994. **Predictors and outcomes of elder-care-based interrole conflict.** *Psychology and Aging* 9(3): 391-397.

A mediational model of role conflict between employment and eldercare is tested (LISREL VII) and supported. Eldercare "involvement" predicts partial absenteeism from work and psychological strain. Psychological strain predicts marital functioning (e.g., anger, withdrawal). However, it is the extent and character of eldercare "involvement" that predict the conflict.

570   Beinecke, R. H., and A. Marchetta. 1989. *Eldercare: The State of the Art.* **Boston, MA: Health Action Forum of Greater Boston.**

The Employee Elder Caregiving Survey was designed to tap the extent of eldercare as well as the impact of caregiving responsibilities on employees' lives. The researchers mailed 6,400 surveys to employees at four Boston area corporations; 1,915 were returned. Key findings demonstrating the extent of eldercare included: 28% of respondents provide eldercare (ranging from 41% to 22% at particular companies); male and female caregivers are in equal proportion (women, however, contribute more hours); and 56% expect the level of care to increase. The impact of caregiving on work is also reported (e.g., over half of the respondents reporting that they had been late or left work early; and a third reporting missed work days). The survey instrument is included.

571   Brody, E. M., M. H. Kleban, P. T Johnsen, C. Hoffman, and C. B. Schoonover. 1987. **Work status and parent care: A comparison of four groups of women.** *Gerontologist* 27(2): 201-208.

Compares working and non-working married daughters providing parent care (n = 150). The "conflicted" workers and the "quit work" nonworkers experienced the most strain and life-style disruptions. In addition, the "quit work" group reported the greatest deterioration in health.

572   Brody, E. M., P. T. Johnsen, M. C. Fulcomer, and A. M. Lang. 1983. **Women's changing roles and help to elderly parents:**

Attitudes of three generations of women. *Journal of Gerontology* **38(5): 597-607.**

Intergenerational comparisons were made about changing roles for women—including responsibilities for eldercare. The sample included three generations of women, elderly women, middle-generation daughters, and young-adult granddaughters (n = 403). Data collected from interviews and an attitudinal likert-scale revealed the following key findings: (1) the elderly women consistently were more receptive to formal services than middle-generation daughters and granddaughters; (2) all three generations agreed the elderly should be able to depend on their children; however, they also agreed that daughters need not quit work.

573   Creedon, M. 1994. **Eldercare and work research in the United States. In** *Working Careers,* **edited by J. Phillips. U.K.: Avebury Press. 93-115.**

574   Creedon, M. 1988. **Elder care.** *Business and Economic Review* **34(2): 8-10.**

575   Creedon, M. 1987. *Issues for an Aging America: Employees and Eldercare.* **Bridgeport, CT: Center for the Study of Aging at University of Bridgeport.**

In one of the first major studies on eldercare and the workplace, employees were surveyed in three companies in Connecticut: People's Bank, Pitney Bowes and Remington Products. Twenty-six percent reported providing eldercare. (Out of Print).

576   Dwyer, J. W., and R. T. Coward, eds. 1992. **Gender and family care of the elderly: Research gaps and opportunities. In** *Gender, Families, and Elder Care.* **Newbury Park, CA: Sage Publications. 151-162.**

Dwyer and Coward emphasize the importance of building a knowledge base for the study of gender and eldercare and suggest the following: application of theory to research, replication of studies, and implementation of longitudinal studies. The authors provide examples of existing data sets on which longitudinal analyses can be performed. Further suggestions for a research agenda are given (e.g., disentangling the effects of gender from other covariates and studying families rather than caregiving dyads).

577   Earhart, K. M., R. D. Middlemist, and W. E. Hopkins. 1993. Eldercare: An emerging employee assistance issue. *Employee Assistance Quarterly* 8(3): 1-10.

Focuses on eldercare as an employee assistance issue. The authors assess the effects of eldercare on worker productivity and organizational performance. The feasibility of using existing programs to accommodate eldercare needs is discussed.

578   Ellis-Sankari, J. 1992. Eldercare belongs in EAP. *Assistance Quarterly Employee* 7(4): 1-16.

Ellis-Sankari examines the advantages of "housing" eldercare programs in Employment Assistance Programs and presents a model of an eldercare programming process.

579   Franklin, S. T., B. D. Ames, and S. King. 1994. Acquiring the family eldercare role: Influence on female employment adaptation. *Research on Aging* 16(1): 27-42.

The authors examine three employment adaptations by elder caregivers: short-term work adjustments, leaves, and quitting. A secondary analysis of data from a study of Michigan families is run at the inception of elder caregiving and three months later.

580   Fredriksen, K. I. 1996. Gender differences in employment and the informal care of adults. *Journal of Women and Aging* 8(2): 35-53.

581   Fredriksen, K. I., and A. E. Scharlach. In press. Caregiving and Employment: The Impact of Job Classification.

582   Gorey, K. M., R. W. Rice, and G. C. Brice. 1992. The prevalence of elder care responsibilities among the work force population: Response bias among a group of cross-sectional surveys. *Research on Aging* 14(3): 399-418.

The authors present their findings from a meta-analysis of 17 surveys on the prevalence of eldercare responsibilities among the employed. The meta-analysis found that two primary methodological characteristics account for half of the variability in reported prevalence rates: the study's response rate and the chosen operational definition of caregiving. High prevalence rates were associated with lower response rates and broader definitions of caregiving. Gorey and colleagues conclude that a more reliable estimate of the prevalence of eldercare in the workplace is between 7.4% and 11.8%. Other methodological issues are discussed.

583   **Kaye, L. W., and J. S. Applegate. 1990. Men as elder caregivers: Building a research agenda for the 1990's.** *Journal of Aging Studies* **4(3): 289-298.**

The authors address the major trends in elder caregiving with an emphasis on the growing trend toward male caregiving. A review of the literature that explores gender differences in caregiving follows. Kaye and Applegate propose a research agenda for studying both quantitative and qualitative dimensions of male caregiving.

584   **Kola, L. A., and R. E. Dunkle. 1988. Eldercare in the workplace.** *Social Casework: The Journal of Contemporary Social Work* **69(9): 569-574.**

The authors discuss the recent awareness of the issue of elder caregiving as a problem in the workplace. A brief analysis of two studies—"Employer Support for Employee Caregivers" by the New York Business Group on Health and a similar exploratory study by the authors—guide a discussion of the perceptions of both employers and employees of the caregiving problem. Implications for policies and practices for Employment Assistance Programs and unions are discussed.

585   **Lechner, V. M. 1993. Support systems and stress reduction among workers caring for dependent parents.** *Social Work* **38(4): 461-469.**

Lechner investigates the impact of support on the perceived stress and health outcomes of employed caregivers. A sample of

133 labor union members and hospital employees was administered questionnaires and a number of measures including The Workplace Flexibility Index and The Relationship with Supervisor Scale (both scales adapted from the Quality of Employment Survey (QES), Quinn and Staines, 1979). The respondents included: women (86%), white (60%), black (25%), Hispanic (8%) and other (7%). Hierarchical Stepwise Regression analyses were conducted on four dependent variables: impact of caregiving, role strain, mental strain, and physical strain. Supportive work environments significantly reduced "unwanted changes in the respondents' health."

586   **Lechner, V. M. 1993. Racial group responses to work and parent care.** *Families in Society: Journal of Contemporary Human Services* **74(2): 93-103.**

This study examines the work and elder caregiving experiences of 113 black and white full-time employees. Findings suggest little difference by race in caregiving demands and levels of work, mental and physical strain. However, white employees received more support in the workplace. And black employees experienced less flexibility in their schedules and perceived their supervisors as less helpful. Hierarchical regression analyses also predicted different responses to work interferences (i.e., late arrivals, early departures, missed days, and extensive telephoning). Work interferences were a predictor for "more fragile physical health" for blacks, and a predictor for "more fragile mental health" for whites.

587   **Lechner, V. M. 1991. Predicting future commitment to care for frail parents among employed caregivers.** *Journal of Gerontological Social Work* **18(1/2): 69-84.**

A purposeful sample of 133 full-time employees with elder care responsibilities was drawn from three New York City unions and three hospitals. A self-administered questionnaire focused on factors that could reduce future committment to caregiving. Statistical analyses revealed that the relationship between the parent and caregiver was the best predictor of commitment. Those less likely to express a future committment were employees who made frequent work scheduling adjustments. The authors discuss policy and clinical implications.

588   Moen, P., J. Robison, and V. Fields. 1994. Women's work and caregiving roles: A life course approach. *Journal of Gerontology* 49(4): S176-S186.

Using a random sample of 427 wives and mothers interviewed in 1956, life history data were gathered for 293 of those individuals using the original interview and a follow up interview 30 years later. Five findings were reported: (1) informal family caregiving is an increasingly common role for women in the United States; (2) caregiving is a short term intermittent role, frequently combined with paid work; (3) caregiving does not necessarily interrupt the caregiver's employment; (4) caregiving seems to be more characteristic of women's lives; and (5) women with higher education are less apt to be in the caregiving role.

589   Mutschler, P. H. 1994. From executive suite to production line: How employees in different occupations manage elder care responsibilities. *Research on Aging* 16(1): 7-26.

This study focuses on patterns of work accommodations made by employees providing eldercare in different occupations. Mutschler draws on data from the 1982 National Long Term Care Survey and classifies working caregivers into four groupings: (1) executive, professional; (2) sales or service; (3) clerical jobs; or (4) production line or other blue collar positions. An analysis of each group leads Mutschler to conclude that demands of eldercare are diverse and vary with membership in an occupational group. Production workers, for example, are most likely to take unpaid leave and least likely to rearrange schedules.

590   Pittman, C. B., S. Neushatz, M. Creedon, G. G. Hunt, and T. Fox. 1991. *The Missing Worker: Caring for Mom and Dad: A Report on Elder Caregiving in Fairfax County.* Fairfax, VA: Fairfax County Office on Aging.

591   Reichert, M. *Eldercare and the Workplace in Germany: A New Challenge for All Social Partners.* Poster presented at the 48th Annual Scientific Meeting of the GSA, Los Angeles. Dr. Reichert, Institute for Gerontology, Schwanenwall 31-35, 44145 Dortmund, Germany.

Reichert summarizes a study on balancing work and elder caregiving in East and West Germany. A secondary analysis was performed on a data set of a representative sample (n = 940) of caregivers. Key findings included: (1) 45% of primary caregivers are employed; (2) the typical "employed caregiver is female, married, higher qualified and between 40 to 55 years old"; and (3) the most frequently used strategy is rearranging schedules for both men and women. Additional data were collected from case studies with 20 working caregivers. The caregivers reported that, not only did caregiving responsibilities impact negatively on the workplaces, but employers offered little support. Differences between East and West Germany are reported.

592   Robison, J., P. Moen, and D. Dempster-McClain. 1995. Women's caregiving: Changing profiles and pathways. *Journal of Gerontology* 50B(6): S362-S373.

The researchers examine variations in caregiving by age and birth cohort using two-wave panel data from a random sample of 293 white women (wives and mothers) in upstate New York. Findings from an event history analysis include: women with more education are less likely to become caregivers; women born in later cohorts are more likely to become caregivers; and timing of other roles is related to being a caregiver (e.g., marrying late and remaining married decreases the chance of caregiving). Sub group analyses suggest that duration of paid work affects education levels differently: women who have a high school education (no college) with a long work history are more likely to become caregivers than college educated women with long work histories. However, better-educated women born in the 1920s and early 1930s, who worked continually from marriage to age 55, are more likely to be caregivers than women who never worked.

593   Scharlach, A., B. F. Lowe, and E. L. Schneider. 1991. Employees, employers, and elder care. In *Elder Care and the Workforce: Blue Print for Action.* Lexington, MA: Lexington Books. 27-41.

A review of the literature provides a framework for the authors' analysis of the impact of eldercare responsibilities on the employees' personal life and work. In addition, the costs of eldercare to employers is examined.

594   **Scharlach, A. E. 1994. Caregiving and employment: Competing or complementary roles?** *The Gerontologist* **34(3): 378-385.**

Interview data from 94 employed caregivers were analyzed using an inductive content analysis approach. For these caregivers, the positive aspects of eldercare responsibilities (e.g., enhanced relationships, sense of accomplishment) "outweighed" the negative aspects. The most helpful workplace options were those that allowed for adapting schedules.

595   **Scharlach, A. E. 1989. A comparison of employed caregivers of cognitively impaired and physically impaired elderly persons.** *Research on Aging* **11(2): 225-243.**

The elder caregiving employees (n = 332) of a large insurance company were surveyed. Thirty-two percent (32%) of survey respondents were caring for cognitively impaired elders. Key findings included: (1) caregivers of the cognitively impaired provided a greater amount of care in all areas; (2) had more strain and experienced more of a negative impact on their social life; (3) had a greater number of days missed from work and experienced more work interference; and (4) were more interested in community programs to help manage stress. The authors discuss the implications.

596   **Scharlach, A. E. 1988.** *Survey of Caregiving Employees.* **Los Angeles, CA: Transamerica Life Companies.**

Scharlach surveyed 3,658 employees of Transamerica Life Companies in Southern California. Of the 1,898 employees who returned the questionnaire (52% response rate), 23% indicated that they were providing eldercare.

597   **Scharlach, A. E., and K. I. Fredriksen. 1992.** *Survey of Caregiving Employees for the University of California at Berkeley.* **Chancellor's Advisory Committee on Dependent Care, University of California at Berkeley, Berkeley, CA.**

598   Scharlach, A. E., and S. L. Boyd. 1989. Caregiving and employment: Results of an employee survey. *The Gerontologist* 29(3): 382-387.

Using data from an employee survey, the authors compare employees who are providing care for an elder with employees who are not. The majority (73.7%) of employed caregivers reported interference between family and work responsibilities. In contrast, 49.1% of other employees reported interference. Workplace programs deemed helpful by the respondents are discussed.

599   Scharlach, A. E., E. L. Sobel and R. E. L. Roberts. 1991. Employment and caregiver strain: An integrative model. *The Gerontologist* 31(6): 778-787.

A multifactorial model of caregiving strain is analyzed (LISREL). Work interference affected strain and increased the liklihood of quitting work. Lower levels of work interference were reported by respondents with greater flexibility with work responsibilities.

600   Scharlach, A. E., M. C. Runkle, L. T. Midanik, and K. Soghikian. 1994. Health conditions and service utilization of adults with elder care responsibilities. *Journal of Aging and Health* 6(3): 336-352.

This article reports on a study of 628 caregivers and a group of 6599 non-caregivers 50 years and older, from Kaiser-Permanente Health Plan in Northern California to assess the effects of caregiving on health and health service utilization. While there was a negative effect of caregiving on employee health, there was no increased utilization of health services. The need for respite care for middle-aged and older adults who have caregiving responsiblities was underscored.

601   Stone, R., and P. F. Short. 1990. The competing demands of employment and informal caregiving to disabled elders. *Medical Care* 28(6): 513-526.

The authors use a work accommodation model (i.e., reduce work hours, take unpaid leave) to analyze data from the Informal

Caregivers Survey, a sample of care providers to the disabled elderly. The findings suggest a profile of the caregiver most likely to make work accommodation: primary caregivers, caregivers to elders with the most needs, and caregivers who are female, white, with "fair to poor health."

602   **Stone, R., G. L. Cafferata, and J. Sangl. 1987. Caregivers of the frail elderly: A national profile.** *The Gerontologist* **27(5): 616-626.**

Presents a descriptive profile of caregivers and disabled adults based on survey information from two major studies. Research findings demonstrate that unpaid assistance to noninstitutionalized disabled elderly persons is being provided by a population that is predominately female. Moreover, a substantial proportion (31%) of the caregivers had competing interests of child care and employment. Work conflict caused 20% of caregivers to alter their work schedules: 20% reduced work hours, 29% rearranged schedules, and 19% took time off without pay. Briefly discusses policy implications.

603   **Stueve, A., and L. O'Donnell. 1989. Interactions between women and their elderly parents: Constraints of daughter's employment.** *Research on Aging* **11(3): 331-353.**

Interviews were conducted with a random sample of 81 women, all of whom were adult daughters. The study focused on the relationship between employment and relationships with elderly parents. Stueve and O'Donnell's analysis suggests that employment somewhat limits women's involvement as caregiver.

604   **Tennstedt, S. L., and J. G. Gonyea. 1994. An agenda for work and eldercare research: Methodological challenges and future directions.** *Research on Aging* **16(1): 85-108.**

This review of the literature on work and eldercare focuses on corporate-based studies. The authors discuss the limitations of the current research and propose strategies for future research.

605   **The Travelers Insurance Companies. 1985.** *The Travelers Employee Caregiver Survey: A Survey on Caregiving*

Responsibilities of Travelers Employees for Older Americans. Hartford, CT: The Travelers Insurance Companies.

In 1985, Travelers mailed 1,412 employees aged 30 or over a detailed survey regarding elder caregiving. Of those responding (739 employees), 28% were elder caregivers. The average duration of caregiving was for five and half years. Women were more likely than men to be caregivers and spent more time caregiving (women spent 16.1 hours, while men spent 5.3 hours). Caregivers indicated that their responsibilities interfered with emotional and social needs.

606   **Wolf, D. A., and B. J. Soldo. 1994. Married women's allocation of time to employment and care of elderly parents.** *Journal of Human Resources* **29(4): 1259-1276.**

The researchers use a structural equations model to study the relationships between married women caring for frail parents and the variables of employment and hours worked. Data from the 1897-1989 National Survey of Families and Households (NSFH) were analyzed. No association was found between married women's care for frail parents and a reduction in work or work schedules. Wolfe and Soldo also discuss caregiving research (e.g., limitations of data sets).

PART 6

WORK-FAMILY WITHIN HUMAN RESOURCES

CHAPTER 19

Diversity Initiatives and Work-Family

607   Bailyn, L.   Issues of work and family in organizations: Responding to social diversity. In *Working with Careers*. New York: Center for Research in Career Development. Ch. 4.

608   Burke, R. J.   1995.   Using an employee attitude survey tounderstand level playing-field issues. *Women in Management Review* 10(7): 15-20.

This paper describes and presents data from an organizational study designed to illuminate the career prospects of professional and managerial women within the organization. The results from an attitudinal survey sent to 1,608 men and women employees in a large professional services firm are presented.

609   Families and Work Institute. 1994. *To Link or Not to Link: The Relationship between Corporate Work-Family and Diversity Initiatives*. New York: The Conference Board and Families and Work Institute. Conference on Linking Work-Family and Diversity Issues.

Reviews and explores the history and theoretical perspectives of both diversity and work-family practices. The authors also outline the similarities and differences both in theory and in implementation. Using interview data from 25 companies, the authors present the similarities, differences, and linkages between the actual implementation of work-life and diversity practices.

610   Francesco, A. M., and C. A. Thompson. 1996. Pregnant Working Women: An Unrecognized Diversity Challenge. Presented at the American Psychological Association in Toronto, Canada.

Francesco and Thompson consider ways companies can effectively incorporate policies concerning pregnant women and their return to work into an overall diversity plan. Those companies that successfully include and support pregnant women, the authors suggest, will benefit by attracting and retaining talented people. Specific suggestions are made.

611   Galinsky, E., J. T. Bond, and D. E. Friedman. 1993. *The Changing Workforce: Highlights of the National Study.* New York: Families and Work Institute.

This report summarizes key findings from this longitudinal study. Telephone interview data from a randomly selected national sample of employed men and women (n = 3,381) were gathered on their work and family lives.

612   Groshen, E. L. 1990. The structure of the female/male wage differential: Is it who you are, what you do, or where you work? *Journal of Human Resources* 26(3): 457-472.

This study attempts to separate segregation by occupation from segregation based on employer (job-cell). The authors examine the wage gap by gender across five industries and control for other forms of segregation. The point is made that although men and women who work in the same job-cell earn basically the same wage (1% difference) it is rare that men and women are in the same job-cell. Put differently, the job-cells are not integrated. Results are summarized and discussed in terms of theory and policy (Table 3, p. 467).

613   Hall, D. T., and V. A. Parker. 1993. The role of workplace flexibility in managing diversity. *Organizational Dynamics* 22(1): 5-18.

Hall and Parker expand the concept of workplace flexibility, that is, they suggest that companies and researchers view flexibility as attention to policies that creatively connect ("fit") people and their work roles. The companies address the whole of the employees' lives; and the workers, in turn, are more engaged. Hall and Parker further suggest that companies that provide flexible workplaces will strategically benefit, that is, they will be competitive and survive.

614   Kossek, E. E., and S. A. Lobel, eds. 1996. *Managing Diversity: Human Resource Strategies for Transforming the Workplace.* Cambridge, MA: Blackwell Publishers.

615   Lobel, S. A. 1996. *Work/Life and Diversity: Perspectives of Workplace Responses.* Boston, MA: Center on Work and Family at Boston University.

In this policy paper, Lobel juxtaposes the experiences of two fields, diversity and work-family, to cull out lessons that have been learned. After discussing some of the history applicable to each field, strategies for evaluating these fields are presented. This paper focuses particular attention on alternative ways to create linkages between business objectives with diversity and work-life strategies.

616   Lobel, S. A., and E. E. Kossek. 1996. Human resource strategies to support diversity in work and personal lifestyles: Beyond the "family friendly" organization. In *Managing Diversity: Human Resource Strategies for Transforming the Workplace,* edited by E. E. Kossek and S. A. Lobel. Cambridge, MA: Blackwell Publishers. 221-244.

The authors review and discuss human resource programs adopted to support employees, including the assumptions that ground them. This chapter also includes a section linking and contrasting employees' work and personal lives and diversity initiatives (Box 9.2, p. 230). Future directions are discussed.

617   Maier, M., C. A. Thompson, and C. C. Thomas. 1991. Corporate responsiveness (and resistance) to work-family interdependence in the U. S. Women in Management: Recent Developments in North America. *Equal Opportunities International* 10(3/4): 25-31.

618   Mattis, M. C. 1995. Corporate initiatives for advancing women. *Women in Management Review* 10(7): 5-14.

Mattis draws on two recent studies concerned with women's advancement in industry and identifies the barriers restricting opportunities, such as attitudinal, structural, and self-selection. The analysis concludes with recommendations and exemplary corporate responses.

619   Morrison, A. M. 1992. The New Leaders: Guidelines on Leadership Diversity in America. San Francisco, CA: Jossey-Bass Publishers.

620   Stroh, L. K., J. M. Brett, and A. H. Reilly. 1996. Family structure, glass ceiling, and traditional explanations for the differential rate of turnover of female and male managers. *Journal of Vocational Behavior* 49: 99-118.

621   Thompson, C. A., and A. M. Francesco. 1996. Valuing diversity: The case of pregnant working women in the United States. *Equal Opportunities International* 15: 1-9.

622   Totta, J. M., and R. J. Burke. 1995. Integrating diversity and equality into the fabric of the organization. *Women in Management Review* 10(7): 32-39.

This paper traces the Bank of Montreal's commitment to workplace diversity and equality from its nascent and visionary beginnings, to the setting up of four task forces, the presentation of task force findings, and the implementation of the findings.

CHAPTER 20

Career Development and Work-Family

623   Brett, J. M., L. K. Stroh, and A. H. Reilly. 1993. Pulling up
        roots in the 1990s: Who's willing to relocate? *Journal of
        Organizational Behavior* 14(1): 49-60.

The authors profile 1000 employees in 20 Fortune 500
companies. Selection was based on willingness to relocate.
Employee willingness to relocate was influenced by their
spouses willingness to relocate. The study also found that
females and minorities were as willing to relocate as their
white male counterparts, but did not have the opportunities.

624   Brett, J. M., L. K. Stroh, and A. H. Reilly. 1992. What is it like
        being a dual-career manager in the 1990s? In *Work, Families,
        and Organizations*, edited by S. Zedeck. San Francisco, CA:
        Jossey-Bass.

Brett and colleagues draw on data from their 1990 Relocation
Study of 1,000 managers transferred by 20 companies in 1987 and
1988. The data informs this analysis of "generalizations" on
work and family managers extracted from the research
literature. The authors conclude that work-family balance
affects dual-career male managers, as well as dual-career
female managers. Conclusions and possible solutions are
discussed.

625   Covin, T. J., and C. C. Brush. 1991. An examination of male and
        female attitudes toward career and family issues. *Sex Roles*
        25(7/8): 393-415.

A Career Issues Survey was designed and distributed to 240
undergraduate and graduate students enrolled in upper level
business courses in a Southern state college. The findings point
to both gender similarities and gender differences in attitudes

towards career issues and in responses to career scenarios. Work-family policy implications are discussed.

626   Cox, T. H., and C. V. Harquail. 1991. Career paths and career success in the early career stages of male and female MBAs. *Journal of Vocational Behavior* 39: 54-75.

Questionnaires were mailed to 502 MBAs (n = 377 males, 125 females) from a business school. Results confirmed hypothesis that women experience lower salary and, overall, experienced somewhat lower levels of career success, even when controlling for comparable education, performance, age, and experience. The effects of career paths, in general, highlight the importance of line job experience and high job mobility. Findings are discussed.

627   Hall, D. T., and P. Lerner. 1980. Career development in work organizations: Research and practice. *Professional Psychology* 11(3): 428-435.

Presents a comprehensive review and evaluation of career development, including related research developments. Hall and Lerner note that there has been little research on career development interventions. In particular, the authors call for field experiments designed to test interventions within specific career stages. Also mentioned is the need to link micro and macro career activity with evaluation of both research and programs.

628   Kahnweiler, W. M., and J. B. Kahnweiler. 1992. The work/family challenge: A key career development issue. *Journal of Career Development* 18(4): 251-257.

The authors consider the changing workforce in terms of work-family issues. Also addressed are innovative employer responses designed to meet the work-family needs of employees. Implications for career development counselors are discussed.

629   Lambert, S. J. 1994. A day late and a dollar short: Persistent gender differences amid changing requirements for

organizational advancement. *Journal of Applied Social Sciences* **18(1): 89-108.**

This study focuses on paths of advancement of male social workers who move into administration posts in greater numbers and earn higher salaries than their female counterparts. A random sample of 607 male and female social work graduates were surveyed (53% response rate). Key findings include: (1) men have higher positions within 3 years of graduation; and (2) more males are involved in external management early in their careers. Lambert concludes that the type of tasks (e.g., external, training, consultation) determines career paths and suggests that social service jobs be restructured to include administrative tasks.

630   **Munton, A. G. 1990. Job relocation, stress and the family.** *Journal of Organizational Behavior* **11: 401-406.**

This study examines the psychological stress involved in job relocation in a sample of employees (n = 111, 96 % male) living in the U.K. Overall, the results underscore job relocation as a stressful event. Indeed, over 75% of the respondents reported the relocation as more than slightly stressful, while 40% reported it as very stressful. Among the factors contributing to relocation stress, are the following: (1) loss of social support or networks; (2) spouse's employment; (3) children's education; and (4) property issues.

631   **O'Connor, D. J., and D. M. Wolfe. 1987. On managing midlife transitions in career and family.** *Human Relations* **40(12): 799-816.**

This study focused on the midlife stage as a crucial transitional career stage. Following a theoretical review, this grounded theory analysis guided the formulation of scales from the interview data. A model of transition containing five steps was established: (1) stability; (2) rising discontent; (3) crisis; (4) redirection; and (5) restabilizing. A discussion of the model and the implications for Human Resource Management concludes the paper.

632   Schneer, J. A., and F. Reitman. In press 1997. The interrupted managerial career path: A longitudinal study of MBAs. *Journal of Vocational Behavior.*

This study examines the impact of early and mid-career employment gaps on career success that the authors operationalize as income, management level, and career satisfaction. Based on statistical analyses of survey data from MBAs (who experienced an employment interruption but are now working full-time), the researchers conclude that employment gaps "appear to have a long-lasting negative impact on career progress."

633   Schneer, J. A., and F. Reitman. 1995. The impact of gender as managerial careers unfold. *Journal of Vocational Behavior* 47: 290-315.

This longitudinal study focuses on the mid-career stage (i.e., 13-18 years post degree) of men and women MBAs. A cohort of MBA graduates from two northeastern universities were surveyed in 1987 and again in 1993. Both surveys questioned employment status, current income, work hours, work experience, employment gaps, primary job responsibility, and career satisfaction. In addition, the 1993 survey "assessed management level, company size, and work significance." Overall, women MBAs at mid-career stage experienced fewer organizational rewards (e.g., pay, management level). Yet the women expressed the same level of satisfaction with their careers as the men.

634   Schneer, J. A., and F. Reitman. 1994. The importance of gender in mid-career: A longitudinal study of MBAs. *Journal of Organizational Behavior* 15: 199-207.

This study provides a comparison of the mid-career work environment of men and women MBAs. The authors surveyed a cohort of MBAs in 1984 and again in 1990 concerning career paths and perceived treatment at work. Reports differed by gender: women were more likely to feel unappreciated by their boss and more likely to face discrimination. The authors note that at mid-career, women earned considerably less than their male counterparts.

635   Schneer, J. A., and F. Reitman. 1990. Effects of employment gaps on the careers of M.B.A.'s: More damaging for men than for women? *Academy of Management Journal* 33(2): 391-406.

This study uses survey data from men and women M.B.A. degree holders who reported "no" or "one" career interruption. Multiple regression analyses reveal a negative association between employment gaps and income. Overall, the negative effects of employment gaps were greater for men. In light of the findings, the authors briefly address issues of discrimination, restructuring, and downsizing.

636   Stephens, G. K. 1994. Crossing internal career boundaries: The state of research on subjective career transitions. *Journal of Management* 20(2): 479-501.

Stephens reviews current research on subjective career transitions and identifies gaps in the literature. An expanded model of career stages is utilized to direct attention to problematic areas of adjustment during career stage transitions (e.g., the influence of nonwork roles and life stages on career transitions, pp. 485-7). Suggestions for further research regarding subjective career transitions are made.

637   Stephens, G. K., and S. Black. 1991. The impact of spouse's career-orientation on managers during international transfers. *Journal of Management Studies* 28(4): 418-427.

The international relocation of a spouse provides the context for an examination of dual-career couples. A random sample of 195 managers registered with the American Chamber of Commerce in Japan were mailed questionnaires. Almost half of the final sample (n = 67) of couples were dual-career couples in America.

638   Stroh, L. K., and A. H. Reilly. In press. Rekindling organization loyalty: The impact of career mobility. *Journal of Career Development.*

639   Stroh, L. K., and J. M. Brett. 1996. The dual-earner dad penalty in salary progression. *Human Resource Management* 35(2): 181-201.

Stroh and Brett investigate wage differences in a sample of 348 married male managers with children at home. The study found that salaries increased 59% over 5 years for dual-earner husbands, while salaries increased by 70% for their counterparts in traditional marriages. Four alternative theoretical perspectives for the wage gap are discussed.

640   Stroh, L. K., J. M. Brett, and A. H. Reilly. 1992. All the right stuff: A comparison of female and male managers' career progression. *Journal of Applied Psychology* 77(3): 251-260.

This study compares the career advancement of male and female managers employed by 20 Fortune 500 corporations. Even though, as the authors put it, the women had done "all the right stuff" (relevant variables are controlled); the women's salary progression and frequency of job transfers were less than the male managers.

641   Swanson, J. L. 1992. Vocational behavior, 1989-1991: Life-span career development and reciprocal interaction of work and nonwork. *Journal of Vocational Behavior* 41: 101-161.

This paper includes a broad-based review of (1) theoretical approaches to life-span career development and the related literature and (2) the interface of work and nonwork activities. Following this comprehensive review, Swanson concludes that the early stages of career development, especially exploration and initial choice, receive most of the attention. Suggestions for research are made. For example, when studying dual-earners, paired or matched samples would help capture the phenomena under investigation.

CHAPTER 21

Strategies and Programs and Work-Family
(annotated by Rachel Kohn)

642   Batt, R., and P. Osterman. 1993. *A National Policy for Workplace Training: Lessons from State and Local Experiments.* Washington, DC: Economic Policy Institute (EPI).

643   Bruce W., and C. Reed. 1994. Preparing supervisors for the future work force: The dual-income couple and the work-family dichotomy. *Public Administration Review* 54(1): 36-43.

By contrasting new work and family roles with traditional theories of workplace, the question of whether "best practice" supervisory guidelines prepare supervisors for an increasingly diverse work force is addressed. Also discussed are the dominant underlying cultural beliefs that worker integrity and commitment are lessened if they are also in a caregiver or spousal role. These underlying beliefs are called into question by the authors who suggest that the role of supervisors (and their training) needs to address the acceptance of workforce diversity.

644   Casey, J. C., and M. Pitt-Catsouphes. 1994. Employed single mothers: Balancing job and homelife. *Employee Assistance Quarterly* 9(3/4): 37-53.

In spite of the presence of single parents at the workplace, researchers have devoted little attention to the work-family experiences of this population. The results of two studies, a series of focus groups and a survey of work-family managers, are discussed. Implications for Employee Assistance Programs are considered.

645   Coshan, M. 1991. Enlarging the concept of employee assistance. *Employee Assistance Quarterly* 7(1): 25-44.

Coshan provides an overview of the role of the Employment Assistant Programs (EAPs) in the public and private sectors and the changing demands for EAPs to expand the range of services provided. Value added services that are needed include: addictions coverage, eldercare, child care, legal services, and trauma response. Also discussed is the need for integration of new services with already existing programs and resources through wellness and health promotion, joint planning, and quality assurance.

646   **Covin, T. J., and C. C. Brush. 1993. A comparison of student and human resource professional attitudes toward work and family issues.** *Group and Organization Management* **18(1): 29-49.**

Perceptions of undergraduate and graduate business students (n = 240) and human resource professionals (n = 229) were compared with regards to work-family issues, such as parental roles, sex-role stereotypes, and employer or government support. Significant differences were found between the groups with regards to these issues. Additionally, gender differences were found on the perceptions of several work-family issues of interest.

647   **Creedon, M., and M. Tiven. 1991. Employees and eldercare: A growing workplace concern.** *Human Resources Horizon* **106: 31-36.**

648   **Feldman, D. C., H. Doerpinghaus, and W. Turnley. 1994. Managing temporary workers: A permanent HRM challenge.** *Organizational Dynamics* **23(2): 49-63.**

Given the increased presence of temporary employment agencies in the U. S., the authors discuss the change in the nature of the psychological contract between temporary workers and employers. The benefits to the temporary worker are explored, as are the key concerns of temporary workers. Suggestions are given for improving management practices in response to the needs of this growing workforce segment.

649   **Friedman, D. E. 1990. Work and family: The new strategic plan.** *Human Resource Planning* **13(2): 79-118.**

This article discusses the trends that have lead businesses to include work-family issues in their organizations strategic plan. Bottom line reasons, such as labor shortages, productivity, and competitiveness have contributed to the strong business response to families. Specific issues addressed are the corporate response to child care, eldercare, flexibility, and the need to change corporate culture.

650   Galinsky, E., and P. Stein. 1990. **The impact of human resource policies on employees: Balancing work/family life.** *Journal of Family Issues* **11(4): 368-383.**

Making use of existing studies of Fortune 500 companies, this article addresses the work-family problems that employees face (e.g., child care, elder care, work time and timing, relocation, job demands and autonomy, supervisory relationships, and organizational culture). Also discussed are the ways productivity is affected by work-family problems, emerging trends in companies and the work-family responses of several scientific companies and universities. Though many leading companies are responsive to work-family problems, the research indicates there remains a lack of awareness and unresponsiveness in many companies.

651   Goodstein, J. D. 1995. **Employer involvement in eldercare: An organizational adaptation perspective.** *Academy of Management Journal* **38(6): 1657-1671.**

Goodstein addresses the particular challenges in responding and adapting to eldercare issues and the increased importance of providing eldercare benefits to employees. Questioning what motivates an organization to become involved in eldercare, it is argued that recognition of environmental changes to which an organization must adapt is the instigator of organizational response.

652   Gorey, K. M., G. C. Brice, and R. W. Rice. 1990. **An elder care training needs assessment among Employee Assistance Program staff.** *Employee Assistance Quarterly* **5(3): 71-93.**

Employee Assistant Program (EAP) staff members in Western New York were surveyed on issues concerning eldercare (e.g., training history, self-perceived competence, and perception of employee's elder care needs). The study found that 75% of the staff members had not received training. Further, these untrained staff members' self-perceived competence scores in elder care issues were low; whereas, the trained staff's self-perceived competence scores were nearly twice as high (only 14% of staff were trained).

653   Gorey, K. M., G. C. Brice, and R. W. Rice. 1990. **An elder care training needs assessment among Employee Assistance Program staff employed by New York State Government: Brief report of a systematic replication.** *Employee Assistance Quarterly* **6(2): 57-93.**

This study replicates the Gorey, D.M. and colleagues 1990 regional study with the exception of the sampling frame. This current study included statewide geographic representation of Employee Assistance Program (EAP) staff members (n = 224). Overall, the findings replicate the regional study underscoring the need for trained EAP staff members to address the needs of employees with elder care responsibilities. For example, although one in five employees provide elder care, a majority of EAP staff members had not received related training (56.9%).

654   Hall, D. T. 1993. **Promoting work/family balance: An organization-change approach.** *Organizational Dynamics* **22(1): 5-18.**

This article points out that work/family balance issues exist for men, as well as for women. Men's accommodations to career and family demands help us understand that a whole continuum of work/family balance possibilities exist. The author suggests that corporate focus should be on end results rather than employee time. Recommendations for evaluating and planning organizational change are made.

655   Herlihy, P. A. 1996. *Examination of Integration and Differentiation of Employee Assistance Programs and Work/Family Programs.* **Ann Arbor, MI: UMI Dissertation Services.**

Dissertation presented to Florence Heller Graduate School for Advanced Studies in Social Welfare, Brandeis University. This dissertation describes a national descriptive survey that focused on the relationship and linkages between Employee Assistant Programs (EAP) and Work-Family Programs within companies with over 1,000 employees. The research goal was to explain and predict when corporations pursue a strategy of integrating or differentiating benefit programs.

656   Jankowski, J., M. Holtgraves, and L. H. Gerstein. 1988. A systemic perspective on work and family units. In *Journal of Social Behavior and Personality: Work and Family: Theory, Research, and Applications,* edited by E. B. Goldsmith. Corte Madera, CA: Select Press. 91-112.

Using illustrative case scenarios, the structural relationship between work and family units is discussed. Also provided is a theoretical rational for possible actions of the worker or family unit, as well as suggestions for interventions and future areas of research.

657   Kalleberg, A. L., D. Knoke, P. V. Marsden, and J. L. Spaeth. 1996. *Organizations in America: Analyzing Their Structures and Human Resource Practices.* Thousand Oaks, CA: Sage Publications.

658   Kline, M. L., and D. L. Snow. 1994. Effects of a worksite coping skills intervention on the stress, social support, and health outcomes of working mothers. Special Issue: Prevention in the workplace. *Journal of Primary Prevention* 15(2): 105-121.

Kline and Snow examine and evaluate worksite interventions (15 sessions) designed to mitigate work- family risk factors and reduce poor health outcomes. Results reveal that the subjects (n = 142, mothers working as secretaries) reported lower stress, and lower use levels of alcohol and tobacco.

659   Kofodimos, J. 1993. *Balancing Act: How Managers Can Integrate Successful Careers and Fulfilling Personal Lives.* San Francisco, CA: Jossey-Bass Publisher.

660   Kossek, E. E., P. Dass, and B. J. DeMarr. 1994. The dominant logic of employer-sponsored work and family initiatives: Human resource managers' institutional role. *Human Relations* 47(9): 1121-1149.

This article discusses two theories—institutional theory and manager dominant logic—to examine human resource managers role in adoption of employer-sponsored child care. Three overlapping components (i.e., management control, environment and coercion) form the orientation for employer-sponsored child care. Positive relationships were found between adoption of employer-sponsored child care and human resource managers global orientation and their interpretation of executive attitudes toward such child care programs.

661   Kram, K. E., and D. T. Hall. 1995. Mentoring in a context of diversity and turbulence. In *Human Resource Strategies for Managing Diversity*, edited by S. A. Lobel and E. E. Kossek. London: Blackwell Publishers. 108-136.

In the context of the expansion of mentoring programs, Kram and Hall spotlight two key issues related to mentoring: (1) the influx of organizational change; and (2) the increased diversity of the workforce. In this "new context" they discuss the nature of developmental alliances, review mentoring, explore diversity and development, and explore strategies to enhance mentoring. Also discussed are implications for human resource research and strategies.

662   Kraut, A. I., ed. 1990. Strategic responses of human resource management to changing work and family issues. *Human Resource Planning* 13(2): 75-77.

Sounding a call for strategic leadership in human resource management, Kraut discusses the current transformation of the workforce. Provided is a brief review of this transformation: the baby boom era; more women in the workforce; increase in divorce rates; and longevity of elders. Also discussed are the hidden costs of work-family conflicts. The above is said in the context of introducing the related articles in this publication.

663   Lambert, S. J. Forthcoming. Occupational Structure and Patterns of Work-Family Involvement.

In consideration of the relationship between the quality of work life and the quality of personal life, Lambert explores occupational conditions and patterns of psychological involvement in the realm of both work and personal life. Using a nationally representative sample of married and working men and women in the U.S., it is indicated that men and women alike face difficulty in being psychologically involved in work and family simultaneously.

664   Lawson, M. B., and H. L. Angle. 1994. When organizational relocation means family relocation: An emerging issue for strategic human resource management. *Human Resource Management* 33(1): 33-54.

665   Lewis, S., and K. Taylor. Forthcoming. *Family Friendly Employment Policies, Sense of Entitlement and the Discourse of Time as a Commodity.*

666   Lobel, S. A., ed. 1992. Editor's note: Introduction to special issue on work and family. *Human Resource Management* 31(3): 153-155.

Lobel weighs the discrepancies that arise when personal values and organizational expectations differ, as well as external factors that influence these values. Definitions of values and how these are expressed in the work environment lead the discussion on managerial strategies to address these value-based conflicts.

667   Milliken, F. J., J. E. Dutton, and J. M. Beyer. 1990. Understanding organizational adaptation to change: The case of work-family issues. *Human Resource Planning* 13(2): 91-107.

The processes that underlie organizational adaptation are discussed, as well as differential organizational attention given to these changing demographics. It is argued that the difference in response is based on the organizational context and how the issues are framed.

668   Mirvis, P. H., ed. 1993. *Building the Competitive Workforce: Investing in Human Capital for Corporate Success*. New York: John Wiley and Sons.

669   Morgan, H., and F. J. Milliken. 1992. Keys to action: Understanding differences in organizations' responsiveness to work-and-family issues. *Human Resource Management* 31(2): 227-248.

Based on a survey of 175 companies, factors that influence a work-family response are discussed. The factors in question are demographics and organizational characteristics. While industry and geographic effects were significant, no relationship was found between gender and organizational response. It was found, however, that companies involved in dialogue with employees via survey were more responsive.

670   Rodgers, F. S., and C. S. Rodgers. 1989. Business and the facts of family life. *Harvard Business Review* 6: 121-129.

The challenge unearthed by the act of combining business and family are discussed. The role of family as a business issue, as well as issues of dependent care and conditions of work, lead to a call for adjustments in corporate missions. Included is a spotlight on companies that are leading the way in work-family responsiveness.

671   Rosen, R. 1991. *The Healthy Company: Eight Strategies to Develop People, Productivity and Profits*. New York: Jeremy P. Tarcher/Pedigree Books.

672   Stroh, L. K., and A. H. Reilly. 1994. *Making or buying employees: The relationship between Human Resource policy, competitive business strategy and organizational structure*. 10: 12-18.

PART 7

TIME AND PLACE

Flexible Work Arrangements

673 Bohen, H. H., and A. Viveros-Long. 1981. *Balancing Jobs and Family Life: Do Flexible Work Schedules Help?* Philadelphia, PA: Temple University Press.

674 Catalyst. 1993. *Flexible Work Arrangements II: Succeeding with Part-Time Options.* New York: Catalyst.

This report provides information gathered from interviews with human resource professionals (from 70 companies) and employees using flexible work arrangements. Middle managers were perceived to be resistant to the use of flexible work arrangements.

675 Christensen, K. E. 1989. *Flexible Staffing and Scheduling in U.S. Corporations.* New York: The Conference Board. 1-21.

The Conference Board and New Ways to Work surveyed 521 companies. Although a majority of the respondents reported using workers hired through temporary agencies, they indicated lower levels of satisfaction with these arrangements than with contractors or in-house temporaries.

676 Christensen, K. E., and G. L. Staines. 1990. Flextime: A viable solution to work/family conflict? *Journal of Family Issues* 11(4): 455-476.

A review of studies which have investigated the outcomes associated with flexible work arrangements is provided. The authors conclude that there is some evidence that the use of alternative work arrangements is associated with a modest increase in time spent on "family needs" but is not associated with increased family satisfaction.

677   Dalton, D. R., and D. J. Mesch. 1990. The impact of flexible
        scheduling on employee attendance and turnover.
        Administrative Science Quarterly 35: 370-387.

When a large public utility company initiated a flexible
scheduling program, it presented the opportunity for a natural
field experiment. One group participated in the flexible
scheduling program; while a control group did not. After a one-
year trial period, the company decided to end the program.
Therefore, it was possible to use an interrupted time-series
design to study the program's effect on employee absenteeism
and turnover. Results indicated reduced absenteeism for the
experimental group but not for the control group. With the
discontinuation of the program, absenteeism increased.

678   Galambos, N. L., and B. J. Walters. 1992. Work hours, schedule
        inflexibility, and stress in dual-earner spouses. Canadian
        Journal of Behavioural Science (3): 290-302.

Dual-earner couples (n = 96 couples) provided information about
work hours, schedule flexibility, role strain, depression, and
anxiety. The study found that longer work hours assumed by
wives were associated with higher role strain among wives and
higher depression among their husbands. Correlations were
noted among spouses' role strain, depression, and anxiety.

679   Golembiewski, R. T., and C. W. Proehl. 1980. Public sector
        applications of flexible workhours: A review of available
        experience. *Public Administration Review* 40: 72-85.

This article presents the findings of a meta-analysis of studies
which have examined flextime arrangements in both the
private and the public sectors. Summaries are provided about
outcome indicators such as absenteeism, tardiness, turnover,
overtime, and productivity.

680   International Labour Office. 1990. The hours we work: New
        work schedules in policy and practice. In *Conditions of Work
        Digest.* Geneva: International Labour Office. Volume 9(2).

Discusses different aspects of work time arrangements as
implemented in different industrialized countries. Case studies

are used to illustrate practices such as part-time work, weekend work, flextime. Public policy issues are discussed.

681   Kim, J. S., and A. F. Campagna. 1981. Effects of flextime on employee attendance and performance: A field experiment. *Academy of Management Journal* 24(4): 729-741.

This study used a quasi-experimental design to examine the relationships between flextime and selected performance measures. Participants (n = 353) worked in a county welfare office. A 45% reduction in long-term absences was reported for the experimental group.

682   Kossek, E. E., A. E. Barber, and D. Winters. 1993. An assessment of individual, work group and organizational influences on the acceptance of flexible work schedules. In *Best Paper Proceedings*. Atlanta, GA: National Academy of Management. 116-120.

The authors highlight the findings of research about employees' perceptions of flexible work arrangements. They conclude that variables at the individual, group, and organizational levels affect employees' acceptance of flexible work options.

683   McGuire, J. B., and J. R. Liro. 1987. Absenteeism and flexible work schedules. *Public Personnel Management* 16(1): 47-59.

A quasi-experimental design was used to compare two flexible schedule options (true flextime and staggered fixed time) as implemented in public sector agencies with 274 employees. The study found that staggered fixed time schedules were associated with lower rates of absenteeism.

684   Parker, V. A., and D. T. Hall. 1993. Workplace flexibility: Faddish or fundamental? In *Building the Competitive Workforce: Investing in Human Capital for Corporate Success*, edited by P. H. Mirvis. New York: John Wiley and Sons. 122-155.

Data from 406 human resource executives participating in the Laborforce 2000 study are explored to consider perceived demand for flexible work arrangements. Statistics are presented about the percentage of companies which had established 10 options for flexible work arrangements. Factors associated with the establishment of more extensive flexibility options included company size, percentage of women in the workforce, and overall human resource philosophy.

685   Shinn, M., N. W. Wong, P. A. Simko, and B. Ortiz-Torres. 1989. Promoting the well-being of working parents: Coping, social support, and flexible job schedules. *American Journal of Community Psychology* 17: 31-55.

Respondents from private firms and public agencies (n = 644) provided information about coping, social support, schedule flexibility, stress and well-being. Associations were found between two coping techniques (problem focused and emotion focused) and outcomes. There was a weak relationship between flexibility and outcomes.

686   Staines, G. L., and J. H. Pleck. 1986. Work schedule flexibility and family life. *Journal of Occupational Behaviour* 7: 147-153.

Using data from the Quality of Employment Survey (n = 1515), the relationships between nonstandard work schedules, flexibility (e.g., workers' control over hours), and quality of family life are examined. The authors found that flexibility acts as a buffer, particularly among women employees.

687   Winett, R. A., and M. S. Neale. 1980. Results of experimental study on flextime and family life. *Monthly Labor Review* 103: 29-32.

This report presents a methodological overview and the results of two exploratory, longitudinal studies that examined the effects of flextime on young families. Two large Federal agencies implemented a flexible work program that gave workers a chance to arrive or leave work early. Winett and Neale present the findings from the log data and questionnaire data, and discuss the effects of flextime on family life.

688   Winett, R. A., M. S. Neale, and K. R. Williams. 1982. The effects of flexible work schedules on urban families with young

children: Quasi-Experimental, ecological studies. *American Journal of Community Psychology* 10(1): 49-64.

This study compared the effects of flexible work schedules on employed parents with children in two separate agencies in Washington, D.C. Using a quasi-experimental design, Agency 1 and Agency 2 each had a control group who changed to a flexible schedule and a group who did not.

689   Wood, S. G., with A. B. Sevison. 1990. **Flexible working hours: A preliminary look at the phenomenon of flexibility in the American workplace.** *American Journal of Comparative Law* 38S: 325-340.

Information from the 1985 Current Population Survey was used to explore national trends in the use of flexible work arrangements. The percentage of companies that reported having flextime doubled from 1977 (15%) to 1989 (30%), with the insurance industry being the sector that offered this option most frequently. Legislative implications are examined.

CHAPTER 23

Alternative Work Arrangements

690   Christensen, K. E. 1993. Eliminating the journey to work: Home-based work across the life course of women in the United States. In *Full Circles: Geographies of Women over the Life Course*, edited by C. Katz and J. Monk. New York: Routledge. 55-87.

Christensen tells the "stories" of women and home-based work by drawing on the women's own words from her case studies. An analysis of the consequences of home-based work concludes the chapter. Two consequences are emphasized: (1) the effects on the workers' health and pension/benefits; and (2) the effects from accommodating work in the home (e.g., space, rituals).

691   Christensen, K. E. 1988. *Women and Home-Based Work: The Unspoken Contract.* New York: Henry Holt and Company.

692   Christensen, K. E., ed. 1988. *The New Era of Home-Based Work: Directions and Policies.* Boulder, CO: Westview Press.

Christensen breaks the myth of home-based work. Using data from the 14,000 women who responded to a *Family Circle* survey and life history data from 20 women who work at home, the author identifies the motivations attracting women to home-based work. The book then examines the consequences of home-based work.

693   Cook, A. H. 1992. Can work requirements accomodate to the needs of dual-earner families? In *Dual-Earner Families: International Perspectives*, edited by S. Lewis, D. N. Izraeli, and H. Hootsmans. London: Sage Publications. 204-220.

Cook argues for "work restructuring as conditioned by the demands of the family" for the purpose of integrating work and family. This chapter presents and evaluates work innovations that restructure the time and place that work is accomplished. Among others, the following topics are discussed: home-based work, flextime, part-time, shift work, and the compressed work week. European comparisons are made.

694   Costello, C. B. 1988. **Clerical home-based work: A case study of work and family.** In *The New Era of Home-Based Work: Directions and Policies,* edited by K. E. Christensen. Boulder, CO: Westview Press. 135-145.

In this chapter, Costello illuminates the experiences and consequences of home-based employment by using interview data from clerical workers and managers. The sample participants were employed by The Wisconsin Physicians Service Insurance Corporation (WPS) who hired clerical workers for part-time home-based work. The chapter concludes with recommendations for successful home-based employment.

695   Dempster-McClain, D., and P. Moen. 1989. **Moonlighting husbands: A life-cycle perspective.** *Work and Occupations* 16(1): 43-64.

The extent or likelihood of moonlighting over the life course is examined in this study. Data on employed husbands (n = 2,118) were drawn from the Michigan Panel Study of Income Dynamics (1976-1977 waves). The research shows that the likelihood of moonlighting changes over the life cycle and interacts with factors, such as low wage rate, sporadic work histories, and ages of children.

696   Gerson, J. M., and R. E. Kraut. 1988. **Clerical work at home or in the office: The difference it makes.** In *The New Era of Home-Based Work: Directions and Policies,* edited by K. E. Christensen. Boulder, CO: Westview Press. 49-64.

Using data from a nationwide survey they conducted, the authors compare office-based and home-based clerical work. A review of the metatheories of home-based work and the previous research on home-based clerical work guides the comparison.

697   Gringeri, C. E. 1995. **Flexibility, the family ethic, and rural home-based work.** *Affilia: Journal of Women and Social Work* **10(1): 70-86.**

This analysis of the flexibility of work in the home is based on the author's interview data gathered from 80 rural home-based workers who were employed by The Middle Company (TMC) in the Midwest. In general terms, the author concludes that women may trade some flexibility for low wages, no benefits, and no job security.

698   Hartman, R. I., C. R. Stoner, and R. Arora. 1991. **An investigation of selected variables affecting telecommuting productivity and satisfaction.** *Journal of Business and Psychology* **6(2): 207-225.**

This study investigates the antecedent variables linked to telecommuting productivity and satisfaction. Selected survey respondents (n = 97 telecommuters) fulfilled the research criteria of working for 40 hours a week or more, with at least 20 hours telecommuting. The study found that performance evaluation and supervisory support (technological and emotional) were linked to both productivity and satisfaction.

699   Heck, R. K. Z., M. Winter, and K. Stafford. 1992. **Managing work and family in home-based employment. In a special edition of At-home Income Generation.** *Journal of Family and Economic Issues* **13(2): 187-212.**

Describes and tests two scales measuring the management of home-based work and the management of family work (see Table 1, pp. 194-195). The respondents in this sample were, therefore, both employed in home-based work and the household manager (n = 899).

700   Kopelman, R. E. 1986. **Alternative work schedules and productivity: A review of the evidence.** *National Productivity Review* **5: 150-165.**

Kopelman reviews the research literature related to alternative or flexible work schedules that use 'hard' measures of productivity (i.e., efficiency or absenteeism). The analysis includes a discussion of the following: (1) application and advantages/disadvantages of the compressed work week; (2) advantages/disadvantages to both employees and organizations of flexible work hours; and (3) evidence of flexible work hours effectiveness (see Table 2, pp. 158-159). Suggestions for implementation are made.

701   **Kraut, R. E. 1988. Homework: What is it and who does it? In** *The New Era of Home-Based Work: Directions and Policies,* **edited by K. E. Christensen. Boulder, CO: Westview Press. 30-48.**

In response to widely disparate estimates and characteristics of home-based workers, Kraut explores and evaluates the variations. He concludes that the methodological and definitional problems inherent in identifying home-based workers lead to disparate estimates.

702   **Norman, P., S. Collins, M. Conner, R. Martin, and J. Rance. 1995. Attributions, cognitions, and coping styles: Teleworkers' reactions to work-related problems.** *Journal of Applied Social Psychology* **25(2): 117-128.**

This study focuses on the stresses and problems that teleworkers experience with their home-based work. Survey data from 192 teleworkers of varying occupational status were analyzed. The results suggest that workers who are prone to self-blame engage in emotional coping strategies. And emotional coping strategies (versus problem-solving strategies) were linked to negative outcomes.

703   **Phizacklea, A., and C. Wolkowitz. 1995.** *Homeworking Women: Gender, Racism and Class at Work.* **London: Sage Publications.**

704   **Pierce, J. L., J. W. Newstrom, R. B. Dunham, and A. E. Barber. 1989.** *Alternative Work Schedules.* **Boston, MA: Allyn and Bacon.**

Presents a review of the research literature and the conceptual perspectives related to alternative work schedules. Following an historical overview, a comprehensive review of alternative work schedules (e.g., part-time, shift work, compressed work week, flexible work hours) is presented. The book also includes a model linking alternative work schedules and both employee reactions and organizational effectiveness. Appendices contain instruments researchers may use.

705   **Pitt-Catsouphes, M., and A. Marchetta. 1991.** *A Coming of Age: Telework.* **Boston, MA: Center on Work and Family at Boston University.**

Four case studies are presented against the backdrop of a review of the literature on telecommuting. Considerations for the design of telecommuting programs are presented.

706   **Shamir, B., and I. Salomon. 1985. Work-at-home and the quality of working life.** *Academy of Management Review* **(3): 455-464.**

In light of recent writings on the technological shift back to the home, the authors explore the implications of working at home. The primary focus is the qualitative nature of the work for the individual, such as the meaningfulness of the work, feedback, and social relations.

CHAPTER 24

Part-Time Work

707 **Adams, S. M. 1995. Part-time work: Models that work.** *Women in Management Review* **10(7): 21-31.**

The experiences of businesses and employees are used to examine some of the characteristics of part-time work. findings Interview findings helped to identify the characteristics of four models which minimize some of the deleterious consequences of part-time work such as restrictions on career advancement: (1) the critical mass model; (2) the diversity model; (3) the individual fit model; and (4) the personal business model.

708 **Appelbaum, E. 1992. Structural change and the growth of part-time and temporary employment.** In *New Policies for the Part-Time and Contingent Workforce,* edited by V. L. duRivage. Armonk, NY: M. E. Sharpe. 1-14.

Appelbaum suggests that the growth in involuntary part-time work arrangements reflects employers' desire to establish these positions. Two of the principal factors which have supported the growth of part-time positions are discussed: changes in technology and new economic conditions. The importance of firm relationships with subcontractors is noted.

709 **Appelbaum, E. 1991. What's driving the growth of contingent employment?** In *New Policies for Part-Time and Contingent Workers,* edited by New Ways To Work. San Francisco, CA: New Ways to Work. 9-11.

Two staffing approaches, static and dynamic flexibility, are contrasted. Static flexibility adopts a short term orientation which reduces worker skills. Dynamic flexibility stresses the importance of training and technology to strengthen worker flexibility through skill enhancement.

710   Appelbaum, E., and J. Gregory. 1988. Union Responses to Contingent Work: Are Win-Win Outcomes Possible? In *Flexible Workstyles: A Look at Contingent Labor, Conference Summary.* ERIC #ED 305471. Washington, DC: U. S. Department of Labor. 69-75.

Although contingent workers currently comprise one-fourth of all workers, unions have only recently begun to consider their needs. The role of unions in negotiating alternative work arrangements, such as job sharing, is discussed. It is suggested that the use of contingent workers can create a two tiered workforce.

711   Barker, K. 1995. Contingent work: Research issues and the lens of moral exclusion. In *Changing Employment Relations: Behavioral and Social Perspectives,* edited by L. E. Tetrick and J. Barling. Washington, DC: American Psychological Association. 31-60.

Barker introduces two models of corporate orientation toward contingent work arrangements: the expense model (which emphasizes profit-incentive strategies) and the flexibility model (focusing on human resource problems). The construct of moral exclusion, or being outside of the rules of fairness, is used to consider contingent work arrangements with adjunct faculty.

712   Barker, K. 1993. Changing assumptions and contingent solutions: The costs and benefits of women working full- and part-time. *Sex Roles* 28(1/2): 47-71.

This study gathered information from 315 women holding jobs in professions which have been male dominated; professions which have been female dominated; and nonprofessional jobs. Part-time workers reported that, in comparison to full-time workers, they were more peripheral to the organization; however they expressed greater satisfaction with their jobs and children.

713   Bennett, S. K., and L. B. Alexander. 1987. The mythology of part-time work: Empirical evidence from a study of working mothers. In *Women, Households, and the Economy,* edited by L. Benería and C. R. Stimpson. New Brunswick, NJ: Rutgers University Press. 225-241.

Interviews conducted with 215 women gathered information about part-time and full-time employment status. There were no overall differences in tenure between the two groups. Furthermore, part-time workers did not demonstrate less commitment to their jobs.

714   Blank, R. M. 1990. Are part-time jobs bad jobs? In *A Future of Lousy Jobs: The Changing Structure of U. S. Wages,* edited by G. Burtless. Washington, DC: The Brookings Institution. 123-164.

Data from the 1988 Current Population Survey were used to explore trends in part-time employment. Blank notes that wage differentials between part-time and full-time workers depends on the occupation and type of job. For example, although part-time workers tend to earn less compared to full-time workers, part-time women service workers actually earn more than their full-time counterparts. Various models for work and wages are presented.

715   Blank, R. M. 1989. The role of part-time work in women's labor market choices over time. *AEA Papers and Proceedings* 79(2): 295-299.

Using data from the 1976-84 Panel Study of Income Dynamics, patterns of the labor market involvement of individual women were examined. Blank concludes that part-time work is not usually used as a transition from non-work to full-time work status but rather part-time work is viewed as an alternative work status.

716   Briar, C. J. 1992. Part-time work and the state in Britain, 1941-1987. In *Working Part-Time: Risks and Opportunities,* edited by B. D. Warme, K. L. P. Lundy, and L. A. Lundy. New York: Praeger Publishers. 75-86.

An historical analysis of women's part-time employment in England is provided. Briar observes that the government encouraged this labor market affiliation in an effort to meet labor shortages during and after World War II. The resultant gender inequalities are noted.

717   Burtless, G., ed. 1991. *A Future of Lousy Jobs? The Changing Structure of U.S. Wages.* Washington, DC: The Brookings Institution.

Trends in the distribution of wages are examined. From 1979-86, wage inequality among men increased (e.g., wage gains by top income earners rose faster than the gains by lower income earners), but the wages earned by women did not exhibit this pattern. Burtless also notes that when baby boomers entered the labor market, older males tended to prosper.

718   Callaghan, P., and H. I. Hartmann. 1991. *Contingent Work: A Chart Book on Part-Time and Temporary Employment.* Washington, DC: Economic Policy Institute (EPI).

719   Carré, F. J. 1992. Temporary employment in the eighties. In *New Policies for the Part-time and Contingent Workforce,* edited by V. L. duRivage. Armonk, NY: M. E. Sharpe. 45-87.

Individuals who work for temporary help services are typically female, young, and black. Forty percent (40%) of temporary workers have part-time schedules. Carré suggests that workers filling temporary positions often find that the possibilities for securing better positions within their firms are limited.

720   Carré, F. J., V. L. duRivage, and C. Tilly. 1995. Piecing together the fragmented workplace: Unions and public policy on flexible employment. In *Unions and Public Policy: The New Economy, Law, and Democratic Politics,* edited by L. G. Flood. Westport, CT: Greenwood Press. 13-37.

721   Christensen, K. E. 1995. *Contingent Work Arrangements in Family-Sensitive Corporations.* Work-Family Policy Paper Series. Boston, MA: Center on Work and Family at Boston University.

This report discusses three corporate models for the use of contingent workers: the traditional personnel model; the crisis-driven model; and the strategic staffing model. Reflecting on the results of a survey of the members of the Work and Family Roundtable, Christensen observes that temporary workers do not typically have access to many of the family-responsive policies and programs.

722   Christensen, K. E. 1987. Women and contingent work. *Social Policy* 17(4): 15-18.

Three factors which have influenced the growth of the contingent workforce are identified: the internalization of the economy, changes in technology, and the shift from an industrial to a service economy. Some of the advantages and disadvantages of contingent work, from the perspective of the workers, are discussed.

723   duRivage, V. L., ed. 1992. New Policies for the Part-Time and Contingent Workforce. In *New Policies for the Part-Time and Contingent Workforce*. Armonk, NY: M. E. Sharpe. 89-134.

Several public policy recommendations are made that could ameliorate many of the problems associated with contingent work arrangements. For instance, duRivage suggests that wage parity between part-time and full-time workers with the same job responsibilities be established. Difficulties with benefits, such as health insurance coverage, are discussed.

724   Feldman, D. C. 1990. Reconceptualizing the nature and consequences of part-time work. *Academy of Management Review* 15(1): 103-112.

Distinctions among the different types of part-time work are made. The interactive nature of the relationships between part-time work status and attitudes toward work is discussed. After reviewing research studies, a number of hypotheses are made.

725   Golden, L., and E. Appelbaum. 1992. What was driving the 1982-88 boom in temporary employment? Preference of workers

or decisions and power of employers. *American Journal of Economics and Sociology* 51(4): 473-493.

Changes in factors such as the labor supply, employer demand for labor, and the bargaining power of unions, are considered for their relationship to the increase in temporary employment. An economic model for permanent and temporary workers is offered. Changes in product demand have provided incentives to firms for increasing the use of temporary workers.

726   Gornick, J. C., and J. A. Jacobs. 1994. *A Cross-National Analysis of the Wages of Part-Time Workers: Evidence from the United States, the United Kingdom, Canada, and Australia.* Working Paper No. 56. New York: Russell Sage Foundation.

International comparisons of the wage differentials between part-time and full-time workers indicate that in the United States, the United Kingdom, Canada, and Australia women part-time workers earn significantly less than full-time workers with the same job responsibilities. The gender gap in wages is discussed.

727   Hartmann, H. I., and J. Lapidus. 1989. Temporary work. In *Investing in People: A Strategy to Address America's Workforce Crises.* Washington, DC: U.S. Department of Labor.

This paper describes the trends in temporary work, including the rapid growth in the temporary help services (THS): (1) one-third of all temporary workers are THS workers; (2) employment in THS grew 10 times faster than total employment; and (3) projected growth through 1999 is 5% annually (Bureau of Labor Statistics). The authors present the costs and benefits of temporary work. Based on their analysis, policy recommendations are made.

728   Hiatt, J. P., and L. Rhinehart. 1993. *The Growing Contingent Workforce: A Challenge for the Future.* Paper presented to American Bar Association Section of Labor and Employment Law. "Daily Report," 23(154), E1-E6.

In the context of the workplace as a whole, the authors consider the nature and growth of the contingent workforce. An exploration of myths associated with the contingent workforce are presented, for instance, the myth that a contingent workforce is enhancing U. S. competitiveness. The authors also address the failure of both the labor movement and our government to protect the contingent workforce. Policy recommendations are outlined.

729   Holden, K. C., and W. L. Hansen. 1987. **Part-time work, full-time work, and occupational segregation.** In *Gender in the Workplace,* edited by C. Brown and J. A. Pechman. Washington, DC: The Brookings Institution. 217-246.

This study addresses occupational segregation among part-time and full-time workers. The authors juxtapose the research on occupational segregation with the characteristics of part-time and full-time work. Since occupational segregation decreased in the years 1971 and 1981, the authors use employment data for these years from the Current Population Study. With the inclusion of part-time data, the authors show that degree of occupational segregation in the total work force is somewhat higher than the full-time workforce.

730   Kahne, H. 1992. **Part-time work: A hope and a peril.** In *Working Part-Time: Risks and Opportunities,* edited by B. D. Warme, K. L. P. Lundy, and L. A. Lundy. New York: Praeger Publishers. 295-309.

Kahne argues that part-time work deserves "attention and innovative experimentation in the workplace." Addressing the potential of New Concept part-time work, Kahne explores the evidence and makes the following points: (1) part-time work should not be limited to low-pay sales and services, but include reduced-hours among professional jobs; (2) productivity gains can be achieved by lowering absenteeism and turnover; and (3) benefit plans can be addressed creatively. Kahne observes that New Concept part-time work deserves the thoughtful attention of labor and management to facilitate the advantage of flexible work scheduling.

731   Kahne, H. 1985. *Reconceiving Part-Time Work: New Perspectives for Older Workers and Women.* Totowa, N.J.: Rowman & Allanheld.

Kahne contrasts the "Old Concept" part-time work, with its inherent low wages, minimal or no benefits and the "New Concept" part-time work, with pro-rated earnings, paid benefits, and opportunities for career progression. This book investigates the rationale, characteristics, context, and costs and benefits of the "New Concept" part-time work.

732   Leo, E. S. 1989. **Working part-time in male professions: Social-Psychological costs and benefits reported by thirty American women with families.** *In The Redesign of Working Time: Promise or Threat?*, **edited by J. B. Agassi and S. Heycock. Berlin: Edition Sigma. 207-226.**

This exploratory, qualitative study is based on interview data and questionnaire data gathered from 30 married women who were employed part-time (currently or within the last three years). The majority of the women (25) were members of the Association of Part-Time Professionals. In this paper, Leo describes these professional part-time workers' job attitudes and commitment, family commitment, job-role strains, and in particular, highlights their part-time professional role strains (e.g., low wages and marginal status).

733   Levitan, S. A., and E. A. Conway. 1992. **Part-timers: Living on half rations.** In *Working Part-Time: Risks and Opportunities*, **edited by B. D. Warme, K. L. P. Lundy, and L. A. Lundy. New York: Praeger Publishers. 45-60.**

Levitan and Conway outline the "bleak economic realities" of part-time employment, such as low wages, and no pension and health care benefits. The characteristics of workers, gender, race, age, and education level, who work part-time for economic reasons are outlined. Policy implications are discussed.

734   Moberly, R. B. 1987. **Temporary, part-time, and other atypical employment relationships in the United States.** *Labor Law Journal* **38: 689-696.**

Moberly outlines the advantages and disadvantages of temporary, part-time, seasonal, and casual employment. Following a discussion of trends and characteristics of atypical employment relationships, the issue of labor law for temporaries is specifically addressed. Moberly concludes that although atypical workers usually receive fewer benefits and experience job insecurity, the workers are generally covered by major social legislation (e.g., collective bargaining, minimum wages, Social Security, and unemployment compensation).

735   Montgomery, M., and J. Cosgrove. 1993. **The effect of employee benefits on the demand for part-time workers.** *Industrial and Labor Relations Review* **47(1): 87-98.**

Drawing from national survey data, the researchers examine the relationship of fringe benefits and hours worked among part-time teachers and teachers aides. The study showed that when fringe benefits rise, hours worked fall. The effect for insurance payments, such as health and dental, is twice as strong. Issues of demand relative to benefits, of cost, and the role of insurance companies are discussed.

736   New Ways to Work, ed. 1992. *New Policies for Part-Time and Contingent Workers.* **San Francisco, CA: New Ways to Work. A Summary of a Conference on the Changing Workforce, held November 1991, sponsored by the Economic Policy Institute.**

737   Polivka, A. E., and T. Nardone. 1989. **On the definition of "contingent work."** *Monthly Labor Review* **112: 9-16.**

Polivka and Nardone consider a precise definition of the contingent workforce, as well as the implications of that definition. They observe that the lack of a consistent definition leads to inadequate measurement for estimating the number of contingent jobs. Measurement issues are discussed.

738   Rebitzer, J. B., and L. J. Taylor. 1991. **A model of dual labor markets when product demand is uncertain.** *The Quarterly Journal of Economics* **106: 1373-1383.**

Dual labor market theory informs this study of dual labor markets, that is, primary and contingent employment contracts. The authors discuss the theoretical underpinnings of the dual labor market model and then presents the model. Implications of the model are presented, as well as directions for research.

739   Rogers, J. K. 1995. Just a temp: Experience and structure of alienation in temporary clerical employment. *Work and Occupations* 22(2): 137-166.

This paper presents an ethnographic account of workers' daily lives in temporary employment based on 13 interviews with women employed as temporary clerical workers. Additional interviews were conducted with branch managers of temporary employment agencies. A grounded theory analysis revealed patterns and themes that parallel alienation theory. Many women and minorities working as part-time workers experience alienation from work, self, and others.

740   Spalter-Roth, R. M., and H. I. Hartmann. 1995. *Contingent Work: Its Consequences for Economic Well-Being, The Gendered Division of Labor, and The Welfare State.* Washington, DC: Institute for Women's Policy Research (IWPR).

Spalter-Roth and Hartmann focus on the relationship between contingent workers and the division of labor by gender. Since women make up a disproportionate share of the contingent work, the implications for income supplements are examined. Specifically addressed are the eventual costs on public welfare programs and the taxpayers.

741   Spalter-Roth, R. M., H. I. Hartmann, and S. B. Shaw. 1993. *Exploring the Characteristics of Self-Employment and Part-Time Work Among Women.* Washington, DC: Institute for Women's Policy Research (IWPR).

742   Steffy, B. D., and J. W. Jones. 1990. Differences between full-time and part-time employees in perceived role strain and work satisfaction. *Journal of Organizational Behavior* 11: 321-329.

Steffy and Jones hypothesize that part-time employees will experience greater role strain than full-time employees. Role strain variables measured were role load pressure, role ambiguity, and job tension. Survey data from employees in a hospital were evaluated to determine differences in work satisfaction and role strain between part-time and full-time employees. The results indicate a moderate relationship between part-time work and greater role-strain. The researchers also found a moderate relationship between part-time workers and dissatisfaction with coworkers and pay. Steffey and Jones discuss the findings, which are somewhat inconsistent with previous research.

743   Tilly, C. 1992. **Two faces of part-time work: Good and bad part-time jobs in U.S. service industries.** In *Working Part-Time: Risks and Opportunities,* **edited by B. D. Warme, K. P. Lundy, and L. A. Lundy. New York: Praeger Publishers. 227-238.**

Tilly uses the theoretical perspective of internal labor markets to explore both the types of part-time employment and the linkages to companies' overall employer relationships. Interview data from 82 managers, union officials, and workers inform Tilly's analysis. Basically the analysis reveals that there are different uses for part-time jobs in the labor markets. Therefore, there are two opposing types of part-time jobs coexisting, secondary and retention. Secondary part-time jobs are low-wage, low-benefit, with no job ladders, whereas retention part-time jobs possess the opposite characteristics.

744   Tilly, C. 1990. *Short Hours, Short Shrift: Causes and Consequences of Part-Time Work.* **Washington, DC: Economic Policy Institute (EPI).**

This report focuses on the growth, characteristics, trends, and consequences of part-time employment. Policy implications are discussed.

745   Williams, H. B. 1989. **What temporary workers earn: Findings from new BLS survey.** *Monthly Labor Review* **112(3): 3-6.**

This report presents information about wages and benefits offered to temporary workers. Data and findings from the Bureau of Labor Statistics study of the temporary help services industry are profiled.

CHAPTER 25

Shift Work

746   Barton, J., and S. Folkard. 1991. The response of day and night nurses to their work schedules. *Journal of Occupational Psychology* 64: 207-218.

This study compares day- and night-shift nurses at a psychiatric hospital on a range of questionnaire measures. At this hospital, the nurses, males and females, were able to choose the shift they wished to work. Although the results reveal some differences between day- and night-shift workers, there appeared to be a more even distribution compared to prior studies. The authors suggest sample composition as one possible explanation, but highlight another explanation, that is, these respondents controlled their schedules. Implications are discussed in the context of work organization.

747   Hood, J. C., and S. Golden. 1979. Beating time/making time: The impact of work scheduling on men's family roles. *Family Coordinator* 28: 575-582.

Hood and Golden juxtapose two case studies as they explore the effects of work schedules through two men's family lives. One man's work scheduling elicited a negative consequence in his family life; while the other prompts a positive consequence. The authors view the cases through both a sociological and psychological lens.

748   Jackson, S. E., S. Zedeck, and E. Summers. 1985. Family life disruptions: Effects of job-induced structural and emotional interference. *Academy of Management Journal* 28(3): 574-586.

This study examines the effects of work-related stress on families. Self-report data for this study were gathered from 95 couples, of whom one partner was a plant operator working on a

28-day rotating shift at a large power and gas utility. Although the study examined structural interference, the results indicate a relationship with job dissatisfaction but no carry over to the employees' families. On the other hand, the results reveal that emotional interference did carry over into the families' interaction.

749   Mott, P. E., F. C. Mann, Q. McLoughlin, and D. P. Warwick. 1965. **Shift work, marital happiness, and family integration.** In *Shift Work: The Social, Psychological, and Physical Consequences.* Ann Arbor, MI: University of Michigan Press. 113-146.

This chapter examines the effects of working shifts on marital happiness and family integration. Among the findings, is the cumulative effect of various work-family conflicts with family and social activities leads to a reduced marital happiness.

750   Presser, H. B. 1995. **Job, family, and gender: Determinants of nonstandard work schedules among employed Americans in 1991.** *Demography* 32(4): 577-598.

Presser examines the effects of job characteristics and family characteristics on nonstandard work schedules, including nonstandard hours and days. Data is drawn from the 1991 CPI (Bureau of Labor Statistics) on nonstandard work schedules. The results reveal that demand for nonstandard employment is high across occupations, especially in the service sectors. Family characteristics affect demand, namely marital status and parental status. For example, being married increases men's chances of working nonstandard hours, but reduces women's. For women, having children and the ages of the children affect days and hours worked.

751   Presser, H. B. 1988. **Shift work and child care among young dual-earner American parents.** *Journal of Marriage and the Family* 50: 133-148.

This study investigates the relationship between shift work and child care among young dual-earner, married couples with children under age five. Data is drawn from the 1984 of the National Longitudinal Survey of Labor Market Experience,

Youth Cohort. The analysis showed that when women work nonstandard hours, they rely primarily on the father for child care. Presser discusses her findings in the context of child care as a work-family issue.

752   **Presser, H. B. 1986. Shift work among American women and child care.** *Journal of Marriage and the Family* **48: 551-563.**

This article presents a detailed analysis of the relationship between shift work and child care. Based on data from the 1982 U. S. Current Population Survey, the analysis shows that many women with young children are engaged in shift work and report that lack of child care restrains them working more hours. Presser discusses the findings and underscores the need to study "when" women work.

753   **Simon, B. L. 1990. Impact of shift work on individuals and families.** *Families in Society: The Journal of Contemporary Human Services* **71(6): 342-348.**

This article discusses the physical, psychological, and sociological consequences of nonstandard work schedules on women, men, and their families. The purpose of the article is to assist human service workers address the needs of shift workers and their families.

754   **Staines, G. L., and J. H. Pleck. 1984. Nonstandard work schedules and family life.** *Journal of Applied Psychology* **69(3): 515-523.**

Staines and Pleck examine the impact of nonstandard work schedules on the family life of married workers with a child under age 18 using data from the 1977 Quality of Employment Survey. Results reveal that working nonstandard hours is associated with a poorer quality of family life. Overall, the study found that working a nonstandard shift was related to more work-family conflict, especially conflict related to schedules.

755   **Weiss, M. G., and M. B. Liss. 1988. Night shift work: Job and family concerns. In** *Journal of Social Behavior and Personality:*

Work and Family: Theory, Research, and Applications, edited
by E. B. Goldsmith. Corte Madera, CA: Select Press. 279-286.

Questionnaire data were gathered from 100 female and 102
male night shift workers concerning job satisfaction, social life
satisfaction, and family interactions. The questionnaire was
designed to elicit information regarding family issues, such as
time spent with children, child care, and marital concerns.
Overall, the respondents viewed their work favorably and
social lives as adequate. The authors discuss the observation
that satisfaction is related to motivation regarding night shift
work.

756   White, L., and B. Keith. 1990. The effect of shift work on the
        quality and stability of marital relations. *Journal of Marriage
        and the Family* 52: 453-462.

This study examines the effects of shiftwork on marital quality
and stability. Panel data from men and women shift workers
were assessed on six measures of marital quality: happiness,
interaction, disagreements, general problems, sexual problems,
and child-related problems. Results of OLS regression analysis
indicate that shift work has a modest negative effect on
marital quality. Also the likelihood of divorce among the
shift workers increased from 7% to 11%.

CHAPTER 26

Time Famine

757 **Gallagher, E., and U. Delworth. 1993. The third shift: Juggling employment, family, and the farm.** *Journal of Rural Community Psychology* **12(2): 21-36.**

Prior research suggests that farm women juggle three shifts: (1) paid employment; (2) child care and housework; and (3) managing and maintaining the farm. Gallagher and Delworth's exploration of the "three shift lives" of farm women is grounded in a review of the literature. They emphasize that other women also are engaged in three shifts (e.g., women with disabled children). Clinical implications are discussed.

758 **Hochschild, A., with A. Machung. 1990.** *The Second Shift.* **New York: Avon Books.**

Hochschild's basic thesis is that many women start a second shift of child care and housework at the completion of their paid work day. She describes the phenomenon of a "leisure gap" separating women and men.

759 **Leete, L., and J. Schor. 1994. Assessing the time-squeeze hypothesis: Hours worked in the United States, 1969-89.** *Industrial Relations* **33(1): 25-43.**

A debate has evolved around the number of hours worked in the U. S. in the last few decades. To estimate hours worked, the authors draw upon data from two sources: The Current Population Surveys and the University of Michigan Time-Use Studies. In response to the debate, the authors identify data and methodological concerns of prior work as they present the rationale and explication of their own approach. They find evidence of a 'time-squeeze.'

760   Presser, H. B. 1989. Can we make time for the children? The economy, work schedules and child care. *Demography* 26(4): 523-543.

In this paper, Presser links broad structural changes at the societal level with work-family policy issues and family responsibilities for child care. The growing diversity of work schedules changes the way parents handle their time with each other and their children. Warning that these diverse schedules may not "fit" with the way formal child care is provided, Presser calls for policy makers and researchers to realistically assess the temporal organization of the workplace with the care of children.

761   Rodgers, C. S. 1992. The flexible workplace: What have we learned? *Human Resource Management* 31(3): 183-199.

Attitudes towards flexibility were examined using data collected from 60,000 employees at 20 Fortune 500 companies. A significant percentage of all employees, particularly women, reported that they have no time for themselves.

762   Schor, J. 1991. *The Overworked American: The Unexpected Decline of Leisure.* New York: Basic Books.

This book exposes a trend that academics missed, that is, the decline of leisure time. Schor posits that Americans are trapped in a cycle of work and spend that precipitates stress, an increased workload, lack of sleep, and stressed familial relationships. To substantiate her argument, Schor quantifies and combines paid work and home work as total working hours, thus defining leisure as a residual.

763   Spitze, G., and S. J. South. 1985. Women's employment, time expenditure, and divorce. *Journal of Family Issues* 6(3): 307-329.

The authors suggest that wives' employment produces a time shortage thus increasing the probability of divorce. Drawing upon data from the National Longitudinal Survey, the authors find that hours worked has an impact on marital dissolution. The relationship between hours worked and marital dissolution is greater for two types of families: (1) middle income families; and (2) families with husbands who disapprove of the wives working.

PART 8

PUBLIC AND PRIVATE PRACTICES AND POLICIES

CHAPTER 27

International Comparisons
(with Irene Fassler)

764   Bailyn, L. 1992. Issues of work and family in different national contexts: How the United States, Britain and Sweden respond. *Human Resource Management* 31(3): 201-208.

A cultural comparison regarding issues of work and family among three countries—United States, Britain, and Sweden—highlights both ideological and institutional differences. While the national responses differ, both in practice and in ideology, occupational segregation by sex continues to exist in all three countries. The author encourages a re-examination of the assumptions about the role of time in high level careers.

765   Borchorst, A. 1995. *Family Policies in Western Europe: Convergence of Divergence?* Working Paper #279. Wellesley, MA: Center for Research on Women at Wellesley College.

The author expands the Esping-Andersen typology of dominant political ideologies (e.g., conservative, liberal and social democratic), to incorporate a gender perspective and uses it to discuss family policies in Western Europe. In addition, the historical origins of various family policies, as well as the position of women in the labor market, are discussed. The concept of European integration is introduced.

766   Bronstein, A. S. 1991. Temporary work in Western Europe: Threat or complement to permanent employment? *International Labour Review* 130(3): 291-310.

Temporary work in Western Europe is gaining legitimacy as a valid form of employment. Efforts continue to ensure that temporary work remains within the limits of its usefulness and that its benefits are shared between users and the workers. The advantages and disadvantages of temporary work as well as the typical profile of a temporary worker are outlined. Temporary work agencies and temporary work's legal context are discussed.

767   Cook, A. H. 1989. **Public policies to help dual-earner families meet the demands of the work world.** *Industrial and Labor Relations Review* **42(2): 201-215.**

American public policies regarding child care, maternity leave and parental leave are reviewed. The author also offers a description of European policies including child allowances, paid leave for care of sick family members, housing allowances, and transportation to and from work.

768   Cook, A. H. 1987. **International comparisons: Problems and research in the industrialized world.** In *Working Women: Past, Present, Future,* **edited by K. S. Koziara, M. H. Moskow, and L. D. Tanner. Washington, DC: The Bureau of National Affairs. 332-373.**

This chapter reviews progress toward achieving a non-sex-biased labor market in the Western market economies. The author discusses work-related issues for women such as work and family roles, job segregation, shorter hours, part-time work, reentry, vocational training and guidance, health and safety, and participation in trade unions. In addition, the author evaluates the research done in these areas and the policy reactions to the research. Suggestions for further research in labor relations are made.

769   Cook, A. H. 1980. **Collective bargaining as a strategy for achieving equal opportunity and equal pay: Sweden and West Germany.** In *Equal Employment Policy for Women,* **edited by R. S. Ratner. Philadelphia, PA: Temple University Press. 53-78.**

A discussion of the concepts of equal pay and equal opportunity for women through collective bargaining in Sweden and West Germany is contained in this chapter. The author reviews the history of equal pay and the unions in both countries and offers a comparison of the two approaches. Further discussion is presented regarding women as union officers, and centralization versus decentralization in union functioning.

770   Cook, A. H. 1978 Revised. *The Working Mother: A Survey of Problems and Programs in Nine Countries.* New York State School of Industrial and Labor Relations, Cornell University, Ithaca, NY.

Each chapter of this book defines a work-family issue set within a country and presents an analysis of related conditions, programs and policies.

771   Cook, A. H., and H. Hayashi. 1980. *Working Women in Japan: Discrimination, Resistance, and Reform.* No. 10. Cornell International Industrial and Labor Relations Report. Ithaca, NY: New York State School of Industrial and Labor Relations at Cornell University.

772   Dowd, N. E. 1989. Envisioning work and family: A critical perspective on international models. *Harvard Journal on Legislation* 26(2): 311-348.

The author critically examines work-family policies in Sweden and France. Through a series of interviews, the author discusses the implications of policies based on principle of equality (Sweden) and policies based on a woman-centered vision (France). Implications for American policies are discussed.

773   Galinsky, E. 1989. *The Implementation of Flexible Time and Leave Policies: Observations from European Employers.* New York: Families and Work Institute.

Methods and consequences of implementation of family policies in the workplace, with a concentration on flexible time and leave, are explored. The author chose to study the leave policies in Sweden and the flexible time policies in West Germany. A comparison of the policies found in these countries was made with the historical progress of work-family policies in the United States. It was concluded that the process of change in attitudes and behavior has the greatest significance for American companies.

774   Haas, L. A. 1993. **Nurturing fathers and working mothers: Changing gender roles in Sweden.** In *Men, Work, and Family,* edited by J. C. Hood. Newbury Park, CA: Sage Publications. 238-261.

The historical context of the official policy of gender equality in Sweden is presented. Also included is a report on the outcomes of that model and an examination of the barriers to the absolute realization of gender equality. The author examines and suggests several reasons for men's minimal use of paid parental leave benefits. Implications for further research are suggested.

775   Haas, L. A. 1990. **Gender equality and social policy: Implications of a study of parental leave in Sweden.** *Journal of Family Issues* 11(4): 401-423.

Data from a mail survey of 319 couples in Gothenburg, Sweden, who were new parents, were analyzed to evaluate the effectiveness of parental leave as a vehicle to reduce gender based division of labor. Findings indicated that fathers who took parental leave were more likely to share in child care tasks and were less satisfied with their employment situation. However, mothers continued to retain primary responsibility for the child and to remain less involved in the labor market. Further suggestions were made for the reduction of gender based division of labor.

776   Haas, L. A., and P. Hwang. 1995. **Fatherhood and corporate culture in Sweden.** *Family Relations* 44: 1-26.

Survey data of the 250 largest Swedish corporations (n = 200, 80% response rate) indicate that while the companies were somewhat father-friendly, most fathers are not taking full advantage of the benefits offered. Corporate culture as a barrier to utilizing father-friendly benefits is explored.

777   Hinrichs, K., W. Roche, and C. Sirianni. 1995. **Working time and employment: New Arrangements.** *International Labour Review* 134(2): 259-272.

The authors report a downward shift in working time and

discuss different work-sharing arrangements and/or policies in Germany, France, and Belgium.

778   Hinrichs, K., W. Roche, and C. Sirianni, eds. 1991. *Working Time in Transition: The Political Economy of Working Hours in Industrial Nations.* Philadelphia, PA: Temple University Press.

779   Hofferth, S. L., and S. G. Deich. 1994. Recent U. S. child care and family legislation in comparative perspective. *Journal of Family Issues* 15(3): 424-448.

The authors examine U. S. child care and family legislation that authorizes new funding to states for child care assistance, for the expansion of Head Start, and to offer tax credits for low-income parents. U. S. child-care and family policies are then compared to those of France, Germany, Hungary, and Sweden. The authors also discuss separate but related current policies in the United States and the four European countries: (1) policies that ease the financial burden of raising children; (2) policies that promote parental choice; and (3) policies that raise the quality of early education and care.

780   Hootsmans, H.   1992.   Beyond 1992: Dutch and British corporations and the challenge of dual-career couples. In *Dual-Earner Families: International Perspectives,* edited by S. Lewis, D. N. Izraeli, and H. Hootsmans. London: Sage Publications. 80-98.

This article presents an overview of corporate practices and public policies regarding work-family issues in the European Community. Specific policies and practices in Britain and the Netherlands are used for illustration.

781   Kamerman, S. B. 1991. Parental leave and infant care: U.S. and international trends and issues, 1978-1988. In *Parental Leave and Childcare: Setting a Research and Policy Agenda,* edited by J. S. Hyde and M. J. Essex. Philadelphia, PA: Temple University Press. 11-23.

Policy trends regarding parental leave and infant care are

examined in the United States and internationally (1978-1988). Specific policy and research agendas are suggested.

782   Kamerman, S. B., and A. J. Kahn. 1988. **What Europe does for single-parent families.** *The Public Interest* **93: 70-86.**

The authors review the different patterns of single parenthood in the following countries: Britain, France, Germany, Norway and Sweden. European policy strategies outlined include: (1) an anti-poverty strategy; (2) a categorical strategy for single mothers; (3) a universal young child strategy for single mothers; (4) a universal young child strategy; and (5) combining labor market and family policy to permit a successful combination of parenting and work. Lessons from European strategies are bought to the reader's attention.

783   Kamerman, S. B., and A. J. Kahn, eds. 1991. *Child Care, Parental Leave and the Under 3s: Policy Innovation in Europe.* New York: Auburn House Publishing.

784   Kramar, R. Forthcoming 1997. *The Processes and Outcomes of Family Friendly Policies in Australian Organizations* Canberra, Australia: **Work and Family Unit, Department of Industrial Relations.**

This report provides an analysis of the implementation of family friendly policies in Australia. Drawing on organizational case studies, the author examines impediments to change, reasons for development (external and internal), and processes involved in implementation. A framework for the analysis of the development of family friendly policies is included in chapter 2.

785   Kramar, R. Forthcoming. **Business Case for a Family-Friendly Workplace. Work and family policies in Australia: Critical Processes.** *Equal Opportunities International.* **Volume 15(8).**

Kramar examines the case studies of five Australian organizations recognized for developing and implementing work-family initiatives. Strategies for overcoming obstacles in development are presented.

786   Kramar, R. 1995. *Work and Family Initiatives in Australia: Purpose and Outcomes.* Unpublished paper. NSW 2109, The Graduate School of Management, Macquarie University, Australia.

After reviewing the official (governmental) support and goals of work-family initiatives, the author discusses specific initiatives being applied in Australia (e.g. flexible working arrangements; paid and unpaid leaves; working time arrangements; and child care services). While it was too early to assess the impact of the policies and programs, the author anticipates that major changes in the labor market would be slow in evolving. Kramar also outlines different frameworks to utilize when analyzing the development and implementation phases of policy initiatives.

787   Leira, A. 1993. Mothers, markets and the state: A Scandinavian 'model'? *Journal of Social Policy* 22(3): 329-347.

The author reviews the state's involvement in child care and leave policies in each of the Scandinavian countries. The existence of a "Scandinavian model" is questioned.

788   Lewis, S. 1992. Work and families in the United Kingdom. In *Work, Families, and Organizations,* edited by S. Zedeck. San Francisco, CA: Jossey-Bass Publishers. 395-431.

This chapter outlines the historical context for work and family issues. The author reviews work-family policies and compares the British system to others in Europe (e.g. Spain, France, Denmark, Ireland). Research on managing work and family in Britain is reviewed, and responses both public and organizational to changing demographics are discussed. Implications for further research are also presented.

789   Lewis, S., and C. L. Cooper. Forthcoming. Balancing the work/home interface: A European perspective. *Human Resource Management Review.*

The authors discuss environmental factors leading to the public debate on work-family issues. The European perspectives of work and family as well as the limitations of how the issues are addressed in Europe are detailed. Suggestions for a shift in perspectives on work and family and implications for further research are offered.

790   Lubeck, S. 1995. **Nation as context: Comparing child-care systems across nations.** *Teachers College Record* **96(3): 467-491.**

Using a "nation as context" model, this article compares the child-care and early education systems of the former German Democratic Republic, France, and the United States. The author developed a model of comparison concentrating on two areas of interest, the degree of administrative and fiscal centralization, and the degree of uniformity. Several points highlighted include: (1) the level of national support toward female employment and extrafamilial child rearing differs by country; (2) policies are social constructions that are able to undergo change; (3) changing patterns of labor participation and family formation may create conditions for change in the United States; and (4) the organizational systems in the United States can learn from cross-national studies.

791   Rosenfeld, R. A., and A. L. Kalleberg. 1990. **A cross-national comparison of the gender gap in income.** *American Journal of Sociology* **96(1): 69-106.**

A comparison of women's and men's income determination in the United States, Canada, Norway, and Sweden is presented. It was found that there was greater income equality in the Scandinavian countries than in the North American ones, but not greater equality by gender across labor market and job positions. In general, family effects on income were found to be relatively low.

792   Rosenthal, M. G. 1994. **Single mothers in Sweden: Work and welfare in the welfare state.** *Social Work* **39(3): 270-278.**

The author explores the topic of single mothers and their families in Sweden and offers suggestions to meet the needs of female headed households in the United States. Lessons to be learned from Sweden include: (1) substituting work for public assistance will not remove single parent families from poverty; (2) universal benefits (e.g., child allowances) will not meet the needs of the poor; and (3) a combination of work and assistance help to provide a "decent standard of living."

793   Ruhm, C. J., and J. L. Teague. 1993. *Parental Leave Policies in Europe and North America.* Department of Economics, University of North Carolina, Greensboro, NC.

Ruhm and Teague describe the international development, efficiency, and incidence of parental leave policies. A longitudinal (1960-1989) data set describes the duration of job protected leave in 17 countries. The authors use econometric techniques to explore the relationship between parental leave, national incomes, and labor market outcomes.

794   Stoiber, S. A. 1989. *Parental Leave and Woman's Place: The Implications and Impact of Three European approaches to Family Leave Policy.* Washington, DC: Women's Research and Education Institute.

The author gives an overview of the development and current status of special leave policies and benefits in Western Europe. More detailed analyses of the leave policies in the United Kingdom, the Federal Republic of Germany and Sweden are also presented. Suggestions for the development of family leave in the United States are made based on the author's analysis: (1) a modest program of family leave can be adopted without seriously burdening employers or putting women at an increased disadvantage in the workplace; (2) a tension between employee security and freedom to manage without unnecessary administrative requirements exists; (3) legislation should be inclusive and universal to minimize fragmented and discriminatory systems; (4) leave entitlements are best utilized as an integral part of a broader policy toward families.

795   Ungerson, C. 1995. Gender, cash, and informal care: European perspectives and dilemmas. *Journal of Social Policy* 24(1): 31-52.

From a feminist perspective, this article explores the concept of payment for both formal and informal care in Britain and other European countries (e.g., France, Germany, the Netherlands, Belgium). Most countries of Western and Central Europe have experienced a shift toward dependence on care services for their elderly and members of the special needs population. The author draws the readers attention to certain policy initiatives that are beginning to blur the boundaries between formal and informal care, especially as it relates to payment. Ungerson posits that the "activities of 'informal care' are being commodified." Suggestions for further study are offered.

CHAPTER 28

Public Policy Analyses

796   Chilman, C. S. 1993. **Parental employment and child care trends: Some critical issues and suggested policies.** *Social Work* 38(4): 451-460.

Chilman reviews and summarizes recent federal legislation affecting working parents of young children. Topics discussed include income supports for the working poor and job-training provisions. In addition, a summary table with the pros and cons of full-time employment for parents of young children is provided (pp. 456-8).

797   Ferber, M. A., and B. O'Farrell, eds., with L. Allen. 1991. *Work and Family: Policies for a Changing Work Force.* **Washington, DC: National Academy Press.**

In this book, The National Research Council's Panel on Employer Policies and Working Families present a historical overview of the family and its relationship to the workplace. The book focuses on the evaluation of policies and programs and the need for further research. Recommendations are comprehensive.

798   Hartmann, H. I., and R. M. Spalter-Roth. 1994. *A Feminist Approach to Policy Making for Women and Families.* **Prepared for the Seminar on Future Directions for American Politics and Public Policy, Harvard University. Washington, DC: Institute for Women's Policy Research (IWPR).**

Hartmann and Spalter-Roth analyze public policies using women's income security as a yardstick. Based on the income security standard, the authors reason that successful policies would reduce poverty, dependency and inequality (Table 3, p. 15). Also discussed are recent trends in work and family including single family trends. Hartmann and Spalter-Roth argue for the need to emphasize commonalties among women.

799   Hartmann, H. I., and R. M. Spalter-Roth. 1990. *Working Parents: Differences, Similarities, and the Implications for a Policy Agenda.* Prepared for a meeting on "Women, Work and the Family: Advancing the Policy and Research Agenda" held by Institute for Research on Women and Gender at Columbia University in the City of New York. Washington, DC: Institute for Women's Policy Research (IWPR).

This paper focuses on the changing family - in particular the working family. Using data from the Current Population Study and the Survey of Income and Program Participation (SIPP), the authors examine family formation, labor force distribution, income distribution, and benefit access. Strategies for private and public policies are addressed.

800   Kamerman, S. B., A. J. Kahn, and P. W. Kingston. 1983. *Maternity Policies and Working Women.* New York: Columbia University Press.

801   Kamerman, S. B., and A. J. Kahn. 1987. *The Responsive Workplace: Employers and a Changing Labor Force.* New York: Columbia University Press.

802   Kingston, P. W. 1988. Studying the work-family connection: Atheoretical progress, ideological bias and shaky foundations for policy. In *Journal of Social Behavior and Personality: Work and Family: Theory, Research, and Applications,* edited by E. B. Goldsmith. Corte Madera, CA: Select Press. 55-60.

Commenting on the state of work-family research, Kingston suggests that researchers have developed "a sophisticated and subtle appreciation" of the linkages between work and family, albeit atheoretical. However, Kingston cautions against overinterpretation and overemphasis of these linkages. Further, he warns that the researchers' feminist and liberal ideologies might obfuscate the "true meanings" individuals ascribe to the linkages; furthermore, ideologies might result in ungrounded policy recommendations.

803   Koziara, K. S. 1987. **Women and work: The evolving policy.** In
       Working Women: Past, Present, Future,   edited by K. S.
       Koziara, M. H. Moskow, and L. D. Tanner. Washington, DC:
       The Bureau of National Affairs. 374-408.

In this chapter, Koziara delineates the course of women
workers and public policy by stages, beginning with early
industrialization (1800s) when the first protective laws
pertaining to women were passed, to the present stage initiated
by the 1963 Equal Pay Act. Includes an analysis of labor market
policies and suggestions for future research.

804   **Lambert, S. J. 1993. Workplace policies as social policy.** *Social
       Service Review* **67: 237-260.**

Lambert defines the difficulties in balancing work and family
not as a business problem, but as a social problem meriting the
engagement of governments, businesses and individuals. In the
context of social policy, Lambert posits that goals of family-
friendly policies are clarified and issues of accessibility, equity
and effectiveness are addressed.

805   **Lerner, S. 1994. The future of work in North America: Good
       jobs, bad jobs, beyond jobs.** *Futures* **26(2): 185-196.**

Lerner addresses the fate of the changing North American
workforce as it faces technological change and globalization.
Following a discussion of workforce trends in the U. K., such as
underemployment and a contingent workforce, policy options
are evaluated in the context of a restructured workforce in the
U. S. and Canada. The basic thesis is that government policies
are needed to mitigate structural unemployment.

806   **Meyers, M. K. 1993. Child care in JOBS employment and
       training program: What difference does quality make?** *Journal
       of Marriage and the Family* **55: 767-783.**

Meyers evaluates child care used by AFDC recipients in their
welfare-to-work process. Analyses were performed using one
year panel data gathered from the GAIN program which
provides child care through a vendor system. Meyers found
that usage of child care alternatives increased after beginning

"job readiness activities." Moreover, she concludes that the convenience and quality of child care are related to the participants dropping out of the program.

807   Osterman, P. 1988. *Employment Futures: Reorganization, Dislocation and Public Policy.* New York: Oxford University Press.

808   Pleck, J. H. 1992. Work-family policies in the United States. In *Women's Work and Women's Lives: The Continuing Struggle Worldwide,* edited by H. Kahne and J. Z. Giele. Boulder, CO: Westview Press. 248-275.

In this chapter, Pleck provides a comprehensive review and assessment of social policies in the United States that address the needs of working families with children.

809   Spalter-Roth, R. M., and H. I. Hartmann. 1991. Science and politics and the "dual vision" of feminist policy research: The example of Family and Medical Leave. In *Parental Leave and Childcare: Setting a Research and Policy Agenda,* edited by J. S. Hyde and M. J. Essex. Philadelphia, PA: Temple University Press. 41-65.

This paper presents the theoretical and methodological underpinnings of the research conducted by The Institute for Women's Policy Research (IWPR), the feminist think tank. Using an IWPR study as an example—"Unnecessary Losses: Costs to Americans of the Lack of Family and Medical Leave"—the researchers document their methodological vision.

810   Spalter-Roth, R. M., H. I. Hartmann, and L. M. Andrews with J. Lindert, C. Andrews, U. Sunkara, and M. Danner. 1992. *Combining Work and Welfare: An Alternative Anti-Poverty Strategy. A report to the Ford Foundation.* Washington, DC: Institute for Women's Policy Research (IWPR).

This study examines the issue of combining welfare benefits and paid work prior to the Family Support Act. The sample—drawn from the Survey of Income and Program Participation (SIPP)—includes 585 single mothers who were

AFDC recipients for a minimum period of 2 months. Based on the findings, the researchers profile types of recipients, of whom 40% are "income packagers," that is, recipients who combine work and benefits (either simultaneously or cycling between). Case studies illustrate the process.

811   **Starrels, M. E. 1992. The evolution of the workplace: Family policy research.** *Journal of Family Issues* **13(3): 259-278.**

The results of research and policy analysis are used to examine three issues from a work-family perspective: corporate culture, gender and class differences, and public policy. A research agenda for these topic areas is proposed.

812   **Stipek, D., and J. McCroskey. 1989. Investing in children: Government and workplace policies for parents.** *American Psychologist* **44(2): 416-423.**

Discusses policies supportive of the changing structure of the family: child care, parental leave, income supports, child support enforcement and flexible schedules. The authors challenge psychologists to produce policy-relevant research, for example, research that examines effects of government and workplace policies on families—including long-term effects.

813   **Wiatrowski, W. J. 1990. Family-related benefits in the workplace.** *Monthly Labor Review* **113: 28-33.**

This retrospective paper examines changes in family structure and characteristics while documenting accompanying responses by government and employers.

CHAPTER 29

Leave Legislation

814   Bond, J. T., E. Galinsky, M. Lord, G. L. Staines, and K. R. Brown. 1991. *Beyond the Parental Leave Debate: The Impact of Laws in Four States*. New York: Families and Work Institute.

This longitudinal study evaluates the impact of leave legislation on employers and includes data on implementation, costs of implementation, leave length, and retention rates of leave-takers. Samples of both employers and employees were randomly selected and surveyed in four states: Minnesota, Oregon, Wisconsin, and Rhode Island. Although formal legislation appeared to have little effect on women, father's leave-taking increased somewhat. However, in Rhode Island where formal legislation included a requirement for temporary disability insurance, lower-income women took longer leaves. Cost impacts on employers are discussed. A key finding was that the majority of employers reported "no increase" in costs with compliance of legislation.

815   Bureau of National Affairs (BNA). 1994. *Majority of Workers Unaware of Rights Provided by Family and Medical Leave Act, BNA Survey Finds*. Washington, DC: BNA.

A nation wide poll conducted by the BNA found that 20 months after President Clinton signed the Family and Medical Leave Act, only slightly more than half of all workers knew about it. When queried about their likely response to leave-taking, women and men differed greatly, many more women than men would take the full 12 week leave. Responses also varied by income level and geographic location. Many workers voiced concern about taking a leave, citing money as the primary reason.

816   Commission on Leave. 1996. *A Workable Balance: Report to Congress on Family and Medical Leave Policies.* Washington, DC: U.S. Department of Labor, Women's Bureau.

This report presents the 1995 data from two major surveys, an Employer Survey and an Employee Survey, on experiences with the Family and Medical Leave Act.

817   England S. E., and B. T. Naulleau. 1991. Women, work and elder care: The Family and Medical Leave debate. *Women and Politics* 11(2): 91-107.

This article provides a background of the debate centering on Family and Medical Leave Legislation.

818   Friedman, D. E., E. Galinsky, and V. Plowden, eds. 1992. *Parental Leave and Productivity: Current Research.* New York: Families and Work Institute.

This report includes a compilation of papers analyzing the impact of parental leave on productivity (e.g., absenteeism, morale, tardiness, recruitment, retention).

819   Hyde, J. S., and M. J. Essex, eds. 1991. *Parental Leave and Child Care: Setting a Research and Policy Agenda.* Philadelphia, PA: Temple University Press.

820   Hyde, J. S., M. H. Klein, M. J. Essex, and R. Clark. 1995. Maternity leave and women's mental health. *Psychology of Women Quarterly* 19: 257-285.

This longitudinal study of 570 pregnant women (The Wisconsin Maternity Leave and Health Study) provides data on the relationship between maternity leave and mental health. Women were interviewed at 3 time points: 5 months pregnant, 1 month postpartum and 4 months postpartum. The study found that women who took a short leave and reported marital concerns scored the highest on depression scales.

821   Hyde, J. S., M. J. Essex, and F. Horton. 1993. Fathers and parental leave: Attitudes and experiences. *Journal of Family Issues* 14(4): 616-641.

The behaviors and attitudes of fathers toward parental leave were examined in a longitudinal study (n = 550). The study found that 71% of fathers take 5 or fewer days. Moreover, most of the leave taken by fathers is in the form of paid vacation days.

822   Marra, R., and J. Lindner. 1992. **The true cost of parental leave: The parental leave cost model.** In *Parental Leave and Productivity: Current Research,* edited by D. E. Friedman, E. Galinsky, and V. Plowden. New York: Families and Work Institute. 55-78

Using the Parental Leave Cost Model (PLCM), the authors compare the cost of parental leave to the cost of turnover in a large high-technology corporation. The authors conclude that the company's liberal parental leave policy of one year is less costly than replacing an employee. There was a 90% retention of leave-taking employees.

823.   Marshall, N. L. 1995. *Women's Experiences with Maternity Leave. The Early Childhood Connection Project.* **Paper #04. Wellesley, MA: Center for Research on Women at Wellesley College.**

Marshall draws from 1991 survey data (n = 4000) to discuss women's experiences with maternity leave. She profiles women workers by the following categories: (1) the full-time-by choice worker; (2) the full-time-because-we-need-the-money worker; (3) the part-time worker; and (4) the conflicted worker.

824   Mercer, W. M., and University of California. 1994. *Survey Results: Family and Medical Leave Act.* **Berkeley, CA: William M. Mercer and University of California.**

This survey was mailed to 908 employers with a 31% response rate (n = 299). The survey was designed to shed light on the potential impact of the Family and Medical Leave Act (FMLA). The analysis revealed that the majority of employers were already complying with the law, although 40% were not in compliance with at least one basic provision. Utilization rates were low and costs were not significant for more than half of the employers. Some differences by size were reported (e.g., smaller employers were more likely to see a positive effect on productivity).

825   National Council of Jewish Women (NCJW). 1987. *Accommodating Pregnancy in the Workplace.* New York: NCJW Center for the Child.

Drawing upon interview data from the Mothers in the Workplace project (n = 2, 620 working women in the third trimester), this report examines the types of accommodations to pregnancy in the workplace and the costs and benefits to the employer. The researchers suggest that employers benefit from policies accommodating pregnancy through increased productivity. For example, pregnant women in "more accommodating workplaces" have fewer sick days, do more work without compensation, and work later into pregnancy.

826   Piotrkowski, C. S., D. Hughes, J. H. Pleck, S. Kessler-Sklar, and G. L. Staines. 1993. *The Experience of Childbearing Women in the Workplace: The Impact of Family-Friendly Policies and Practices.* New York: National Council of Jewish Women.

This secondary analysis of Mothers in the Workplace (MITW) 1986 and 1987 panel data focuses on the effects of workplace policies on childbearing women. Findings confirm prior research suggesting that specific employment characteristics, such as being a new hire, doing shift work, working part-time, receiving a low-wage, or working for a small organization, inhibit access to family-friendly benefits. In contrast, the authors point out several themes that contribute to the well-being of women in the workplace; namely, availability of health benefits, flexibility of scheduling, and a healthy supervisor/employee relationship.

827   Pleck, J. H. 1992. Fathers and parental leave: A perspective. In *Parental Leave and Productivity: Current Research,* edited by D. E. Friedman, E. Galinsky, and V. Plowden. New York: Families and Work Institute. 17-20.

This article reviews research data on the leave-taking behaviors of fathers after having a child. Rather than taking formal leave, a majority of fathers take paid sick or vacation days off.

828   Pleck, J. H. 1991. *Employer Policies and Working Mothers of Infants: An Overview.* Working Paper Series, No. 243. Wellesley, MA: Center for Research on Women at Wellesley College.

In this working paper, Pleck reviews the literature on employer policies and working mothers of infants. Topics discussed are parental leave, flexible work schedules, and race, ethnicity and class effects. Pleck notes little research has been done on the latter.

829   Pleck, J. H. 1988. Fathers and infant care leave. In *The Parental Leave Crisis,* edited by E. Zigler and M. Frank. New Haven, CT: Yale. 177-191.

This chapter presents a background review of parental leave policies in the United States. In addition, the author examines the availability, utilization and effects of parental leave in both the United States and Sweden.

830   Scharlach, A. E. 1995. *The Family and Medical Leave Act of 1993: Analysis and Appraisal.* Work-Family Policy Paper Series. Boston, MA: Center on Work and Family at Boston University.

Scharlach provides a comprehensive review and analysis of leave legislation. Several case studies are presented (e.g., Polaroid, Apple Computer). Following an in-depth analysis of the implications of the research and current status of leave legislation, recommendations for employers and public policy are presented. An appendix contains summaries of major studies on leave legislation (pp. 37-40).

831   Scharlach, A. E., and J. Stranger. Mandated Family and Medical Leave: Boon or Bane? Unpublished Manuscript.

832   Scharlach, A. E., S. L. Sansom, and J. Stanger. 1995. The Family and Medical Leave Act of 1993: How fully is business complying? *California Management Review* 37(2): 66-79.

Examines company compliance with The Family and Medical Leave Act of 1993. Based on survey data from companies (n = 302) predominately in California, Scharlach and colleagues conclude that implementation is "limited." While 6% of the companies were not in compliance on any provisions of the law, 40% were not in compliance with at least one basic requirement (e.g., did not offer health care).

833   **Shaller, E. H., and M. K. Qualiana. 1993. The Family and Medical Leave Act - Key provisions and potential problems.** *Employee Relations Law Journal* **19(1): 5-22.**

The authors discuss the Family and Medical Leave Act, describe its provisions and outline potential problem areas.

834   **Spalter-Roth, R. M., and H. I. Hartmann. 1988. *Unnecessary Losses: Costs to Americans of the Lack of Family and Medical Leave.* Washington, DC: Institute for Women's Policy Research (IWPR).**

This study quantifies losses that occur to workers, to taxpayers, and to the nation resulting from the lack of parental and medical leave legislation. Estimates are drawn from PSID survey data (Panel Study of Income Dynamics). Using a cost-benefit analysis, the researchers present costs of no parental leave, by gender and race, taxpayers, and society. Policy recommendations are made.

835   **Towers Perrin 1993. *Family and Medical Leave Programs: Before and After the New Federal Law.* New York: Towers Perrin.**

Readers (employers) of the "Towers Perrin Monitor" were surveyed on family leave policies. The study found that not many people take family leave, and those who do are mostly women at the time of childbirth. In terms of cost, more than 90% said that the costs were not significant, even though many policies continued health benefits. Overwhelmingly (97%), the employers agreed that benefits from family leave included increased employee morale and loyalty as well as retention of employees.

836   Trzcinski, E., and M. Finn-Stevenson. **1991. A response to arguments against mandated parental leave: Findings from the Connecticut survey of parental leave policies.** *Journal of Marriage and the Family* 53: 445-460.

The authors refute three major arguments put forth by opponents of parental leave. In response to the argument that "mandated parental leave will raise costs of doing business", empirical findings are presented from the Yale University Study which surveyed a random sample of 1,990 Connecticut firms. This study compared the cost of providing leave with the cost of permanently replacing the worker. The researchers concluded that firms should not incur substantial costs from parental leave policies.

837   Trzcinski, E., and W. T. Alpert. 1992. *Job Guaranteed Medical Leave: Reducing Termination Costs to Business.* **Paper presented at the World Congress on the Family, Columbus, OH.**

838   Trzcinski, E., and W. T. Alpert. 1991. **Handling work during leave: Strategies and costs.** *Journal of Managerial Issues* 3(4): 403-426.

The authors propose a conceptual model for strategies to handle an employee's leave. In brief, it involves an analysis of responsibilities and a decision-making strategy to handle the leave-taker's responsibilities: wait until return, give to coworkers, or hire temporary help.

839   Trzcinski, E., and W. T. Alpert. 1990. *Leave Policies in Small Business: Findings from the U. S. Small Business Administration Employee Leave Survey.* **Washington, DC: Small Business Administration, Office of Advocacy.**

Using a nationally representative sample (n = 2732), the authors examined employee utilization of family leave and its impact on employers. The study found that the incidence of leave-taking increased when formal policies were in place and health care coverage was offered. Another key finding was that the cost of covering for a worker on leave was approximately the same as the worker's wages and benefits. Overall, parental leave policies were found to have a cost saving effect on businesses. Based on the enactment of the Family and Medical Leave Act, this study projects a cost savings to businesses of $244 million.

840   Zigler, E. F. and M. Frank, eds. 1988. *The Parental Leave Crisis: Toward a National Policy.* New Haven, CT: Yale University Press.

PART 9

LINKAGES TO CORPORATE STRATEGIES AND GOVERNANCE

CHAPTER 30

Downsizing/Restructuring/
Reengineering and Work-Family

841   Agassi, J. B., and S. Heycock, eds. 1989. *The Redesign of Working Time: Promise or Threat?* Berlin, Germany: Edition Sigma.

Four of the most pressing challenges associated with work experiences are discussed in this book: unemployment, stress, gender gap, and the low level of worker autonomy. Experiences in a number of European countries are examined.

842   Appelbaum, E. 1987. Technology and the redesign of work in the insurance industry. In *Women, Work, and Technology,* edited by M. D. Wright, et al. Ann Arbor, MI: University of Michigan Press. 182-201.

Interview data, site visits, and secondary data were used to consider how changes in the insurance industry might affect the work experiences of women, such as the number of jobs, the redistribution of occupations, the levels of skills, the nature of clerical work, and opportunities for upward mobility. Appelbaum notes that the skill levels required for women clerical workers in the insurance industry are rising.

843   Appelbaum, E., and R. Batt. 1994. *The New American Workplace: Transforming Work Systems in the U.S.* Ithaca, New York: ILR Press.

Business innovations in management, human resources, the organization of work, and industrial relations have become widespread. This book uses data from surveys and case studies to explore these innovations and consider the extent to which they represent fundamental changes in business strategies.

844   Appelbaum, E., and R. Batt.   1993.   *High-performance Work Systems: American Models of Workplace Transformation.* Washington, DC: Economic Policy Institute (EPI).

845   Bailyn, L. 1992. *Breaking the Mold: Women, Men, and Time in the New Corporate World.*   New York: The Free Press.

Bailyn argues that work-family programs will have a limited impact unless businesses "break the mold" of traditional assumptions, such as assuming a conflict between private and organizational needs. Additionally, Bailyn urges a change in the way work is organized and rewarded, particularly in terms of time, commitment, and career success.

846   Barling, J. 1994. Work and family: In search of more effective workplace interventions. *Trends in Organizational Behavior* 1: 63-73.

Several key assumptions about work-family conflicts and family-responsive supports are examined. A review of empirical studies is used to consider factors such as quality of work experiences and the quality of parent-child interactions. A model linking different aspects of work experiences and family functioning is suggested.

847   Blau, D. M. 1987. A time-series analysis of self-employment in the United States. *Journal of Political Economy*   95(3): 445-467.

Ever since industrialization during the mid to late 19th century, there has been a steady decrease in the proportion of self-employed workers in the United States as well as other countries. Using a time series analysis, Blau examines the factors associated with a reversal in this trend, for both men and women, starting in 1970. He observes, "This rather remarkable simultaneous occurrence strongly suggests that a change of a fundamental nature has occurred in the advanced industrial economics that has made self-employment more attractive and/or competitive."(p. 447) Blau concludes that two sets of factors, changes in industrial structure and technology, have precipitated these changes.

848   Bowman, J. L. B., G. M. Couchman, and S. W. Cole. 1994. Midlife and older displaced workers: A comparison of predisplacement and new earnings. *Journal of Family and Economics Issues* 15(2): 93-115.

849   Brief A. P., M. A. Konovsky, R. Goodwin, and K. Link. 1995. Inferring the meaning of work from the effects of unemployment. *Journal of Applied Social Psychology* 25(8): 693-711.

Using data collected from 148 unemployed persons, questions about the economic and experiential functions of work were explored. Statistical analyses revealed a relationship between the length of unemployment and perceptions of both economic and experiential deprivation. Although economic deprivation was related to subjective assessments of well-being, this relationship was not noted between experiential deprivation and perceptions of well being. Subjective well-being was measured using the Satisfaction and Life Scale.

850   Brockner, J., M. A. Konovsky, R. Cooper-Schneider, R. Folger, C. Martin, and R. J. Bies. 1994. Interactive effects of procedural justice and outcome negativity on victims and survivors of job loss. *Academy of Management Journal* 37(2): 397-409.

This study asked individuals who had been laid-off to assess the "fairness" of the lay off procedures (termed "procedural justice"). These ratings were then compared to the presence of three dimensions measuring "negative outcomes": severance pay; extension of life insurance; and extension of medical insurance. The results of three studies with different samples (e.g., first time registrants for unemployment insurance; lay-off survivors from a single workplace; employees at a manufacturing company scheduled for lay-off) showed that relationships between procedural justice and outcome negativity were observed.

851   Broman, C. L., V. L. Hamilton, and W. S. Hoffman. 1990. Unemployment and its effects on families: Evidence from a plant closing study. *American Journal of Community Psychology* 18(5): 643-659.

Data were collected from 1,579 workers to explore the impact of unemployment on employees' families. The sample included 831 at a plant scheduled to close (some of whom had already been laid-off and others scheduled for lay-off) and 766 at a plant not scheduled to close. Family stress was higher among employees of the plant scheduled for closing than among those working at the plant not scheduled for closing. The analyses confirm that the resultant financial stresses have negative effects on families. Family stress was mediated by financial hardship.

852   **Burkhardt, M. E. 1994. Social interactions effects following a technological change: A longitudinal investigation.** *Academy of Management Journal* **37(4): 869-898.**

Network analysis techniques were used to collect information about sources of social influence and the role of interpersonal relationships in the dispersion of beliefs and behaviors throughout an organization following the introduction of technological change, use of computers for data analysis. This study builds on theories of interaction, information processing theories and social process theories. The findings of this longitudinal study, which collected data from 99 employees a t three time intervals, suggest that interpersonal interactions affected beliefs concerning mastery of the new technology, but relationships with coworkers had more impact on attitudes and behaviors related to the new technology.

853   **Carter, V. J. 1994. The family, the workplace, and work technology: An integrated model of class identification among women office workers.** *Work and Occupations* **21(3): 308-334.**

This study explores relationships between the class identity of female office workers and factors related to individual characteristics, family characteristics, and characteristics of their work environment. Survey data were collected from 292 respondents in 101 offices at a public university. Among the respondents, 35.6% identified themselves as "working class" and 59.9 % as "middle class." The findings suggest relationships between middle class identity and both job autonomy and intrinsic job rewards, and the duration of office automation.

854   Crouter, A. C., and B. Manke. 1994. The changing American
        workplace: Implications for individuals and families. *Family
        Relations* 43: 117-124.

        The authors review the findings of previous studies to explore
        how three important workplace changes (employee
        involvement teams, use of computer technologies for
        communication, and downsizing) may affect employees and
        their families. It is suggested that these changes are related to
        other workplace factors, such as stress. The linkages between
        organizations, expectation for increased employee involvement,
        and workplace commitment to flexible policies and practices
        are considered.

855   Dresser, L., N. Colan, L. C. Litchfield, R. Meringer, C. Yeager,
        R. Elliot, and R. Darveau. 1996. *The Displaced Family: Job
        Loss, Family Supportiveness, and the Role of Outplacement
        Services.* Boston, MA: Center on Work and Family at Boston
        University and Jandl Associates.

        This exploratory study examined the impact of unemployment
        on families who mediate the experiences of the unemployed
        family member, and also experience some of the experiences of
        unemployment themselves. The study sample included 155
        respondents (115 unemployed persons; 30 spouses; and 10
        children). Five standardized scales were used: The Quality of
        Life Scale, the Marital Satisfaction Scale; the Child-
        Adolescent Communication Scale; the Perceived Stress Scale;
        and the Family Environment Scale. The researchers report that
        the most important predictors of stress were the unemployed
        worker's age, family environment, and the number of months
        unemployed.

856   Flanagan, C. A. 1990. Change in family work status: Effects on
        parent-adolescent decision making. *Child Development* 61:
        163-177.

        Three groups of families with adolescents were studied to
        examine the relationships between changes in family employ-
        ment status and parent/child decision making patterns. The
        data were collected at four time periods from mothers and their
        adolescent children who were members of 504 families. The

families were placed in three groups: those where a family member had been laid-off or demoted at the first and last points of data collection; where no layoff or demotion was reported; and where a lay-off or demotion was reported at Time 1 but that status was changed by Time 4. No relationships were noted between family employment status and family integration. Among boys, relationships were noted between family employment status and the adolescents' perceptions of parent-child conflict.

857   Goldstein, N. 1992. **Gender and the restructuring of high-tech multinational corporations: New twists to an old story.** *Cambridge Journal of Economics* 16: 269-284.

858   Hanks, R. S. 1990. **The impact of early retirement incentives on retirees and their families.** *Journal of Family Issues* 11(4): 424-437.

Qualitative and quantitative data from interviews with 60 early retirees and their spouses (n = 51) were used to examine relationships between early retirement incentives and outcome measures related to satisfaction with retirement (using the "Satisfaction with Retirement Scale"). The findings suggested relationships between satisfaction with retirement and health, as well as expectations for future health and productivity.

859   Larson, J. H., S. M. Wilson, and R. Beley. 1994. **The impact of job insecurity on marital and family relationships.** *Family Relations* 43: 138-143.

Data were collected from 111 spouses (n = 222) about perceptions of stress (using the 14 item Perceived Stress Scale) associated with job insecurity and family function (e.g. subscale of the McMaster Family Assessment Device). The researchers used spillover theory and systems theory to hypothesize that job insecurity would be related to decreased family and marital functioning. Among women, job insecurity was associated with lower functioning in nine dimensions (e.g., overall family functioning, family communication, problem solving, role clarity, affective involvement, behavior control, marital adjustment, and marital/family problems) but among men, this stress was related to five of the variable sets (e.g., role clarity, affective involvement, overall family functioning, marital adjustment, and number of marital/family problems).

860   Mirvis, P. H., A. L. Sales, and E. J. Hackett. 1991. The implementation and adoption of new technology in organizations: The impact on work, people, and culture. *Human Resource Management* 30(1): 113-139.

The introduction of technology at two workplaces were contrasted. Data were collected from a total of 2,400 workers through surveys which were distributed before and after the introduction of computer technologies. The researchers examined four sets of factors (technology strategy and plan; implementation; user attitudes and experience; and organizational culture) and concluded that two factors affected the success of the technology: training and the pursuit of a participative change strategy. Differences among user groups were noted.

861   Shaw, L. B., D. P. Champlin, H. I. Hartmann, and R. M. Spalter-Roth. 1993. *The Impact of the Glass Ceiling and Structural Change on Minorities and Women.* Washington, DC: Institute for Women's Policy Research (IWPR).

Shaw and colleagues examined the effects of restructuring on minorities' and women's opportunities to enter and/or advance beyond entry-level positions in management and the professions. The researchers considered two types of restructuring, corporate restructuring and industrial restructuring (i.e., the shift toward a service-producing economy). An extensive review of the literature uncovered many problems for minorities and women resulting from restructuring. Some of the identified problems follow: (1) the loss of routes to management (i.e., supervisory and low-level managerial positions); (2) the loss of well-defined career ladders; and (3) the use of independent contractors.

862   Targ, D. B., and C. C. Perrucci. 1990. Plant closings, unemployment and families. *Marriage and Family Review* 15(3/4): 131-146.

This paper reviews findings of previous studies to discern relationships between unemployment among married persons and marital relationships, impact on family members, and the quality of family life. Policy implications, such as advance notification of planned facility closings, financial assistance, and severance pay are considered.

863   Vosler, N. R. 1994. **Displaced manufacturing workers and their families: A research-based practice model.** *Families in Society: The Journal of Contemporary Human Services* **39**: 105-117.

The ecological perspectives and systems theory frameworks were used to consider the impact of plant closing on employees and their families. Reflecting on the findings of previous studies, Vosler proposes a conceptual models: characteristics of plant closings; resources available to families; family coping; employment status; family financial status (and changes in this status); perceptions of changes in family roles; family relationships; health/mental health of employee and spouse; and health/mental health of children.

CHAPTER 31

Workplace Culture and Values and Family Responsive Programs

864   Blanchard, M. L. 1991. Linking work and family issues to the corporate mission. *Human Resource Horizons* 106: 15-18.

865   Bowen, G. L. 1988. Corporate supports for the family lives of employees: A conceptual model for program planning and evaluation. *Family Relations* 37: 183-188.

Bowen proposes a conceptual model to examine the outcomes associated with employer-supported family benefits for employees and their families. This model is comprised of four primary sets of factors: (1) corporate culture and philosophy; (2) work environment (i.e., structure and dynamics); (3) employees' perceptions and circumstances (personal significance and need and expectations and beliefs); and (4) outcomes (i.e., outcomes at home and outcomes at work).

866   Bureau of National Affairs (BNA). 1989. *Corporate Work and Family Programs for the 1990's: Five Case Studies.* Special Report No. 13. Washington, DC: Bureau of National Affairs.

This report presents case studies from companies actively involved in providing a comprehensive range of work/family benefits, or in other words, "stage two" companies. The case studies chosen illustrate a variety of benefits and experiences: Warner-Lambert Co., NCNB Corp., Campbell Soup Co., Hallmark Cards, and IBM.

867   Chatman, J. A., and K. A. Jehn. 1994. Assessing the relationship between industry characteristics and organizational culture: How different can you be? *Academy of Management Journal* 37(3): 522-553.

The differences in characteristics of organizational culture a t

15 firms representing four service sector industries were examined. The researchers report relationships between cultural values and the industry technology and growth. Using the 54-item Organizational Culture Profile (O'Reilly et al., 1991), seven dimensions of organizational culture were examined, among them: innovation, stability, respect and aggressiveness (all with eigenvalues greater than 1.0). The median within firm correlations among the study participants ranged from .257 to .664.

868   Crouter, A. C., and S. M. MacDermid. 1990. Into the lion's den: Methodological issues for work-family research inside the corporation. *Marriage and Family Review* 15(3/4): 59-74.

The authors consider the methodological challenges and constraints associated with conducting workplace-based research on work-family issues. A review of different research traditions (needs assessment; case studies; program evaluations) is provided. Three research design elements are explored and critiqued: access and entry to the site; need for multiple data sources for triangulation; and elements of program evaluation. Crouter and MacDermid discuss the need to pursue longitudinal designs, studies that span multiple organizations, and research that collects data on variations in the intra-organizational environments.

869   Families and Work Institute. 1993. *An Evaluation of Johnson & Johnson's Work-Family Initiative.* New York: Families and Work Institute.

This executive summary prepared by the Families and Work Institute describes and evaluates the Johnson and Johnson, Balancing Work and Family Program. The company's basic goal was to create a family-friendly workplace where employees and supervisors work together to lessen conflict between work and family responsibilities. This paper identifies and evaluates the eleven programs Johnson and Johnson initiated.

870   Friedman, D. E. 1990. Corporate responses to family needs. *Marriage and Family Review* 15(1/2): 77-98.

This article provides an overview of corporate responses to employees' work and family experiences. Information about the growth of employer-supported child care assistance is included.

871   Friedman, D. E. 1987. *Family-Supportive Policies: The Corporate Decision-Making Process.* New York: The Conference Board.

This Conference Board report uses data gathered from interviews conducted with 75 companies and 50 community organizations to map out many of the key planning decisions associated with the development of work-family programs. Issues such as forming task forces and assessing family needs are addressed.

872   Galinsky, E. 1988. *The Impact of Supervisors' Attitudes and Company Culture on Work/Family Adjustment.* Paper presented at the Annual Convention of the American Psychological Association, August 1988 Atlanta, Georgia.

This study, in which 733 employees participated, collected data about employees' perceptions of their supervisors' support (for both task and work-family issues) as well as job satisfaction, stress, stress-related health problems, and work-family interface. The extent of supervisor support was identified as a key variable which was related to the outcome measure.

873   Galinsky, E. *Labor Force Participation of Dual-Earner Couples and Single Parents.* New York: The Families and Work Institute.

This paper focuses on company cultures that have responded to the changing workforce, such as dual-career and single-parent families. Programs and policies designed to facilitate employees' ability to handle work and family responsibilities are discussed.

874   Galinsky, E., D. Hughes, and J. David. 1990. Trends in corporate family-supportive policies. *Marriage and Family Review* 15(3/4): 75-93.

This report considers corporate responses to work-family issues from a developmental perspective. The characteristics of companies in Phase I and Phase II are presented. Organizational predictors of response to work-family issues, such as company size, industry, and workforce demographics, are identified.

875   Goldberg, C. R., A. P. Gorman, and K. B. Hansen. 1990. **Issues in the corporate workplace.** *New England Journal of Public Policy* **6(1): 65-73.**

This article discusses three issues relevant to contemporary work-family issues: understanding the business implications, designing responses which fit with organizational culture, and establishing supports which respond to the needs of employees.

876   Gonyea, J. G. 1993. **Family responsibilities and family-oriented policies: Assessing their impacts on the workplace.** **Employee Assistance Quarterly 9(1): 1-29.**

This article provides an overview of research exploring the impacts of eldercare and child care policies and programs on six dimensions of work experiences: stress; morale and job satisfaction; absenteeism and tardiness; job performance; job search and job acceptance; and career development and turnover.

877   Goodstein, J. D. 1994. **Institutional pressures and strategic responsiveness: Employer involvement in work-family issues.** *Academy of Management Journal* **37(2): 350-382.**

This article reviews theoretical perspectives and empirical studies that provide insight about the factors which predict organizational response to work-family issues. Using a framework about institutional environments and pressures developed by Oliver (1991), Goodstein uses five sets of motivating factors: cause, constituents, content, control, and concerns. Survey data from 1,239 organizations found relationships between organizational size, proportion of female employees, and industry groups with organizational response.

878   Googins, B. K., R. B. Hudson, and M. Pitt-Catsouphes. 1995. *Strategic Responses: Corporate Involvement in Family and Community Issues.* Work-Family Policy Paper Series. Boston, MA: Center on Work and Family at Boston University.

This paper presents a framework for corporate decision makers to consider complex social issues. Information about the challenges facing families and communities is presented. Discussion is focused on four alternative private sector strategies: market response, employee programs, corporate philanthropy, and volunteerism.

879   Greenberger, E., W. A. Goldberg, S. Hamill, R. O'Neil, and C. K. Payne. 1989. Contributions of a supportive work environment to parents' well-being and orientation to work. *American Journal of Community Psychology* 17(6): 755-783.

The employed men and women (n = 321) in this sample expressed similar levels of job satisfaction and organizational commitment. Women reported more role strain and associated health problems. Whereas the presence of formal supports (e.g., policies and programs) were more important to women's well-being, the level of informal social support was more important to the men. Higher levels of role strain were associated with higher usage of work-family programs and benefits.

880   Hughes, D., and E. Galinsky. 1988. Balancing work and family lives: Research and corporate applications. In *Maternal Employment and Children's Development: Longitudinal Research,* edited by A. E. Gottfried and A. W. Gottfried. New York: Plenum Press. 233-268.

The Bank Street College Corporate Work and Family Life Study gathered information about stress and satisfaction from 732 respondents. Working mothers reported higher stress levels and greater work-family conflicts than working fathers. The stress reported by these working mothers was positively correlated with breakdowns in child care arrangements. Recommends employer responsiveness to employee needs, especially child care.

881   Ingram, P., and T. Simons. 1995. **Institutional and resource dependence determinants of responsiveness to work-family issues.** *Academy of Management Journal* 38(5): 1466-1482.

Data from the National Organizations Study were used to consider Goodstein's model of organizational responsiveness to work-family issues which was based on Oliver's theory about institutional pressures and strategic responses. Among the findings reported, Ingram and Simons indicated confirmation that organizations that "pay attention to other organizations" are more responsive to work-family issues.

882   Judge, T. A., J. W. Boudreau, and R. D. Bretz. 1994. **Job and life attitudes of male executives.** *Journal of Applied Psychology* 79(5): 767-782.

Data were collected from 1,309 males executives about job satisfaction, life satisfaction, job stress, work-family conflicts and organizational policies. The study found positive relationships between job satisfaction and life satisfaction and inverse relationships between job stress and job satisfaction. Work-family conflicts were associated with decreased job satisfaction.

883   Kingston, P. W. 1990. **Illusions and ignorance about the family-responsive workplace.** *Journal of Family Issues* 11(4) :438-454.

This articles challenges some of the optimism in the work-family field that we are at the beginning of a trend toward the expansion of employer-sponsored work-family supports. Discussion is focused on the lack of reliable, documented data about the outcomes of work-family policies and programs.

884   Kofodimos, J. 1995. *Beyond Work-Family Programs: Confronting and Resolving the Underlying Causes of Work-Personal Life Conflict.* Greensboro, NC: **Center of Creative Leadership.**

Examines the rationale behind the current work-family programs and identifies their problems. The basic thesis is that the companies' executive(s) psychological processes are mirrored in the company culture (e.g., mastery, competitiveness, control, time-focused). Such characteristics of the culture serve as barriers to successful work-family programs. Strategies for a shift in cultural values are discussed.

885   **Kossek, E. E., and V. Nichol. 1995.** *Understanding the Immediate Climate for Work/Family Integration: Assessing Congruence in the Supervisor and Subordinate Relationship Affecting Work/Family Outcomes.* **Paper presented at the National Academy of Management Meetings, Vancouver, British Columbia.**

Kossek and Nichol propose, " ... congruence in the supervisor subordinate relationship predicts an employee's work and family outcomes." Data such as supervisor support for work-family conflicts and attitudes toward managing work and child care responsibility were collected from 132 pairs of supervisors and employees. Supervisors, in general, rated themselves as being more supportive of work-family conflicts than did the employees.

886   **Kraut, A. I. 1990. Some lessons on organizational research concerning work and family issues.** *Human Resource Planning* **13(2): 109-118.**

Summaries of studies conducted at six companies are presented: Dupont, Merck, IBM. BellSouth, Honeywell, and Mobil. Some of the challenges associated with workplace-based research are discussed.

887   **Lambert, S. J. Forthcoming 1996. Expanding theories of occupational structure: Examining the relationship between employer responsiveness and worker well-being. In** *The Integration on Social Work and Social Science,* **edited by D. Tucker, R. Sarri, and C. Garvin. New York: Greenwood Press.**

Lambert postulates that well-designed jobs are the foundation for successful family-responsive programs and policies (which cannot, by themselves, overcome the negative impacts of poorly designed jobs). Surveys were collected from 599 employees at Fel-Pro, Inc. The study found that, overall, the relationship between benefit appreciation and worker well-being depends on the quality of workers' jobs.

888   Lewis, S., and K. Taylor. 1996. Evaluating the impact of "family friendly" employer policies: A case study. In *The Work Family Challenge: Rethinking Employment*, edited by S. Lewis and J. Lewis. Newbury Park, CA: Sage Publications.

889   Lobel, S. A. 1992. A value-laden approach to integrating work and family life. *Human Resource Management* 31(3): 249-265.

Lobel suggests that people experience work-family conflict when there is a discrepancy among values, for example: (1) when organizational expectations and values differ; and (2) when individuals express different values in work and family roles. Specific strategies to reduce work-family conflict are presented.

890   Lobel, S. A., B. K. Googins, and E. Bankert. 1994. *Work-family initiatives: Visioning the future.* Paper presented at the Drexel University 5th Annual Stein Conference, Philadelphia, PA.

891   MacDermid, S. M., and D. B. Targ. 1995. A call for greater attention to the role of employers in developing, transforming, and implementing family policies. *Journal of Family and Economic Issues* 16(1): 145-170.

The linkages between work-family policies established in the public and the private sectors are explored. In spite of the increase in the numbers of firms offering work-family policies, programs and practices, the authors note that a very small percentage of workers actually have access to corporate-sponsored supports. The experiences of low income workers, women workers, and employees of small businesses are examined.

892   MacDermid, S. M., M. Williams, S. Marks, and G. Heilbrun. 1994. Is small beautiful? Work-family tension, work conditions and organizational size. *Family Relations* 43: 159-167.

Interviews were conducted with 60 working women to examine relationships among size of the workplace and work conditions, interpersonal relationships, and work-family tension. The respondents working at small firms reported that the closeness of their work relationships reduced negative work to home spillover. Demanding work schedules were associated with difficulties managing work-family conflicts.

893   McRae, S. 1994. **Labour supply after childbirth: Do employers' policies make a difference?** *Sociology* 28(1): 99-122.

The data from two surveys (n = 4,991 and 500) were used to compare two sets of independent variables, the characteristics of workplace policies and the characteristics of female employees who have given birth, with three aspects of women's labor market activities after birth (e.g., return to labor market; hours of work; and choice of employer after birth). McRae found that the characteristics of the women and factors in the local labor market were more predictive of the women's labor market attachments than either employer policies or characteristics of the workplace.

894   Nelson, P. T., and S. Couch. 1990. **The corporate perspective on family responsive policy.** *Marriage and Family Review* 15(3/4): 95-107.

Using the results of two surveys, employers' attitudes toward the establishment of family-oriented services and benefits were assessed. Although employers expressed positive attitudes about possibilities for employer-sponsorship of these programs, the researchers noted the gap between these favorable attitudes and their workplace practices.

895   Pitt-Catsouphes, M., J. Joseph, M. Rountree, and J. C. Casey. 1995. *Lessons Learned: Corporate Diversity Initiatives and Workplace Inclusion.* Boston, MA: Center on Work and Family at Boston University.

Interviews were conducted with diversity managers from 14 companies to determine linkages between disability-related issues and approaches to valuing diversity. An annotated bibliography is included in the report.

896   Pitt-Catsouphes, M., P. H. Mirvis, and L. C. Litchfield. 1995. *Behind the Scenes: Corporate Environments and Work-Family*

Initiatives. Boston, MA: Center on Work and Family at Boston University.

The Corporate and Work-Family Initiatives study surveyed 93 firms about their work-family policies and practices. Data were collected about organizational characteristics and corporate culture. The respondents provided information about expectations and attitudes relevant to work-family issues manifested at four levels of the company: organizational policies; priorities of top leaders; supervisory practices; and employee experiences.

897 Pleck, J. H. 1993. Are "family-supportive" employer policies relevant to men? In *Men, Work, and Family,* edited by J. C. Hood. Newbury Park, CA: Sage Publications. 217-237.

In this chapter, the relationship between men and family-supportive policies is explored both from a research and an organizational perspective. Pleck reviews and critiques studies exploring work-family issues that fail to document changing trends in men's participation in family roles. While offering evidence of changing trends, Pleck makes a case for the growing need and use of family-supportive policies by men. Suggestions for changes in organizational culture conclude the article.

898 Putti, J. M., S. Aryee, and T. K. Liang. 1989. Work values and organizational commitment: A study in the Asian context. *Human Relations* 42(3): 275-288.

This study gathered information from 175 Asian employees in Singapore about their work values and their organizational commitment. Using standardized scales, the study found relationships between these two sets of variables, particularly between intrinsic (versus extrinsic) work values and commitment.

899 Raabe, P. H., and J. C. Gessner. 1988. Employer family-supportive policies: Diverse variations on the theme. *Family Relations* 37: 196-202.

Interviews were conducted with 30 directors of human resources selected randomly from a sample of businesses in the New

Orleans area employing at least 750 workers. These interviews surfaced a number of methodological challenges to work-family research, such as the respondents' interpretations of the existence of formal and informal policies. Information was collected about a range of work-family policies and practices. Policy implications are discussed.

900   Thompson, C. A., C. C. Thomas, and M. Maier. 1992. Work-Family conflict and the bottom line: Reassessing corporate policies and initiatives. In *Womanpower: Managing in Times of Demographic Turbulence,* edited by U. Sekaran and F. Leong. Sage Publications. 59-84.

This chapter addresses corporate initiatives for assisting employees handle work-family conflict and the barriers impeding their effectiveness. The link between changing corporate policies and corporate culture is explored.

901   Thompson, C. A., L. Beauvais, and H. Carter. Forthcoming 1997. *Work-Family Programs: Only Slow-Trackers Need Apply? An Investigation of the Impact of Work-Family Culture.*

The authors investigate the relationship between a supportive work culture and the utilization of work-family benefits, organizational commitment, and intention to continue working with the company. This paper describes the development of a scale to tap these issues.

902   Warren, J. A., and P. J. Johnson. 1995. The impact of workplace support on work-family role strain. *Family Relations* 44: 163-169.

Employed mothers (n = 116) with preschool children reported on their perceptions of their work environments, their use of work-family benefits, and levels of role strain. The results suggest supervisor support and, to some extent corporate culture, are related to work-family stress.

903   Zedeck, S., ed. 1992. *Work, Families, and Organizations.* San Francisco, CA: Jossey-Bass Publishers.

The introductory chapter to this edited volume provides highlights about key work-family topics. Summaries for key research studies are included. Zedick includes a discussion of the variables which have been addressed by work-family studies.

904   Zimmerman, T. S., and R. J. Fetsch. 1994. **Family ranching and farming: A consensus management model to improve family functioning and decrease work stress.** *Family Relations* 43: 125-131.

This pilot study explored the role of communications strategies associated with family involvement in the operations of ranches and farms. Eight intergenerational families participated in this project, which used the Consensus Management Model. Increases in family coping skills were reported.

CHAPTER 32

Employee Involvement and Work-Family

905   Goff, S. J., M. K. Mount, and R. L. Jamison. 1990. **Employer supported child care, work/family conflict, and absenteeism: A field study.** *Personnel Psychology* 43: 793-809.

Survey data were collected from 253 employees (62 users of onsite child care and 191 nonusers). Data related to absenteeism, work-family conflict, care for sick children, satisfaction with child care arrangements, and supervisor support were collected. One of the findings reported was that employees who had spouses caring for children did not experience less work-family conflict.

906   Grover, S. L., and K. J. Crooker. 1995. **Who appreciates family-responsive human resource policies: The impact of family-friendly policies on the organizational attachment of parents and non-parents.** *Personnel Psychology* 48: 271-288.

Information from the 1991 General Social Survey (n = 745) indicate that employees who had access to work-family policies and programs reported greater organizational commitment. The researchers suggest that the benefits of workplace based supports extend beyond just the users of such programs.

907   Guzzo, R. A., G. L. Nelson, and K. A. Noonan. 1992. **Commitment and employer involvement in employees' nonwork lives.** In *Work, Families, and Organizations,* edited by I. L. Zedeck. San Francisco, CA: Jossey-Bass Publishers. 236-271.

Using several case studies, a historical perspective on employer involvement in the nonwork lives of employees is examined. Theoretical insights and the findings of empirical studies are used to explore the relationships between work-family issues and employees' organizational commitment.

908 Lambert, S. J. 1997. Workers' use and appreciation of supportive workplace policies. In *Work Force Diversity,* edited by A. Daley. NASW Press. An earlier version of this paper is included in the Proceedings of the Academy of Management, NASW Press.

Data from a survey of employees (n = 599) working for Fel-Pro, a company with family-responsive policies and programs, reveal relationships between demographic characteristics, utilization of work-family policies and programs, and employees' appreciation of these benefits. It is reported that, overall, the rates of using the available work/life supports were similar for men and women.

909 Lambert, S. J. 1996. In Review.. *The Symbolic Effects of Employee Benefits: The Relationship between Family-Responsive Policies and Extra-Role Performance.* This research was funded by the Fel Pro/Mecklenburger Foundation and the Lois and Samuel Silberman Fund.

Data from the Fel-Pro study (n = 325 employees) are used to consider the direct and indirect relationships between the availability of family-responsive programs and policies and extra-roles aspects of employee performance. Reported findings include the direct positive relationships between perceptions of benefit usefulness and both self-reported citizenship as well as the submission of suggestions.

910 Lambert, S. J. 1991. The combined effects of job and family characteristics on the job satisfaction, job involvement, and intrinsic motivation of men and women workers. *Journal of Organizational Behavior* 12: 341-363.

Data from the 1977 Quality of Employment Survey were used to explore two theoretical perspectives about job satisfaction among men and women: job expectations and job values. The findings related to the permeability of work and family responsibilities indicated that spouse's job security has a positive effect on women's job satisfaction.

911   Marsden, P. V., A. L. Kalleberg, and C. R. Cook. 1993. Gender differences in organizational commitment: Influences of work positions and family roles. *Work and Occupations* 20(3): 368-390.

Information about the organizational commitment of workers selected from the 1991 General Social Survey (n = 912) was used to consider gender differences. The data suggest that women manifest slightly lower organizational commitment due to characteristics of the positions which they hold that are less likely to have "commitment-enhancing features" rather than other factors, such as family affiliations.

912   Orthner, D. K., and J. F. Pittman. 1986. Family contributions to work commitment. *Journal of Marriage and the Family* 48: 573-581.

This study explores the linkages between organizational support for families and employee commitment to work. Results from a LISREL analysis of survey data from air force personnel suggest that commitment to work is related to perceived support from organizations. That is, when the organization is perceived as supportive, the families are more supportive of the employee, and the employee is more committed to work.

913   Thompson, C. A., and G. Blau. 1993. Moving beyond traditional predictors of job involvement: Exploring the impact of work-family conflict and overload. *Journal of Social Behavior and Personality* 8(4): 635-646.

Data were collected from 234 employees from several different organizations about work-family conflicts, role overload, job satisfaction, and job involvement. Work-family conflicts (e.g., work-family and work-parent conflict) were associated with job involvement.

914   Youngblood, S. A., and K. Chambers-Cook. 1984. Child care assistance can improve employee attitudes and behavior. *Personnel Administrator* 29: 45-46, 93-95.

The experiences of employees at two textile companies were compared to explore organizational climate, job satisfaction, absenteeism, and turnover. Employees with children at the company which provided on-site child care expressed lower intention to leave the company.

CHAPTER 33

Productivity/Performance and Work-Family

915   Aldous, J. 1990. Specification and speculation concerning the politics of workplace family policies. *Journal of Family Issues* 11(4): 355-367.

Aldous reviews information that links changes in the female labor participation rates with employer-supported family benefits. The author considers some of the factors, such as women's economic and political power, that may have contributed to the relatively limited response of employers to this demographic shift. This article provides an introduction to this special issue of the *Journal of Family Issues* and offers an overview of research documenting the outcomes of work-family benefits.

916   Clegg, C. W. 1983. Psychology of employee lateness, absence, and turnover: A methodological critique and an empirical study. *Journal of Applied Psychology* 68(1): 88-101.

Clegg identifies and discusses a methodological flaw in empirical studies investigating employee unauthorized absences, lateness, and voluntary turnover. The problem, argues Clegg, is that researchers have failed to identify and consider the range of plausible rival hypotheseses, specifically the analytic consideration of reverse causation and control of third variables. The argument is supported by a review of the literature (Table 1, pp., 90-92) and an empirical study. Clegg proposes research and theoretical approaches to redress weaknesses.

917   Fernandez, J. P. 1986. *Child Care and Corporate Productivity: Resolving Work/Family Conflicts.* Lexington, MA: D.C. Heath.

This book presents and examines survey data from 4,971 management and crafts employees in five companies located in the Midwest.

918   Friedman, D. E. 1991. *Linking Work-Family Issues to the Bottom Line.* Report No. 962. New York: The Conference Board.

Presents a comprehensive review of work and family research literature that links family issues to companies' focus on the bottom line. Friedman integrates data from corporate studies with her analysis.

919   Friedman, D. E., and E. Galinsky. 1992. Work and family issues: A legitimate business concern. In *Work, Families, and Organizations,* edited by S. Zedeck. San Francisco, CA: Jossey-Bass Publishers. 168-207.

In this chapter, the authors explore the issue of company policies that are responsive to the changing needs of families. The authors review the literature supporting bottom-line advantages for companies that pursue work-family policies. Also discussed are the range of corporate responses and the corporate culture conducive to effective family-supportive policies.

920   Galinsky, E. 1988. *Child Care and Productivity.* Prepared for the Child Care Action Campaign, March 1988. New York: Bank Street College.

Galinsky uses data from research studies to establish the need for child care. The solutions that responsive companies have instituted are discussed and linked to corporate productivity.

921   Gonyea, J. G., and B. K. Googins. 1992. Linking the worlds of work and family: Beyond the productivity trap. *Human Resource Management* 31(3): 209-226.

The authors explore how corporate family-responsive initiatives affect the workplace with a review of the work-family and productivity research. Based upon identified challenges for work-family researchers, recommendation for future research are made: (1) employ broad assessment measures of organizational effectiveness, rather then a narrow focus on corporate productivity; and (2) frame the research questions within an organizational culture context.

922   Googins, B. K., J. G. Gonyea, and M. Pitt-Catsouphes. 1991. *Linking the Worlds of Family and Work: Family Dependent Care and Workers' Performance.* Boston, MA: Center on Work and Family at Boston University.

A final report to the Ford Foundation. This report presents a review of the literature about productivity and work-family issues and proposes a research agenda which could explore the linkages between family dependent care and worker productivity. Some of the key methodological challenges that have hampered previous studies are discussed.

923   Kamerman, S. B., and P. W. Kingston. 1982. Employer responses to the family responsibilities of employees. In *Families that Work: Children in a Changing World,* edited by S. B. Kamerman and C. D. Hayes. Washington, DC: National Academy Press. 144-208.

The authors review the findings of a number of studies to consider factors that have affected: (1) the extent of employer response to employee's family responsibilities; and (2) the outcomes of employer response. The policy analysis includes a discussion about compensation, benefits, and employer-sponsored services (e.g., pensions, health and medical coverage, maternity benefits/parental leaves, vacations, family benefits, relocation, child care services, and work schedules).

924   Kossek, E. E. 1991. *The Productivity Impact of Employer-Sponsored Child Care. Child Care Challenges for Employers.* Proceedings from the Governor's Conference on Employer-Sponsored Child Care, held in Detroit, MI, 1990. Horsham, PA: LRP Publications.

Kossek explores the issue of employer-sponsored child care from a research-oriented perspective. Suggestions for ways companies might measure productivity effects of child care programs are made based upon a review of the literature.

925   Kramar, R. Forthcoming. *Business Case for a Family-Friendly Workplace.*   Unpublished Draft.   NSW Department of Industrial Relations, Australia: Women's Equity Bureau.

Kramar analyzes the costs and benefits for companies that implement family-friendly policies to assist employees balance their work and family responsibilities.

926   Lambert, S. J., K. Hopkins, G. Easton, J. Walker, H. McWilliams, and M. S. Chung. 1993. *Added Benefits: The Link Between Family-Responsive Policies and Work Performance at Fel-Pro Incorporated.*   Chicago, IL: University of Chicago.

This study investigated the success of work-family programs at Fel-Pro, an auto gasket company in the Midwest. Data were collected from two sources: an employee survey data and data from employee records. Employees who used the work-family programs had the highest job evaluations and the lowest reported intent to leave the company. The positive effect, a sense of comfort, from the policies even reached employees who rarely used them. The researchers concluded that the work-family programs positively affected work performance and openness to change.

927   Perlow, L. A. 1995. Putting the work back into work/family. *Organizational Studies Conference, Best Papers Group and Organization Management* 20(2): 227-239.

This study used interview data from engineers (n = 30) and from managers (and support staff) from a Fortune 100 company. The results reveal barriers to successful work-family programs. The results are discussed from an organizational perspective (e.g., changing the organization's reward system).

928   Phillips, J. D., and B. Reisman. 1992. Turnover and return on investment models for family leave. In *Parental Leave and Productivity: Current Research,* edited by D. E. Friedman, E. Galinsky, and V. Plowden. New York: Families and Work Institute. 33-45.

Data from three studies were used to calculate costs associated with turnover. Two categories of variables were considered:

"hidden variables" (e.g., incoming employee inefficiency; inefficiency of departing employee; inefficiency of supervisor and coworkers closely associated with incoming employee: inefficiency while position is vacant) and "visible variable" (e.g., processing cost; relocation costs). The authors provide strategies for calculating turnover costs and concluded that this cost is approximately 1.5 times annual salary for exempt employees.

929   **Raabe, P. H. 1990. The organizational effects of workplace family policies: Past weaknesses and recent progress toward improved research.** *Journal of Family Issues* **11(4): 477-491.**

Raabe identifies weaknesses in evaluation research on work-family policies within organizations. This critical review of the research addresses the following topics: methodological improvements, conceptual refinements, characteristics of work-family policies, and organizational outcomes.

930   **Scott, K. D., and E. L. McClellan. 1990. Gender differences in absenteeism.** *Public Personnel Management* **19(2): 229-253.**

This study examines the characteristics and attitudes of secondary school teachers in a county school system in the mid-Atlantic region. Survey data were matched with absenteeism data from employee records. Variables measured included: job satisfaction; central life; job involvement; and role conflict. In addition to absenteeism data, the survey included a measure designed to tap the "real" reason for absenteeism. Overall, there were few gender differences, however women took more days off and perceived some work-related factors differently. For both men and women, role conflict and job involvement were significantly related to absenteeism.

931   **Shellenbarger, S. 1993. Lessons from the workplace: How corporate policies and attitudes lag behind workers' changing needs.** *Human Resource Management* **31(3): 157-169.**

Shellenbarger argues that work-family practices do not meet the needs of workers' with consequences on several fronts: loss of productivity; reduced quality of life; and a loss of workers.

Shallenbarger charges that employees face antifamily discrimination.

932   Staines, G. L., and E. Galinsky. 1992. **Parental leave and productivity: The supervisor's view.** In *Parental Leave and Productivity: Current Research*, edited by D. E. Friedman, E. Galinsky, and V. Plowden. New York: Families and Work Institute. 21-32.

This study incorporated the supervisor's perspective to investigate the validity of assumptions about parental leave. Survey data were gathered from 331 supervisors at a high technology company with a year-long leave policy. The study shows popular assumptions (e.g., pregnant women disrupt productivity in workplace and change their minds about leaves) did not hold true. Supervisor data revealed that (1) women gave supervisors long time to plan for leaves; (2) two-thirds of women kept to leave plans; and (3) when changes in leave plans occurred, the majority of supervisors said they did not affect performance. The authors note that problems were most likely when a supervisor was not supportive or unknowledgeable about the programs.

933   The Conference Board. 1993. *Work-Family: Redefining the Business Case.* New York: The Conference Board.

934   Witt, L. A. 1988. **Breadwinner vs. non-breadwinner differences in married women's job satisfaction and perceptions of organizational climate.** *Human Relations* 41(6): 483-491.

Relationships between employees' family status, job satisfaction and perceptions of the organizations were examined in this study which included 46 married, full-time employees. Standardized instruments (Job Description Index; Organizational Climate Questionnaire; Survey of International Values) were incorporated into the survey instruments. Respondents who were breadwinners reported more job satisfaction and had more favorable perceptions of organizational climate.

Author Index

(Entries are citation numbers rather than page numbers.)

About the Compilers

TERI ANN LILLY, MARCIE PITT-CATSOUPHES, and BRADLEY K. GOOGINS are affiliated with The Center for Work & Family at Boston College. The Center was founded in 1990 as the first academic center which focused on research and policy assessments of work and family issues.

ISBN 0-313-30322-3

90000>

EAN

9 780313 303227

HARDCOVER BAR CODE